Reversals of Fortune

GARY MUCCIARONI

Reversals of Fortune

Public Policy
and
Private Interests

THE BROOKINGS INSTITUTION
Washington, D.C.

About Brookings

The Brookings Institution is a private nonprofit organization devoted to research, education, and publication on important issues of domestic and foreign policy. Its principal purpose is to bring knowledge to bear on current and emerging policy problems. The Institution was founded on December 8, 1927, to merge the activities of the Institute for Government Research, founded in 1916, the Institute of Economics, founded in 1922, and the Robert Brookings Graduate School of Economics, founded in 1924.

The Institution maintains a position of neutrality on issues of public policy. Interpretations or conclusions in Brookings publications should be understood to be solely those of the authors.

Copyright © 1995

THE BROOKINGS INSTITUTION

1775 Massachusetts Avenue, N.W., Washington, D.C. 20036

Library of Congress Cataloging-in-Publication data:

Mucciaroni, Gary.
    Reversals of fortune : public policy and private interests / Gary Mucciaroni.
        p. cm.
    Includes bibliographical references and index.
    ISBN 0-8157-5876-6 (cl)—ISBN 0-8157-5875-8 (pa)
    1. United States—Economic policy—1993-   2. United States—Commercial policy.   3. Tax incentives—United States.
    4. Deregulation—United States.   5. Protectionism—United States.
    6. Agricultural subsidies—United States.   7. Pressure groups—United States.   8. Lobbying—United States.   I. Title.
    HC106.82.M83   1995
    338.973—dc20   94-22353
                                              CIP

9 8 7 6 5 4 3 2 1

The paper used in this publication meets the minimum requirements of the American National Standard for Information Sciences—Permanence of paper for Printed Library Materials, ANSI Z39.48-1984.

Typeset in Times Roman

Composition by Harlowe Typography
Cottage City, Maryland

Printed by R.R. Donnelley and Sons Co.
Harrisonburg, Virginia

To
the memory of
my father

Preface

THE origins of this study reach back to my days as a graduate student when I read Grant McConnell's *Private Power and American Democracy* and Theodore Lowi's *The End of Liberalism*. Their analyses of American politics fascinated me as a student; as a citizen, however, they shook my faith in democratic government. In a nutshell, what they argued was that private interests, many of them rather narrow, dominated much of the American polity. Public policy had no authentic public-interest rationale and instead was the handmaiden of private power. Group theorists had recognized the importance and influence of organized interests in the American polity for years, of course. What was new was the negative conclusions reached about the effects of private interests on American democracy. Neither majoritarian nor pluralist versions of our politics seemed valid any longer.

Many of the policy breakthroughs of the 1970s that came under the rubric of social regulation—environmental and consumer protection, affirmative action, occupational health and safety—were at odds with the clientelism described by McConnell and Lowi. Whether and how much these measures succeeded in achieving their objectives or hampered the economy, or both, remain in dispute. More certain is that they were widely viewed as political defeats for a wide range of industries. Furthermore, the cozy triangles and subgovernments through which private interests thrived and were protected appeared to be breaking up or opening up into more nebulous and unstable "issue networks." The McConnell-Lowi image of American politics seemed obsolete or at least exaggerated.

But what followed was Mancur Olson's *The Rise and Decline of Nations*. His concern was less with how private interests corrupt democracy than with their effects on economic growth. Yet Olson's portrayal of the polity was similar to that of the earlier authors: interest-group liberalism had run rampant. Olson and the other public-choice practitioners employed a theoretical apparatus different from that of the traditional political scientists, but they arrived at an identical conclusion. Broader, more "public" interests operated at a distinct disadvantage in the policymaking process compared with more narrow private ones.

Even as Olson was formulating his analysis, a remarkable policy reversal was occurring in Washington. Regulatory agencies, many of which were either established to protect industries or eventually became captured by them, came under attack for their pro-industry, anticompetitive behavior. In several instances these attacks succeeded, and the regulated industries were vanquished under the banner of deregulation. Then, in the mid-1980s came a second remarkable turnabout: tax reform. Again, reputedly powerful and entrenched interests were defeated in their attempt to retain valuable tax subsidies. I would have been much less interested in these cases had they simply reflected the increased pluralism that began when public-interest groups and social movements confronted producers by demanding greater social regulation in the early 1970s. What intrigued me about these cases was that mass-based groups played at most a subsidiary role, and that the policy changes withdrew benefits producers already had gained from government, rather than levying new costs producers could pass on to consumers.

As important and interesting as these changes were in substantive policy terms, my interest in them lies in what they can tell us broadly about the shifting fortunes of producer groups—industries and sectors of the economy that organize to promote their interests in Washington. For at the same time that such groups were suffering these dramatic reversals of fortune, the same or similar groups were holding their own, or even gaining, in other policy areas. A study of group fortunes over time and across different policies seemed to be in order.

Hence the central questions of this study: Why do policymakers bestow benefits on these groups in some areas of public policy but refrain from doing so in others? Why are benefits given to these industries in one period but revoked at a later time? What conditions and processes shape policymakers' postures toward particular interests, and why do they sometimes change?

In addressing these questions, I argue that producer-group fortunes are not shaped so much by the groups themselves or their political activities as they are by the policymaking process, or what I call the issue and institutional contexts. The kinds of issues that become salient, how they are defined in policy debates, and the different institutional arrangements for making policy choices all have a powerful impact on group fortunes.

My vehicle for pursuing the analysis is an examination of the development of public policy in four areas: taxation, regulation, trade, and agriculture. Aside from their intrinsic importance and diversity, these are all areas where it is possible for producers to gain substantial benefits while paying little of the costs. The comparative case study approach allows me to build generalizations about the relationships among issues, institutions, interests, and policy without sacrificing the rich and nuanced insights found in single case studies.

This book is less about uncovering new facts than it is about analyzing and interpreting in a comparative framework what is known about these four policy areas. For most of these cases there already exists a voluminous literature. My use of secondary sources was supplemented by primary research that, depending on the particular case, includes roll-call data, press accounts, personal interviews, and statistical data.

For its generosity in allowing me the time to pursue this project, I thank the Russell Sage Foundation, where I spent 1990–91 freed of the usual professorial obligations. The foundation's president, Eric Wanner, along with my fellow visiting scholars, created a stimulating environment for fruitful intellectual work. I also want to acknowledge the many useful comments I received when I presented my research at Dartmouth, Massachusetts Institute of Technology, North Carolina, Syracuse, Temple and Vanderbilt. For their helpful advice after reading the manuscript, I thank Chris Bosso, Martha Derthick, and especially John Tierney. Any shortcomings that remain are exclusively my responsibility. I appreciate the attention paid to my manuscript by the Brookings publications staff. In particular, my editor, Nancy Davidson, mixed patience, encouragement, and coaxing all in their proper measure. Donna Verdier took a somewhat verbose and awkward prose and made it much less so. For their research assistance I thank Ed Muir, Steve Pirozzi, and Norberto Terrizas. David Bearce verified the manuscript for factual accuracy.

GARY MUCCIARONI

Contents

Tables

Figures

Reversals of Fortune

CHAPTER ONE

Group Fortunes and the Policymaking Process

IN THE mid-1980s, after years of bestowing ever more lucrative tax benefits on corporations and investors, the U.S. Congress reversed course, undoing much of its earlier beneficence. Until then, the curtailment of tax breaks had been considered almost as unlikely as the fall of the Soviet Union. Similarly, starting in the 1970s, industries that had previously enjoyed valuable regulatory protection from the vicissitudes of the competitive market experienced much less precipitous, but no less striking, reversals of fortune.

At the same time, and in contrast, many domestic producers found Washington increasingly receptive to their petitions for relief from foreign competition—after decades in which policymakers had labored to make the U.S. market one of the world's most open and had held firm against most entreaties for protection. Meanwhile, agricultural producers continued to harvest a bounty of subsidies—a bumper crop in the 1980s—and prevailed against efforts to remove them from the government dole.

This book examines the fluctuating fortunes of producer groups over time and across policy areas at the federal level.[1] What accounts for change and continunity in the public policy fortunes of producers? Why do policymakers in Washington give these groups particularized benefits in some areas of public policy but refrain from doing so in others? Why do they bestow such benefits in one period but revoke them sometime later? What conditions and processes shape policymakers' postures toward producer-group interests, and why do they sometimes change?

"Producer groups" are industries, firms, and occupations that provide goods and services consumed by the public. Although the size and resources of these groups vary, even the largest among them constitute only a small proportion of the overall financial assets, productive capacity, and labor force of the national economy. Yet they include some of the most highly organized and resourceful groups represented in Washington.[2]

Multiple, competing interests are a fact of modern political life, especially in a nation as large and diverse as the United States. Reflecting our various roles and affiliations, "each individual man," as Arthur F. Bentley put it, is "a component part of very many groups."[3] A fundamental, albeit crude, distinction among these interests is that some are more or less private and specific while others are more or less public and diffuse. E. E. Schattschneider, for instance, distinguished between those "common interests shared by all or by substantially all members of the community" and those special interests "shared by only a few people or a fraction of the community," which "exclude others and may be adverse to them."[4] Making public policy frequently means choosing between relatively narrow, exclusive, and private interests, on the one hand, and those that are broader, inclusive, and more public, on the other.

As consumers, we share an interest in lower prices and greater availability of goods and services. As taxpayers, we seek lower tax burdens as well as efficient provision of many public goods, such as adequate national defense and highway systems. To be sure, these collective goals call for trade-offs, and citizens are certain to disagree about which goal is more important. But the fact that common interests are shared by most members of the community alone sets them apart from the particular interests of producer groups, which seek to protect or advance their specific economic interests.[5]

The enterprises and individuals that make up producer groups do not always agree with one another, of course: owners, managers, and workers often clash over important matters. They nevertheless frequently share an interest in using governmental power and resources to promote and protect their economic destinies. The same firms that compete for customers in the marketplace often work together to gain special tax or regulatory treatment. The trade union representatives and corporate managers who struggle with each other over compensation and working conditions usually unite when seeking relief from foreign competition.

Some answers to the questions posed in this book lie in an examination of a set of policies that enable groups to engage in "rent-seeking" behavior: through government intervention, the owners of resources can command incomes higher than they could earn through a competitive market or other means.[6] Policies that promote rent-seeking make (or seem to make) a discernible trade-off between particular economic interests and those of the broader public. The benefits of these policies are perceived to be concentrated (that is, producer groups receive most of the benefits), whereas their costs are diffuse (that is, everyone or large groups in society pay most of the costs).[7] Clearly, producer groups and other narrow, highly organized groups have a strong incentive to pursue such policies, and their relatively small size and homogeneity make it easier for them to organize to do so. Their small numbers mean that the per capita benefits gained from collective action are often sizable. Conversely, the large groups that shoulder the costs of the benefits are unlikely to resist rent-seeking behavior because per capita costs are small.[8]

Efforts to contain or reduce policies that benefit producer groups, particularly those efforts undertaken since the 1970s, are the focus of this book. The core of the work is a comparative analysis of four areas in which policymakers have enacted, refrained from enacting, or revoked policies with concentrated benefits and diffuse costs: economic regulation, tax policy, agricultural subsidies, and trade protection.

Several considerations recommend the choice of these cases over others. First, each is an important area of public policy in its own right. It *matters* to both consumers and producers who pays more taxes and who pays less, whether major industries enjoy anticompetitive regulations or trade barriers that dampen competition, and what farm subsidies do to the supply and price of food. Second, although these four cases are not a representative sample of all policies, they do constitute the three major kinds of policy instruments (taxes, spending, and regulation) that any government has at its disposal.[9] Third, the chosen cases present clear distinctions between the interests of producer groups and those of the broader public.[10] Policymakers in these areas have to decide whether to adopt policies with concentrated benefits and diffuse costs; in other words, they must decide whether to redistribute billions of dollars to taxpayers and consumers or to owners, managers, and employees of particular industries and firms. Although substantively quite different, each of these policies—a tax loophole, an anticompetitive regulation, a trade barrier, a subsidy payment—affords groups the opportunity to gain substantial benefits while paying little of the cost.

A central argument of this book is that there is considerable variation over time and across policy areas in the propensity of policymakers to adopt policies with concentrated benefits and diffuse costs, that is, policies favorable to producers. These variations are at least as important as overall trends. Other observers have either ignored changes in these policies across space and time, or they have assumed that producer-group fortunes change in the same direction across all areas. Thus sweeping generalizations about the "rise and fall of special interest politics" are exaggerated.[11]

In two of the cases examined here, tax policy and anticompetitive economic regulation, producer groups were major beneficiaries of government largesse for many years after World War II, but their fortunes declined dramatically in the 1970s and 1980s, when the government adopted policy reforms meant to benefit diffuse publics. Despite their adamant and vigorous opposition to reform in most cases, the groups were unable to defend themselves against the strong challenges to the status quo launched by reform forces. A third case, trade policy, likewise demonstrates how producer-group fortunes can decline, as occurred when tariffs were reduced sharply from the mid-1930s onward and when most demands for new protection were rejected in the three decades following World War II.

That producer interests sometimes suffer reversals of fortune is less surprising, of course, when one considers that since the late 1960s public-interest groups and other citizens have challenged business and agricultural groups over environmental protection, consumerism, and civil rights; the producers often lost.[12] More recent challenges to producer interests, which are the focus of this book, differ from those earlier ones in two important ways.

First, public-interest groups and social movements have played only a minor role. The key battle lines have been drawn not between producer groups and mass-based groups in society but instead between producers and government. The subsidies and protections from the market that are granted to producers appear more and more problematic to those in public authority. The claims that producers make complicate the efforts of public officials to govern (and, ultimately, to stay in power). Officials do not necessarily feel pressure from the public to curtail policies that benefit producers, but producers' claims make it more difficult to grapple with two sets of problems.[13] One set has to do with managing the public household: getting government costs under control in an age of resource tempting to account for how virtually all policy choices are made, no matter how much their particular political and institutional contexts vary, they are pitched at too high a level of analysis. They can therefore "explain" why producer-group fortunes are either rising, declining, or remaining the same, but as James Q. Wilson has argued in the context of regulation, "A single-explanation theory of regulatory politics is about as helpful as a single explanation of politics generally. . . . Distinctions must be made, differences examined."[19] Instead of general models, analytical tools are needed to distinguish and isolate the critical variables that account for different outcomes. The garbage-can model, for instance, cannot by itself predict what kinds of problems are likely to be coupled with what kinds of solutions or, consequently, what kinds of political conditions make it likely that producer-group fortunes will decline (or rise). What is needed are specific propositions or hypotheses that logically relate issues to solutions and to political and institutional conditions.

At the other end of the analytical spectrum are myriad richly detailed case studies, some of which offer insightful speculation on the generalizability of their findings and conclusions. Whereas the general models of policymaking try to explain too much, studies of single cases are limited by a lack of systematic comparison with other cases. Without explicit comparison with other cases, it is difficult to determine whether the descriptions and explanations these studies offer apply to more than one case.

Take, for example, Christopher J. Bosso's excellent study of the politics of pesticides policy.[20] Bosso analyzes the transformation of this arena from a classic "subgovernment" dominated by producer groups to a much more permeable, pluralistic, and competitive "issue network."[21] The chemical industry, agricultural producers, and their allies in government—once guaranteed mild and self-serving regulation of pesticides—were challenged by environmental and health interests and a variety of other outsiders in Congress and in the bureaucracy, beginning in the 1970s. The result was a new pesticides policy that, more than ever before, balanced competing interests. Bosso weaves together an explanation that includes a proliferation of scientific information about the hazards of pesticide use and its impact on a public previously unaffected by or unaware of the consequences of pesticides; the mobilization of new interests in response to an upsurge in participation on the part of a "post-materialist" generation as well as to the dissemination of information;

and the institutional reforms, particularly in Congress, that have made policymaking more open and unstable.

Bosso's analysis raises a host of questions: Do producer-group interests have an advantage in policy areas in which scientific knowledge is less relevant or central to agenda setting and policymaking? Can producers thrive outside the protection of the subgovernment structure? Did congressional reforms similarly affect other policy areas, with similar consequences for producer-group fortunes? How critical for producers' fortunes is the mobilization of an organized opposition? In short, how generalizable are Bosso's findings?

What this book seeks to establish are middle-level generalizations about the relationships among interests, issues, institutions, and public policies. Rather than try to explain the entire public policy universe, this work focuses on explaining variations in policymakers' propensity to enact policies with concentrated costs and diffuse benefits. The set of cases analyzed here includes ones in which producers' fortunes are rising, declining, or remaining the same. The limited number of cases and the variety of outcomes permit the development of rich, nuanced insights that are the strength of detailed case studies as well as valid generalizations that help to explain variations observed in policymakers' responses to group interests.

The comparative case-study approach employed here has most often been used to construct typologies of different policies.[22] Perhaps the most important contribution of these typologies has been to show how policies determine politics, and not only the reverse, since certain properties of different policies (for example, how their benefits and costs are distributed or perceived) determine the kinds of actors and coalitions that join the political conflict. The next step, however, is to try to explain how and why some policymaking arenas change—becoming conducive to new patterns of politics and new policies—and why others stay the same for long periods. Policies of benefit to producer groups reflect what Wilson calls client politics and what Theodore J. Lowi calls distributive policy,[23] but the questions remain: What makes these policies undergo transformations, and why do they sometimes continue unchanged?

The Analysis in Brief

Variations in policies—and therefore in the fortunes of producer groups—over time and across policy areas are not random outcomes.

Rather, they reflect a predictable logic that emerges from analysis of two broad categories, or contexts, of policymaking: the kinds of issues that become salient in the political arena and how those issues are defined, and the capacities, incentives, and behavior of key institutional actors in government.[24]

The *issue context* has to do with the agenda-setting stage of the policymaking process, when certain issues are seriously considered within government and other issues are ignored or given little attention. The issue context, in which perceptions of producer groups and their claims are established in the minds of policymakers, is shaped by short- and long-term economic conditions experienced by producers and previous policy choices and their consequences, as well as by historically and culturally rooted predispositions toward producers and their policies.[25]

The *institutional context* is concerned with what occurs after an issue reaches the agenda. Cases examined for this book show that institutional arrangements, capacities, and incentives prevalent in the policy arena determine policymakers' disposition of agenda items, whether favorable for producer groups or not. Most important, producer-group fortunes are much more likely to decline when institutional leaders are actively committed to resisting policies with concentrated benefits and diffuse costs. Leaders' decisions about whether to resist or challenge such policies depend upon their calculations of the likelihood that their challenge to the groups will succeed and upon the magnitude of the expected payoff (in terms of some long-term political goal), given limited political resources and whatever opportunity costs are entailed. In addition, policy arenas that are centered in the executive branch, feature greater bureaucratic autonomy, and come under the jurisdiction of nonconstituency-oriented committees in Congress are also less advantageous for producer interests than those that are otherwise.[26]

Nothing guarantees that the issue and institutional contexts will be synchronized for favorable (or unfavorable) outcomes for producer interests. A highly favorable issue context may encounter an institutional context that is not, or vice versa. Issues change without lockstep changes in institutional actors or arrangements. Institutional arrangements established to address one kind of issue often persist long after new issues have entered the agenda. Occasionally a major shift in a particular issue context produces a shift or reform in the corresponding institutional arena, but institutions generally evolve over time without regard to change in any particular issue context. Such lags and disjunctures give rise to a more rich and complicated pattern of producer-group fortunes than can be captured by simple dichotomies like whether fortunes are rising or declining.

The Issue Context

Two assumptions about producer-group interests are common but fallacious. The first is that there is inevitably a zero-sum relationship between the interests of producers and those of the broader public, and that consequently policies with concentrated costs and diffuse benefits entail sacrificing the broad public interest to private interests. The second assumption is that those seeking to advance producer-group interests succeed by their sheer political and organizational advantages—that is, their superior ability vis-à-vis large publics to organize, to engage in collective action, and to mobilize resources (such as expertise, campaign contributions, and votes) in order to reward their friends in government and punish their enemies.

Either or both of these assumptions may be valid some of the time, but neither captures the full interplay of the political process. First, it is quite possible for the pursuit of producer interests to be consonant with that of some broader public interest. At the very least, it is possible for the producer interests to be perceived as consistent with those of the public ones. Indeed, at the core of many policy debates over whether to adopt policies with concentrated benefits and diffuse costs is a genuine argument about whether policies that clearly serve producer groups will also serve the public interest. What counts as the public interest and whether it can be reconciled with or advanced by benefiting private interests are themselves politically and intellectually contested questions. Second, raw political pressure may often matter less in the resolution of the debate than the ability of one side or another to influence the perceptions of the nature of a public issue, the legitimacy of the groups and their claims, and the consequences that might be expected from providing (or denying) benefits to producers. "Persuasiveness," it has been argued, "is the most underrated political resource."[27]

Policies pursued for the seemingly exclusive benefit of particular groups can be sustained, usually, only if they receive broad support (or at least acquiescence) from policymakers and the public. "A political conflict among special interests is never restricted to the groups most immediately interested," argued Schattschneider. "Instead, it is an appeal . . . for the support of vast numbers of people who are sufficiently remote to have a somewhat different perspective on the controversy."[28] Producer groups succeed when they convert their special-interest claims into convincing public-interest arguments. Not only do such policies often tap widely shared values in American society, but they must continue to do so to ensure their long-term survival.

In some cases this consensus rests upon equity considerations, as when the group seeking benefits is deemed "deserving." It is not a coincidence, for instance, that trade protection has increased just as the perception (whether accurate or not) has grown widespread that American industry is the victim of unfair foreign competition and that those bearing the costs of economic dislocation should be compensated and given time to readjust to economic changes. Similarly, it is unlikely that the subsidy budget for farmers would have grown so rapidly in the 1980s if the family farmer had been perceived as a rich, undeserving corporation or a lazy "welfare cheat." Industries seeking regulatory or tax advantages may argue that other industries, no more important to the economy than theirs, receive favorable treatment. Or, like farmers, they may plead "special circumstances," such as exposure to the unusually high risks of work in the natural environment.

In other cases, policies of direct benefit to producers may be perceived as producing secondary benefits that are spread widely throughout society. Tax incentives were defended for many years on the grounds that the jobs and incomes they would generate would stimulate the economy,[29] just as economic regulation was often justified in terms of nurturing infant industries critical to the nation's interest or protecting consumers and small firms from monopolies and chaotic markets. Similarly, agricultural producers point to the paramount importance of a dependable food supply and the reputation of American agriculture as the most productive in the world. In all these instances, the group portrays itself as a kind of conduit through which worthy economic and social goals can be achieved. Hence producer groups and their allies claim the need for inducements on the grounds that some broader public interest will be served—that is, the benefit produced will be more diffuse.

Issue context, then, refers to the kinds of problems that become salient and to how those problems get defined. *Issue salience* means the degree to which people are aware of a problem and care about it. *Issue definitions* refer to the meanings and interpretations people attach to problems.[30] The issue context is critical for determining producer-group fortunes because within it the perceptions of the groups and the legitimacy of their claims are established. In some contexts participants in the policymaking process will perceive producer groups positively, as advancing legitimate claims in accord with some public interest. In others they will see them negatively, judging their claims to be illegitimate and inimical to the public interest.

An issue context unfavorable to producers or to the policies that benefit them increases producers' vulnerability to attempts to reduce benefits and makes it more difficult for benefits to rise. Conversely, an issue context favorable to the groups or to their policies makes it easier to increase benefits and virtually ensures that efforts to reduce benefits will be defeated or perhaps not even attempted.

Schattschneider stated that "political conflict is not like an intercollegiate debate in which the opponents agree in advance on a definition of the issues. . . . The antagonists can rarely agree on what the issues are because power is involved in the definition."[31] Just as producers and their allies will frame issues in terms of the dire need for an inducement or compensation, producers' opponents will attempt to define the issue in terms of the lack of need for inducements, the diffuse costs that society will bear, and the effects on equity for citizens generally. Whose issues and issue definitions will gain greater currency, and thus become the prevailing perception of producer groups and their claims, depends on a variety of factors, including objective events and trends as well as the subjective predispositions of political actors. Not only do objective and subjective influences change over time, but also the perceptions that they give rise to are somewhat malleable.

Certainly among the most important influences are economic conditions. David Vogel has argued that national economic trends affect the political fortunes of business interests. When conditions are adverse, producer-group fortunes rise as policymakers and the public become more concerned about the plight of business.[32] Yet general economic trends may have differential effects across policy areas, helping producers in one area but hurting them in others. Likewise, just as important as national economic conditions may be those experienced by particular sectors that are represented by producer groups.

Policies benefiting particular producer groups are much more difficult to resist or reduce when those groups are experiencing economic distress. Distress does not guarantee that producers' fortunes will rise or that they will avoid decline; it does, however, make such outcomes more likely.

When groups are seen as hapless victims of economic misfortune, a presumption of need is established that is not accorded producer groups in healthy economic sectors. For instance, the claims of farm groups and many domestic industries have been regarded as legitimate, for the most part, because these groups are perceived as victims of economic forces beyond their control. The economic crisis in agriculture helped immunize farm groups from pressures to cut subsidies throughout the 1980s, just as the increasing penetration of domestic markets, a strong dollar, and unfair trade barriers erected by foreign competitors lent urgency to demands for protectionism in that decade. Similarly, the great growth in tax expenditures for industry that occurred from the early 1970s to the early 1980s coincided with heightened concern about the performance of American business. While scores of industries lost benefits under tax reform in 1986, oil and gas interests escaped nearly unscathed because the energy industry was in deep trouble at that time.

Groups may be accorded a presumption of need if they are suffering from short-term economic distress or long-term structural decline. Those in the latter category, however, will be hard-pressed to justify continuation of policies that are judged to be ineffective or unfair. Declining industries being beaten by foreign competition may be able to make the case that trade protection will give them the breathing room they need to restructure and reinvest, but they may be less persuasive if they demand the retention of tax incentives that for years have failed to make them more competitive.[33]

In contrast to industries experiencing economic problems, those that enjoy relative prosperity are accorded no presumption of need. They may even be perceived as victimizers if their good fortune apparently comes at the expense of consumers and taxpayers. Regulated industries and those that received tax benefits were perceived as privileged, greedy interests when regulation and the growth of tax expenditures came to be seen as contributors to the diffuse financial burdens of the American public. Regulation and tax policy were implicated in the financial squeeze caused by inflation, taxes, and stagnant real incomes. By the mid-1980s the U.S. economy was in the midst of its longest peacetime boom in decades. Attention shifted from the need of business to invest in the economy to the inequity of a tax system that allowed many profitable companies to escape paying their fair share. In short, the hypothesis is that the public policy fortunes of producer groups are inversely related to their economic fortunes.

The kinds of policies that are already in place (or not in place) also will affect policymakers' estimations of whether economic distress justifies increasing, or at least maintaining, benefits. Previous policy choices, their consequences, and the ideas that they embody shape the issue context, too, as discussed above regarding industries' efforts to preserve tax incentives that did not produce their intended policy objectives. Experience with the Smoot-Hawley law of the 1930s, whose tariffs were eventually faulted for worsening the Great Depression, led to widespread support for free trade and to resistance against protectionist pressures for many decades. Scandalous reports of profitable corporations paying little or no taxes followed the great growth in tax loopholes in the early 1980s under the Economic Recovery Tax Act of 1981, which lent credence and visibility to the criticism that the income tax had become unfair; producer groups thus were put in a vulnerable position. Farm programs also came under greater scrutiny in the 1980s when their costs skyrocketed, mostly because the entitlement features of the programs in place automatically led to cost escalations with bumper crop yields and falling market prices. In addition, because the amount of subsidy received by each farm is tied to its level of production—with the largest farms receiving the bulk of subsidies—farm programs came to be seen as highly inequitable. On the other hand, by 1990 the urgency to reduce subsidies substantially was dampened by incremental reforms in the 1985 farm law that reduced the cost of farm subsidies in the latter part of the decade.

Objective trends and events do not strictly determine the issue context, however. Because such things as economic conditions and the effects of previous policy choices are frequently complex and ambiguous, political actors can, within limits, read into them what they wish and choose which aspects of reality comport best with their political objectives. Public officials, experts, journalists, and interest-group representatives all choose which issues to push and dramatize, deploying resources and pursuing strategies that advance their preferred definitions. Industries that benefited from regulation were threatened only when reformers gleaned mounting empirical evidence that showed the costs of regulation and the benefits that could accrue from deregulation, and only then when they linked their solution to problems such as inflation and the energy crisis. By the same token, the mass media helped create positive perceptions of farm interests by choosing to dramatize the plight of family farmers while largely ignoring the issue of the cost and inequitable distribution of farm subsidies.

Perceptions of groups as conduits to promote a diffuse societal interest, victims of maltreatment and impersonal market forces, or victimizers of the public are created through politics, as participants in the political process create and reshape perceptions by stressing certain issues and issue definitions rather than others. The so-called facts are constantly reinterpreted, selectively highlighted, or completely ignored by contenders in the political arena who seek to persuade the public and one another that the issue or issue definition they champion is the most valid and important one.

Therefore it should not be surprising that, although changes in objective conditions correspond proximately to changes in the salience and definitions of issues, the correspondence is not precise. This is particularly the case concerning the timing of what goes on and off the issue agenda. For example, in the second half of the 1980s the trade deficit shrank, economic growth was strong, and other economic indicators signaled a brighter picture for U.S. exporters, but the issue context continued to be as hospitable to industries complaining of unfair competition from abroad as it had been earlier in the decade, when economic conditions were much less favorable.

Another reason for looking beyond objective conditions in seeking to understand how the issue context is shaped is the fact that longstanding myths and symbols sometimes bolster (and sometimes undermine) perceptions of groups and their claims. For instance, farm interests often tap the agrarian myth of a virtuous yeomanry that valiantly struggles against natural disasters and economic exploitation. Industries seeking trade protection invoke patriotism and perhaps veiled appeals to xenophobic impulses. Those seeking tax benefits inveigh against high taxes and portray industry as the source of the nation's wealth and material progress. Advocates of tax reform and deregulation depict the political process as a battle between average American taxpayers and consumers and selfish, powerful, "big business" lobbyists wearing Gucci loafers.

In all of these cases, symbols and images rooted in history and culture and transmitted through the mass media were manipulated to raise the salience of particular issues and issue definitions. Hence perceptions are partially subjective and malleable. As Bosso puts it, "Problems are artificialities, defined through decidedly subjective interpretations of real-world conditions. A condition does not produce 'a problem' but a whole host of *possibilities* awaiting someone's perceptual linkages."[34]

Changes in the issue context directly and significantly affect the kinds of coalitions that emerge in the policy arena. In issue contexts that are unfavorable to producer groups, opposing coalitions will emerge and perhaps flourish. Conversely, favorable contexts work to strengthen producer-group coalitions and their claims.

Political parties serve as key instruments for building coalitions, and a long-standing maxim of political science is that where interest groups are strong, political parties are weak, and vice versa.[35] According to Mancur Olson, groups that are large and inclusive ("encompassing") have different incentives than ones that are small and exclusive. It is rational for smaller groups to push for policies that grant them most of the benefits and impose most of the costs on others. On the other hand, larger groups (approaching the size of society as a whole) have an incentive to avoid such policies and to push instead for those that more equally distribute costs and benefits. Since political parties, particularly party leaders, seek to represent large constituencies with diffuse interests, they have incentives to appeal to that broader, more inclusive national audience. Competition between two parties should encourage both to expand the scope of conflict to capture the support of a majority of voters.[36] Consequently parties, unlike producer groups, have to be concerned with the aggregate national consequences of the policies they propose.[37]

The most prevalent and effective coalitions that emerge to oppose policies benefiting producer groups are bipartisan, including both Republicans and Democrats, liberals and conservatives, and the executive and legislative branches of government. These coalitions are much looser and less permanent than disciplined party majorities found in parliamentary systems, but they are effective nonetheless. Although it is theoretically possible for a single party to offer effective resistance to producer interests, bipartisan coalitions are more likely to emerge and they stand a greater chance of success. First, the separation of powers, weak party discipline, and, often, divided party control of the legislative and executive branches of government make it very difficult for single-party majorities to govern in the United States. Second, producer groups and their allies frequently seek the support of both parties by, for example, making campaign contributions to incumbent officeholders, be they Democrats or Republicans. For most of these groups ideology and partisanship (if they figure at all) are subordinated to pursuit of material benefits from those in power, regardless of party. Because lobbying activity is nonpartisan, so to speak, producers' opponents also will seek a broad coalition. Third, it makes sense for opponents of producers to build a highly inclusive coalition because such coalitions have an incentive to resist policies that benefit narrow groups at society's expense.

A broad, bipartisan coalition was at the heart of resistance to demands for trade protection in the decades following World War II. American presidents of both parties supported free trade, as did bipartisan majorities in Congress. The leading champions of deregulation were liberal Democratic Senator Ted Kennedy and conservative Republican President Gerald Ford. Nor could tax reform have been accomplished without support from both sides of the political spectrum and both branches of government. Tax reform was backed by conservative Republicans like Ronald Reagan and Representative Jack Kemp as well as by Democrats like Senator Bill Bradley and the labor union–funded Citizens for Tax Justice.

There is no guarantee, however, that political parties will always defend diffuse interests against those of producer groups. Groups' benefits can rise or be maintained when parties are largely irrelevant in a policy arena; when producer groups are able to maintain close links with one of the two parties; or when the two parties compete with each other to gain the support of the groups. Economic regulation persisted for many years, in part because most Democrats and Republicans paid little attention to it and in part because some Democrats wanted the support of the regulated industries or continued to believe in regulation as a sound policy idea. Farm interests continue to receive the support of most House Democrats, and in the Senate they receive substantial support from both parties. The erosion of resistance to trade protection is centered among congressional Democrats, many of whom have abandoned their commitment to free trade in response to pressures from domestic industries and organized labor.

When both parties respond favorably to the interests of producer groups, resistance thoroughly breaks down, paving the way for a rise in the fortunes of producer groups. The most vivid example is the accelerated growth of tax expenditures from the early 1970s to the early 1980s, which reached a crescendo in 1981 when Democrats and Republicans in the administration and in Congress bid against each other to see which party could be more generous to those seeking benefits. In the Senate (where party competition for control of the chamber is keen and where rural interests are overrepresented), support for the rise in farm subsidy payments also was bipartisan. Certain trade protection episodes demonstrate this pattern as well.

These coalitions emerge and break down at two levels: ideas and partisan electoral strategy. Traditional Democratic, liberal support for regulation was based on the notion that the public needed to be protected against monopolies and the chaos of unregulated markets. This support eroded when it became apparent that regulatory agencies were often captured by industry and that deregulation was an issue that could be used to appeal to the consumer movement of the 1970s. Traditional Republican, conservative support for tax incentives was grounded in the idea that they would provide added resources for business investment (capital formation) and that the tax code could be used to provide for social needs (for example, health insurance) that would otherwise drain government resources. These ideas were supplanted by supply-side economic theory, which rejected capital formation and social engineering as rationales for tax incentives. By eliminating tax incentives and using the savings to cut tax rates for taxpayers as a whole, conservatives sought to appeal to voters as a diffuse group rather than to satisfy their corporate constituents.

By the same token, bipartisan support for free trade has broken down as (mainly) Democrats have embraced fair trade as a new policy rationale and as they seek to appeal to workers in specific industries displaced by international competition. A strong bipartisan coalition in favor of reducing farm subsidies has yet to emerge, because many Democrats continue to believe that subsidies are needed to protect farmers and because most Democrats continue to pursue an electoral strategy of appealing to farm interests and the groups allied with them.

The Institutional Context

Institutions are a staple of political analysis, including studies of public policy, and they have become all the more so with their recent "rediscovery."[38] There are many examples of institutional arrangements and actors initiating, facilitating, modifying, and blocking policy changes. Certain institutional arrangements and actors will be more likely than others to resist or challenge demands for policies with concentrated benefits and diffuse costs.

EXECUTIVE BRANCH AUTONOMY. First, the absence of or reduction in such policies is associated with bureaucratic autonomy.[39] This refers to the degree to which policymaking authority is lodged in the executive branch and to which executive agencies have incentives and capacities for resisting and challenging producer groups. Bureaucracies have a great advantage in challenging producer interests for the obvious reason that, unlike elected officials, bureaucrats are not subject to the immediate threat of being removed from office by disgruntled constituencies. Furthermore, the formal structure and organizational missions of bureaucratic agencies may give them both the autonomy and the capacity to pursue courses of action that are adverse to producer groups.

The independent status of regulatory commissions and the broad, flexible mandates they have to regulate in the public interest enabled pro-reform commissioners to undertake deregulation. Although it was impossible to accomplish tax reform administratively, the Treasury Department played a major role in getting the issue on the agenda. Treasury's mission, to guard the revenue base, is consistent with reform. By contrast, the Department of Agriculture historically has been a constituency-oriented agency, explicitly established to advance the economic interests of farm producers. There has been little push for reform from the department's professional staff, as evidenced by its absence from the reform battles of the 1980s. In the case of trade policy, Congress assigned to the executive branch several decades ago the authority to grant or withhold relief, precisely to shield itself from protectionist pressures. Trade protection can be granted only if the executive branch finds, through a structured process of fact-finding and adjudication, that certain conditions exist to justify relief. But in more recent legislation Congress has changed this process in ways that make it more difficult for the executive branch to withhold relief from petitioners.

This does not mean that relatively autonomous agencies will always oppose policies with concentrated benefits and diffuse costs or that bureaucratic opposition will always result in the defeat of those policies. It does mean, however, that wherever we find effective governmental resistance to such policies, we should find bureaucrats playing an important role in bringing it about.

STRONG CONGRESSIONAL COMMITTEES. Second, resistance to policies benefiting producers is associated with policies that come under the jurisdiction of "policy" or "prestige" committees in Congress—that is, committees that attract members whose primary goal is making "good" public policy or gaining influence with their colleagues rather than providing constituency service.[40] Tax reform and deregulation were undertaken by committees that do not exist exclusively, or even primarily, for gaining their members' reelection. By contrast, the dominant goal of members of the agriculture committees is to enhance their chances for reelection by promoting the interests of their rural constituents.

As with the bureaucracy, this does not mean that policy or prestige committees always resist policies that benefit producers or that such resistance will result in their defeat. The House Ways and Means Committee and Senate Finance Committee were the source of the growth of tax expenditures; the Senate and House Commerce committees were hardly unfriendly to the regulated industries for many years. It only means that nonconstituency-oriented committees have the potential for resisting or reversing producer-group policies when other conditions in the arena are hospitable to that course.

One condition, of course, is the issue context. An issue context that is unfavorable to producer interests should embolden these committees to resist and challenge producers and make it easier for them to succeed in doing so. The capacity of institutions to resist and challenge producers also varies over time (although, obviously, more slowly and less frequently than do issues). Committee rules and procedures, membership, and leadership, as well as relations between committees and the parent chamber, shift over time. To the extent that these shifts increase the autonomy and respect given to committees, the capacity to resist and challenge producers should increase accordingly.

STRONG, COMMITTED LEADERSHIP. Perhaps the greatest institutional bulwark against policies that benefit producers is active and committed leadership in defense of diffuse publics perceived to be injured by the claims of producer groups. Without the resolve of the president, heads of executive agencies, and key legislators, producer interests cannot be successfully resisted or challenged. The personal skills and devotion of leaders is especially critical in the U.S. policymaking process because the institutional constraints on central authorities are comparatively great. Presidents, for instance, do not enjoy the luxury of party discipline in Congress, the parliamentary fusion of legislative and executive leadership, or necessarily the allegiance of the bureaucracy.

It was leaders like Presidents Gerald Ford, Jimmy Carter, and Ronald Reagan and former Ways and Means Committee chairman Dan Rostenkowski who pushed and persuaded reluctant majorities in Congress to address tax reform and deregulation and to approve the measures. It was they who put the producer groups under stress and on the defensive, breaking down their internal cohesion. It is leaders, primarily in the executive branch, who have been among the greatest proponents of free trade and the shepherds of legislation to negotiate and conclude tra'e agreements with other nations. Not all of these individuals hold formal leadership positions, but those who have not yet attained that status often aspire to it. Tax reform and deregulation reached the agenda through the efforts of Senators Bradley and Kennedy and Representative Jack Kemp and other legislative entrepreneurs who adopted these issues to appeal to broad national audiences.

Leaders have a greater capacity and stronger incentives than others to champion reforms that benefit diffuse interests over special interests for several reasons. They are better positioned to resist group pressures because they are more insulated than other officials. Access to the president is limited, committee chairmen enjoy seniority and safe seats, and heads of executive agencies need not worry about reelection.

They also have resources at their disposal that nonleaders rarely have, such as greater access to the mass media, control over procedures, the wherewithal to grant and withhold favors, and, in the case of the president, high symbolic status. In the hands of a skilled president, the symbolism of office can build support based upon emotion and widely shared values like patriotism. Access to the media provides the opportunity to shape the agenda by raising the salience of certain issues and issue definitions. Control over procedure allows leaders to influence which alternatives will be debated, the order in which they will be considered, and the timing of decisions. Control over appointments to the executive branch, assignments to legislative committees, and other rewards and penalties can be used to influence nonleaders and build coalitions in favor of diffuse interests.

Moreover, leaders' actions are more visible and in many cases their constituencies are larger than those of nonleaders. Well-organized and relatively narrow interests—producer groups, for example—will have more influence in smaller jurisdictions than in larger ones, where their influence is likely to be diluted and counterbalanced. The president and party leaders may be expected to direct their reelection appeals to broad, national audiences, because those leaders represent broad, inclusive interests.[41] Thus, unlike interest-group politics, presidential and party politics tend to expand the scope of conflict beyond the exclusive control of producers.

Leaders also seek to gain the respect of colleagues and other elites who expect them to act responsibly (that is, to take broad and long-term perspectives on policy issues) and to be skilled and effective. Defeating reputedly powerful interests is one way for leaders to gain respect, because doing so demonstrates skill and effectiveness, which enhances their reputations as influential players in Washington. At the same time, producer interests present leaders with a major test of their influence and their commitment to broad public interests. Meeting and topping challenges posed by other leaders—in other words, imitating and competing—are other incentives prompting leaders to work for reform.[42]

Not all leaders at all times will choose to champion diffuse over specific interests, of course, but they are more likely to do so than nonleaders, and their support is necessary (although not sufficient) for successfully resisting policies with concentrated benefits and diffuse costs. Some producer interests in Congress or in the party may be so critical and powerful that a leader must compromise with them. Or leaders may simply pursue a coalition-building strategy of gaining support from multiple specific producers. But since concessions to specific interests entail diffuse costs, such a strategy is almost certain to be less attractive than one that appeals to the diffuse interests of the general public. Satisfying citizens or failing to satisfy them is, after all, what will make or break national leadership.

Under what conditions will leaders become actively committed to resisting or challenging policies benefiting producers? Leaders must choose carefully, calculating which challenges offer the best chances of success and which ones offer the greatest payoff in terms of achieving some goal (such as influencing colleagues or making good policy). A challenge must be deemed both feasible and worthwhile as an investment of scarce political resources, given the potential payoff and the opportunity costs from forgoing investment in other political contests from which they might also reap rewards. Leaders will take into account, first of all, the issue context. A context that creates positive perceptions of producer groups will deter leaders from mounting a challenge because they realize that the chances for success are reduced and the risks of political injury to themselves are increased. One of the main reasons for the lack of reform leadership in agriculture, for instance, is the salience of the prolonged farm crisis and the sympathy that was evoked for the plight of farmers. These circumstances were likely to deter potential reform leaders who understood that the chances of achieving reform would be slim and the risks of a political backlash great.

The intensity of leaders' commitment to challenging producer groups also varies with features of the policies themselves. Taxation and regulation constitute major functions of government. Along with international trade negotiations, these policy instruments have distributive impacts that cut across several economic sectors and greatly affect the performance of the national economy. By contrast, because farm policy is sector-specific, it is hived-off from the central concerns of the president, congressional leaders, and Congress as a whole. In addition, unlike most tax expenditures and regulations, the cost (and thus salience) of farm subsidies rises when farmers experience economic distress (with the attendant sympathy for farmers blunting efforts directed at reducing subsidies). As the farm economy improves, the cost of subsidies declines, and thus so does the urgency to launch reforms. Leaders do not face such a constraint in the other policy areas.

Trade and agriculture have international dimensions that may either constrain or enhance policymakers' capacity to resist producer interests. American agriculture and many other industries point to the supposed unfair advantages enjoyed by their foreign competitors, such as trade barriers that keep out U.S. products and subsidies that foreign governments provide to their firms. American farmers argue that giving up their own subsidies without comparable concessions from producers abroad amounts to "unilateral disarmament." The Reagan and Bush administrations hoped to buy political support for cutting subsidies by promising American farmers greater access to export markets. Efforts to negotiate reductions in European and Japanese barriers to American farm commodities have failed, however. On the other hand, President Bill Clinton helped gain adoption of the North American Free Trade Agreement over the objections of organized labor by defining NAFTA as a foreign-policy issue.

Issues, Institutions, and Policy Fortunes

Chapters 2, 3, and 4 provide data on trends in benefit levels for tax expenditures, trade barriers, and agricultural subsidies.[43] These trends—

that is, rises, declines, or standstills in benefit levels—reveal much about the propensity, over time, of policymakers to adopt policies with concentrated benefits and diffuse costs. They tell only part of the story, however. It is also important to examine actual policy decisions, including decisions to do nothing, because looking only at benefit levels may mask as much as it reveals about trends in producer-group fortunes. For example, benefit levels may indicate that certain producers maintained the same level of benefits over a ten-year period. However, over that same period, attempts to reduce benefits may have failed. Examining what did *not* happen, then, tells more about producer-group fortunes than do benefit trend lines by themselves. Hence periods of benefit maintenance denote times when efforts to reduce benefits reached the agenda but failed to gain adoption as well as times when benefit levels simply remained unchallenged and unchanged.

Conversely, it is quite possible for rising benefit levels to mask a significant degree of resistance to such policies. For example, even when the issue context is hospitable to major rises in producers' benefits, sufficiently strong resistance by institutional actors may result in only modest rises. In such instances policy fortunes are best described as contained rather than rising. Containment therefore denotes periods in which benefits rise only incrementally but significant rises fail to materialize.

Figure 1-1 shows how different combinations (variations) of issue and institutional contexts produce different policy outcomes (that is, producer-group fortunes that *rise*, *decline*, are *contained*, or are *maintained*). When the issue context favors producers, and institutional actors' commitment to resisting or challenging producer groups is low, the political climate is ripe for group fortunes to rise. Rising fortunes were typical, for instance, in tax policy during the 1970s, in anticompetitive regulation before the 1970s, and in agriculture in the 1980s.[44] At the opposite extreme, when the issue context favors producers' opponents and institutional actors' commitment to resisting or challenging groups is high, producer-group fortunes should decline.[45] Examples here include tax reform in the 1980s, deregulation in the 1970s, and trade policy from the end of World War II to the 1970s.

When the issue context favors producers but institutional actors are committed to challenging policies of benefit to producers, producers' fortunes are contained. The major case here is trade policy from the 1970s to the present. Finally, when the issue context favors producers' opponents but institutional actors' commitment to reducing benefits is

Figure 1-1. *Issues, Institutions, and Producer-Group Fortunes*

Institutional actors' commitment to resisting or to challenging groups

	High	Low
Producers	*Fortunes contained* Trade protection (1970s to present)	*Fortunes rose* Tax expenditures (before 1982) Agricultural subsidies (1980s) Anticompetitive regulations (before 1970s)
Producers' opponents	*Fortunes declined* Tax expenditures (1980s) Trade protection (before 1970s) Anticompetitive regulations (1970s)	*Fortunes maintained* Agricultural subsidies (1990s)

Favored by
issue context

low, groups are able to maintain their benefits. In these instances, the issue context works against rises in benefits and provides opportunities for reducing benefits, but institutional actors do not muster a sufficiently strong attack on producer interests. Agricultural policy in the 1990s is the example.

Organization of the Book

The chapters that follow explore in some depth each of the four types of policy outcomes. Chapter 2 examines the transition from rising group fortunes in the tax arena to a dramatic decline in such fortunes in the 1980s. Similarly, the fortunes of groups benefiting from anticompetitive regulation rose for decades until their dramatic decline in the 1970s. Trade policy, discussed in chapter 3, is more complicated than the other three cases. Protectionism declined in the postwar era but began to rise gradually during the last twenty years as resistance to it eroded, yet the recent increase in protection has been more modest (that is, contained) than changed economic and political circumstances might have produced.

The rise and then maintenance of programs benefiting farm producers is the topic of chapter 4.

An obvious alternative to the analysis presented here would be one that focused on the producer groups themselves. Perhaps group fortunes vary with the levels of mobilization of the groups, with some producer groups better equipped to promote and defend their interests than others. Group-based explanations of politics do, after all, have a long and venerable tradition. According to this perspective, government tends to enact (and maintain) policies with concentrated benefits and diffuse costs when the level of pressure from producers rises; government tends to avoid such policies (or revoke them) when the pressure subsides or disappears.[46] Other aspects of groups may be as important as well in determining their political effectiveness—their resources, size and organizational characteristics, and ability to build alliances with other groups—and consequently, their policy fortunes.

To wholly substitute such an explanation for the one presented here, however, would require some dubious assumptions about policymaking. Policymaking institutions would be reduced to a black box, and public policies would merely reflect the degree of pressure being exerted by organized interests. How institutional structures shape and channel demands, how policymakers bring their independent judgments to bear on policy issues, and how actors and forces other than groups influence policymakers would all have to be ignored.[47]

Of course, producer-group characteristics and behavior do shed some important light on the outcomes in the four policy areas, as discussed in chapter 5. Nevertheless, the contention in this book is that we learn more about the political fortunes of interest groups by looking at the policymaking process in which they must operate than by looking at the groups themselves. It should also be kept in mind that a group-based explanation and one stressing issue and institutional dynamics are not mutually exclusive. The former, however, should be viewed as an adjunct rather than an alternative to the explanation developed in chapters 1 through 4.

Finally, and perhaps most important, producer-group influence is *contingent* rather than automatic. Although it certainly may help groups if they are mobilized, resourceful, and have other advantages, there is no guarantee that these attributes will translate into rising fortunes or success at staving off declines. By the same token, groups that are less mobilized or resourceful will not necessarily see their fortunes decline or fail to see them rise. Specifically, different issue contexts and institutional arrangements can either facilitate or impede groups' activities and influence in the policymaking process.

Chapter 6 summarizes the findings from the earlier chapters, explores the relative importance of the issue and institutional contexts, and discusses the linkages between them. It goes on to discuss how the findings regarding institutions relate to recent work on the "rediscovery of institutions" in the political science literature. It cautions against adopting institutionally determinist explanations for public policy outcomes, stressing the contingent nature of their impacts instead. The chapter concludes with a discussion of the broader implications of the book's findings for national politics. It argues that neopluralist images of contemporary American politics—which lament the inability of Washington to come to a consensus on major national issues and achieve closure— appear exaggerated.

CHAPTER TWO

Tax Expenditures and Anticompetitive Regulation

FEDERAL TAX and regulatory authority offer producer groups ample opportunities to secure a bounty of economic benefits. Tax expenditures—the fiscal equivalent of spending programs—reduce the amount of income taxes industries and individuals owe the government and provide incentives for investing in particular kinds of economic activities.[1] They include revenue lost because of tax law provisions that allow a special exclusion, exemption, or deduction from gross income or that provide a credit, preferential rate, or deferral of tax liability. Congress legislates these provisions to give tax relief to constituents and to achieve various social objectives. The American middle class is the intended beneficiary of many of the most important provisions (for example, deductions for interest paid on home mortgages). But a wide range of producer groups—from steel companies and real estate developers to kiwi growers and horse breeders—also reaps benefits.

Many "anticompetitive" regulations, such as rate setting and imposition of barriers to entry, shield producers from market competition. When price competition is thwarted and new competitors are blocked from entering markets, regulated industries receive higher profits and market shares than they would without such government intervention.

Tax expenditures have been legislated and anticompetitive regulations promulgated for decades. Both were seemingly permanent fixtures on the nation's policy landscape. Not surprisingly, in most cases, the affected producers opposed reform and fought hard against it.[2] Scholars, politicians, and pundits alike thought prospects for reform in these areas were remote, at best. Regulatory commissions were described as captured by industries that considered doing business without regulation both economically irrational and politically improbable. Similarly, without major institutional change, the incentives of the political marketplace dictated that politicians would be unable or unwilling to revoke all but perhaps the most abusive tax preferences.[3] Reforms of a sort were legislated in 1969 and 1976, but they were modest; they made little progress in removing tax loopholes, and they added as many new provisions as they eliminated.[4]

Yet these policy areas underwent major transformations in which the fortunes of producer groups declined and many of their most prized policy benefits were repealed. Beginning in the mid-1970s, the courts, Congress, and regulatory commissions successfully launched deregulation in several industries, including trucking, telecommunications, airlines, railroads, financial services, and natural gas. The Tax Reform Act of 1986 ushered in the most sweeping tax changes seen in decades. Although the act affected all aspects of income tax law, it is perhaps best known for the curtailment or wholesale elimination of many tax expenditures, which had benefited insurance, banking, real estate, heavy manufacturing industries such as steel and automaking, and other economic interests. A summary of key provisions of the act is included in appendix 2A-1.

Most of this chapter is devoted to understanding the rise and fall of producer group fortunes in the income tax arena. A briefer treatment of deregulation follows the tax case. As the chapter shows, very similar, although not identical, forces were at work in bringing about change in both cases.

Tax Expenditures: From Rising to Declining Fortunes

Congress began legislating tax expenditures during the early part of this century when it created the income tax. Table 2-1 shows that tax expenditures were added and expanded incrementally over several decades. Congress legislated about the same number of such provisions in each of four periods from 1909 through 1982, with the most growth coming after World War II. These increments added up to a massive

Table 2-1. *Number and Period of Enactment of Tax Expenditures, 1909–82*

Type of tax expenditure	Period enacted				
	1909–19	1920–45	1946–69	1970–82	Total
Need based[a]	5	8	5	3	21
Tax equity[b]	5	0	1	1	7
Special group[c]	6	3	3	2	14
General economic incentives[d]	2	2	4	2	10
Specific economic incentives[e]	7	4	10	13	34
Miscellaneous	1	1	1	1	4
Total	26	18	24	22	90

Source: Adapted from John F. Witte, *The Politics and Development of the Federal Income Tax* (University of Wisconsin Press, 1985), p. 289.

a. Provisions designed to take into account presumed economic need. "Need" includes conditions imposing restraints on income-earning potential, extraordinary expenses, situations of economic hardship, and conditions affecting the elderly.

b. Provisions designed either to eliminate taxes on taxes or to take into consideration expenses accrued in earning income.

c. Provisions affecting reasonably permanent, identifiable demographic or occupational groups; the economic conditions adressed by the provision cannot be assumed to be exclusive to that group, and there is no overriding presumption that the benefit is being granted primarily on other grounds.

d. Provisions designed to induce investment and, at least theoretically, to enhance economic growth; these are not exclusive to a particular industry or class of economic producers.

e. Provisions designed to create economic incentives to encourage specific forms of desirable behavior other than general economic investment.

change over time, especially during the last two decades, when revenue losses attributable to tax expenditures rose dramatically (see figure 2-1). They rose as a proportion of income tax receipts from 38 percent to about 74 percent from 1967 to 1982, and they almost doubled as a proportion of gross national product (GNP), going from 4.4 percent to 8.2 percent.[5] As table 2-2 shows, tax expenditures rose from $159 billion in 1975 to $486 billion in 1985 and as a proportion of federal budget outlays rose from 21 percent to 45 percent over the same period.

John F. Witte categorizes tax expenditures with an eye to identifying those provisions for which organized groups have particular interests at stake. As shown in table 2-1, the most numerous tax expenditures have been in the category of specific economic incentives, the very kind of tax benefits producer groups might be expected to seek. These provisions led the postwar growth of tax expenditures. Adding to that number those provisions intended to aid special groups yields a total of forty-eight—53 percent of all tax expenditures—targeted toward specific interests in the economy by the mid-1980s. In addition, coalitions of industries also supported many of the "general economic incentives" (for example, investment credits, capital gains, and depreciation write-offs). The picture for size is a close copy of the one for number (see table 2-3). Specific eco-

Figure 2-1. *Revenue Losses from Tax Expenditures, 1967–81*

Billions of dollars

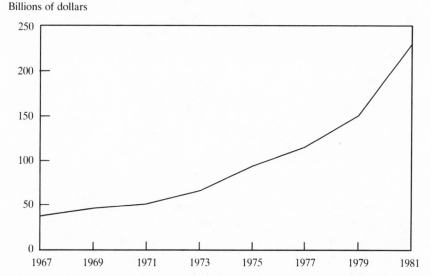

Source: Timothy J. Conlan, Margaret T. Wrightson, and David R. Beam, *Taxing Choices: The Politics of Tax Reform* (Washington: CQ Press, 1990), p. 23.

nomic incentives are the largest category, representing 41 percent of all revenue losses from tax expenditures and 29.5 percent of tax receipts in 1982.

The Tax Reform Act of 1986 also had considerable effect in reversing the growth of tax preferences. Several provisions benefiting businesses and well-to-do individuals were either eliminated or made less generous.[6] Closing loopholes saved roughly $300 billion over a five-year period.[7] Tax expenditures fell from more than $486 billion in 1985 to $373 billion in 1989, or from more than 45 percent of budget outlays to about 33 percent

Table 2-2. *Growth of Federal Tax Expenditures, Selected Fiscal Years, 1975–89*

Billions of 1989 dollars unless otherwise specified

Tax expenditure	1975	1979	1985	1989
Total amount	159.1	267.0	486.3	373.0
Change over previous year shown	. . .	107.9	219.3	− 113.3
Percentage change over previous year shown	. . .	67.8	82.1	− 23.3
As a percentage of federal budget outlays	21.2	31.4	45.2	33.3

Source: Author's calculations, using data from Charles H. Stewart III, "The Politics of Tax Reform in the 1980s," in Alberto Alesina and Geoffrey Carliner, eds., *Politics and Economics in the Eighties* (University of Chicago Press, 1991), p. 153.

Table 2-3. *Tax Expenditure Growth, by Category, 1975–82*

Category[a]	As a percentage of tax expenditures		As a percentage of tax receipts	
	1975	1982	1975	1982
Need-based provisions	16.8	12.3	8.2	8.8
Tax equity provisions	22.7	16.2	11.1	11.6
Special group benefits	4.2	2.0	2.0	1.4
General economic incentives	18.4	23.0	9.0	16.6
Specific economic incentives	36.2	41.0	17.7	29.5
Miscellaneous	1.8	5.6	0.9	4.0
All tax expenditures	100.1[b]	100.1[b]	48.9	72.0[b]

Source: Witte, *Politics and Development*, p. 294.
a. See table 2-1 for descriptions of the types of tax expenditure provisions.
b. Totals are rounded.

of outlays (see table 2-2).[8] Even these aggregate figures understate the effect of the 1986 act on producer groups, however. Provisions favoring business and other organized sectors of the economy bore the brunt of the loophole closing. Provisions benefiting individuals fared better, especially those with highly diffuse benefits.[9] Corporations, on the whole, were the major losers: they had to pay about $120 billion more in taxes. Individual taxpayers paid an equivalent amount less.

Unfortunately, figures for Witte's categories are not available for the post-reform years. However, table 2-4 offers an alternative categorization, according to budget function. It shows that the largest dollar loss of benefits occurred in the area of commerce and housing credit, which, since the home mortgage interest deduction was preserved in the 1986 act, affected primarily industries and investors. Benefits lost by the energy industry, combined with those lost by commerce and housing credit, made up about 63 percent of the total losses.

The Issue Context: From Tax Expenditure Growth to Tax Reform

Two problems dominated policymaking during the period when tax expenditures grew: middle-class restiveness over perceived high taxes and the presumed need for capital formation. In the first instance, rising tax expenditures were seen as a way to reduce tax burdens on the middle class. In the second, tax expenditures were legislated to spur investment and economic growth generally as well as in particular industries.

By the mid-1980s, the issue context had changed. The U.S. economy was into its longest peacetime boom in decades. The need for business

Table 2-4. *Federal Tax Expenditures, by Selected Outlay Functions, Selected Fiscal Years, 1975–89*

Billions of 1989 dollars unless otherwise specified

Function	Fiscal year			Change from 1985 to 1989	Percentage change from 1985 to 1989	Decrease as percentage of total decrease, 1985 to 1989
	1975	1985	1989			
Energy	7.1	28.6	1.0	−27.6	−96.5	19.6
Natural resources and environment	0.8	2.3	2.9	0.6	26.1	. . .
Commerce and housing credit	0.2	213.8	153.1	−60.7	−28.4	43.1
Education, training, employment, and social services	4.2	31.6	21.4	−10.2	−32.3	7.2
Health	12.7	39.3	46.7	7.4	18.8	. . .
Income security (includes social security)	37.0	137.2	94.7	−42.5	−31.0	30.1

Source: Author's calculations, using data from Stewart, "Politics of Tax Reform," p. 153.

investment in the economy got less attention than questions about the equity of a tax system that allowed profitable companies to escape paying their fair share. In the debate over tax reform, middle-class tax relief remained an important issue, but it was married to the issue of fairness and the desire to stem special-interest tax abuses. Both fairness and relief could be achieved not by expanding tax expenditures but by reducing them. If those provisions that benefited producer groups were closed, the resultant revenue gains could be transferred to individual taxpayers as rate reductions. Other issues that were compatible with reform, although they were less salient than relief and fairness, also came to the fore: the effect of tax expenditures on economic efficiency and growth and the increasing complexity of a tax code crammed with special provisions.

The changed issue context was principally the result of economic conditions, the effect of previous policy choices, and the interaction between the two. In the immediate post–World War II period, more and more personal income became subject to taxation. The broadening of the tax base, plus expanding incomes during the prosperity of the 1950s and 1960s, created a fiscal dividend for the federal government. Not only was it possible to increase government spending; it was also possible to legislate tax cuts and increases in exemptions, standard deductions, and more narrowly based tax expenditures.

With the increase in incomes, however, first from real growth and then from inflation, exemptions and standard deductions began to lose their sheltering effect on middle-class incomes. At the same time, because tax rates were not indexed for inflation, taxpayers moved into higher tax brackets. This bracket creep was a boon to Congress because it automatically increased revenue, avoiding the political pain of legislating tax increases. Instead, Congress could take the popular route of tax reduction. Between 1954 and 1981 Congress adopted sixteen major tax bills. Of these, eleven reduced taxes, only four increased them, and one left revenues unchanged.[10]

During the 1970s, the growth in real disposable income slowed, inflation accelerated, and bracket creep worsened. In inflation-adjusted dollars, the median after-federal-tax (including social security withholdings) income of one-earner families dropped from $7,743 in 1972 to $6,523 in 1981. This decline in real disposable income was accompanied by rising tax burdens. By 1981 individual income tax receipts had reached a record high of 9.6 percent of GNP.[11] Table 2-5 shows the changes in average and marginal tax rates at five-year intervals from 1965 to 1980. Taxpayers in all income categories saw their average and marginal rates jump between 1965 and 1980.

The squeeze on middle-class incomes generated considerable political pressure for reducing taxes and increasing tax expenditures.[12] Tax revolts erupted in several states late in the 1970s, most notably in California. The immediate target of Proposition 13 was the property tax, but the grass roots campaign signaled voters' broader dissatisfaction with their financial situation.[13]

If people were frustrated with their own tax burdens, they were also becoming more sympathetic to complaints from the business community. Ironically, the shift of an increasing proportion of the income tax burden away from corporations—and toward individuals—contributed to taxpayers' frustration with income tax law. Corporate tax payments had fallen from 25 percent in the 1950s to 6 percent in 1983.[14] Despite this trend, business argued that taxes and other forms of government intervention discouraged investment and raised the cost of doing business. Not only could taxpayers identify with complaints about high taxes, but, along with policymakers, they were increasingly worried about the economy's long-term performance. Hence business demands for tax relief and incentives seemed not so much pleadings for special treatment for special

Table 2-5. *Average and Marginal Tax Rates for Four-Person Families at Multiples of the Median Family Income, Selected Years, 1965–84*

Percent

Income level	1965	1970	1975	1980	1984
One-half median income					
Average rate	2.5	6.0	2.7	5.4	6.0
Marginal rate	14.0	16.8	26.0	16.0	14.0
Median income					
Average rate	7.9	10.0	9.6	11.6	10.3
Marginal rate	17.0	19.5	22.0	24.0	22.0
Twice median income					
Average rate	12.0	14.7	15.2	18.3	16.0
Marginal rate	22.0	25.6	32.0	43.0	33.0
Five times median income					
Average rate	20.4	25.0	28.1	32.4	26.1
Marginal rate	39.0	49.2	53.0	59.0	49.0
Ten times median income					
Average rate	30.9	33.9	37.8	41.4	33.3
Marginal rate	53.0	59.5	62.0	68.0	50.0

Source: Allen Schick, *The Capacity to Budget* (Washington: Urban Institute Press, 1990), p. 139.

interests as reasoned arguments to regenerate noninflationary economic growth.[15]

The fervor to cut rates and expand tax incentives resulted in the Revenue Act of 1978 and culminated in 1981 with the passage of the Economic Recovery Tax Act (ERTA). The 1978 legislation began as a proposal to reform the tax code by cutting back tax expenditures; it became instead an exercise in lowering taxes. President Jimmy Carter, who called the tax code a "disgrace to the human race" and campaigned on a pledge to overhaul it, floated a plan to eliminate the preferential treatment for capital gains and several other provisions; his final proposal, however, boiled down to a modest attempt to cut back such notorious loopholes as the three-martini lunch. Congress ignored even this mild reform, instead enacting new tax benefits and generously expanding many existing ones. Debated in the midst of the furor over Proposition 13 and after almost a decade of academic and official concern with the nation's long-term economic decline and the need for investment, the revenue act ended up stuffed with new tax credits and exemptions intended to spur capital formation.[16]

ERTA began in 1981 as the Reagan administration's proposal for substantial cuts in tax rates for corporations and individuals. Added to the rate cuts were costly new and expanded tax incentives, the result of a bidding war that broke out between congressional Democrats and the Republican administration. Liberalized depreciation, the sale of tax credits through leasing, oil tax reductions, and other provisions caused huge revenue losses.[17] As David Stockman, the administration's budget director, put it: "The hogs were really feeding. The greed level, the level of opportunism, was just out of control."[18]

Rather than diminish public discontent with federal tax policy, ERTA exacerbated the already prevalent perceptions of unfairness. Tax expenditures diminish both vertical and horizontal equity. Proponents of the first (progressivity) argue that special tax provisions benefit mainly corporations and affluent individuals who are able to take advantage of them. Marginal (statutory) rates might be progressive—that is, the wealthy pay more—but *effective* rates (what is actually paid) reflected essentially a flat tax rate. Horizontal equity is the notion that those with the same income should pay the same taxes; tax expenditures permit taxpayers at the same income levels to pay widely varying effective rates. By the late 1970s a majority of the public felt that the federal income tax was unfair; unfairness was cited as the biggest problem with the tax system, almost to the exclusion of other tax issues.[19]

Perceptions of unfairness had worsened over time. Since 1972 the federal income tax and the property tax had contended closely for the label "the worst tax—the least fair," but by 1980 the income tax had become the least popular. Most of the public, not surprisingly, felt that federal income taxes were "too much" for "middle-income families," for "people whose incomes all come from salaries," for those "who own their homes," and for "low-income families." Large majorities also felt that income taxes were "too low" for two groups—"high-income families" and "large business corporations."[20]

Probably no single person did more to heighten the visibility of the fairness issue than Robert McIntyre, director of the lobby group Citizens for Tax Justice. A little-known disciple of Ralph Nader, McIntyre spent endless hours ferreting out corporate tax abuses and publicizing them. McIntyre's efforts were important because they dramatized and reinforced preexisting perceptions of the system's lack of fairness.

Nothing provided more grist for McIntyre's mill than the aftermath of ERTA. As corporations and the rich engaged in a tax-sheltering frenzy, perceptions of unfairness grew sharply. A stream of reports flowed out about corporations and affluent individuals paying little or nothing in taxes.[21] ERTA practically ended corporate taxpaying: business paid just over 6 percent of the total income tax revenue in 1983.

Corporate tax avoidance set off a storm of protest in Congress beginning in 1982, when an ERTA provision allowing profitless firms to sell their tax breaks to profitable ones—a transaction called "safe harbor leasing"—led to a flurry of bizarre deals advantageous to both buyers and sellers. McIntyre found that 128 out of 250 large, profitable, well-known companies paid no federal income tax in at least one year between 1981 and 1983. Seventeen paid no taxes in all three years. According to McIntyre, whose findings were widely reported in the press, "Americans are wondering why the federal government is incurring the largest deficits in history even while they are paying the highest taxes ever. . . . This study documents one important answer: the demise of the corporate income tax."[22] Predictably, the findings served as a means to pillory corporations. On national television Senator Robert Byrd of West Virginia, for instance, reported that one woman raising three children in Milwaukee on a $12,000 salary paid more taxes than Boeing, General Electric, Du Pont, and Texaco put together.

If the fairness issue was the problem that had the greatest political impact in the debate over reform, it was by no means the only one.[23] Critics had long complained of four other undesirable consequences of the growth of tax expenditures. One is complexity. The tax code began as an eight-page piece of legislation in 1913, but it eventually came to occupy entire shelves in libraries. It was (and remains) incomprehensible to the average citizen. Another problem is that the growth in tax expenditures coincided with—some argued it even contributed to—the decline in economic growth and productivity in the United States. At the very least, the record of tax expenditures in stimulating investment was dubious. By distorting investment decisions, capital was not allocated to its most efficient uses. The expansion of such provisions as the investment tax credit and accelerated depreciation write-offs coincided with declining investment and competitiveness in many of the same industries for which the provisions were enacted (steel and auto manufacturing are two). The effects of ERTA confirmed arguments that tax expenditures misallocated resources. Generous shelters for investing in commercial real estate, for example, led to an oversupply of office space, prompting press reports that new office buildings were standing empty in metropolitan areas.

Tax expenditures also contribute to the erosion of the tax base, especially when personal income is not growing rapidly. Raising revenue, of course, was the original objective of the income tax. With more and more personal income excluded from taxation, losses in revenue can be offset only if tax rates are raised. Raising tax rates intensifies the political pressure for providing more generous outlets to shelter income. This means that tax rates must rise on a smaller proportion of income subject to taxation, which completes the vicious circle. Moreover, if tax expenditures are not accompanied by a commensurate rise in revenue from other sources or by spending cuts, they contribute to the federal deficit. They represent revenue that would otherwise be collected by the Treasury. When the deficit became a critical issue in the 1980s, tax expenditures came to be seen as more problematic.

The American public is decidedly ambivalent toward the income tax, however. Americans support many of the most expensive provisions that provide particularized benefits and incentives; they also consider the overall system deeply flawed (especially in terms of fairness), and they endorse tax reform in the abstract. Support for specifics thus coexists with disaffection with the overall system. It is plausible to think that one or the other side of this dichotomy in opinion prevails at different times. When the issue context is filled by a stream of media reports that point up abuse and unfairness, discontent with the system is amplified. The passage of ERTA, the act's troublesome excesses, and the publicity that attended them focused people's attention and reinforced the preexisting perception of unfairness, inefficiency, and complexity, which fueled the widespread perception in Washington that "things had gotten out of hand."[24] This turn of events opened a policy window. Reform proponents, waiting for an auspicious moment, had an opportunity to push their issue onto the agenda.[25]

Reformers not only called attention to fairness and other issues but also framed them in ways guaranteed to augment the political appeal of eliminating tax expenditures as a solution to the problem. They focused the policy debate on the unfairness and irrationality of the system as a whole rather than on the merits (political or economic) of specific provisions. Second, they focused their efforts on provisions that benefited producer groups, while leaving largely untouched the more popular (and expensive) provisions that benefited the middle class.

With tax reform framed as a struggle between specific and diffuse interests, members of Congress who might have been tempted to vote against reform risked having challengers at the next election point out that they had denied their constituents a diffuse benefit and that they were captives of privileged interests. In other words, their opponents could assert that they had had the opportunity to vote for greater fairness and efficiency and less government, and they had shied away from it.[26] In the end their fear and the media glare that attended their vote compelled many members to support reform.

The progression to final congressional action involved more than media attention and reelection anxiety, however. To be sure, the salience of the fairness issue and discontent with what was perceived as greed and abuse set the stage for change. The time was ripe for reform, and it had advanced part of the way to the agenda. Nevertheless, tax reform could not have proceeded without the formation of a coalition strong enough to overcome formidable opposition from those who benefited handsomely from the status quo.

The coalition that supported tax expenditure growth was bipartisan. Both parties shared responsibility for the creation and modification of these provisions.[27] From 1946 to 1981, 70 percent of House and Senate roll-call votes to originate tax expenditures were bipartisan. For modifications, the figure is 63 percent on floor votes.[28] As Witte put it, "Whatever partisan differences exist are outweighed by the common incentives that operate in tax politics. And these bipartisan incentives generate constant pressures . . . [that] bias the system in favor of conferring specific tax benefits at the expense of general revenues."[29] Republicans were comfortable with that outcome. Expanding such provisions was consistent with their belief that the tax burden on business was a major drag on the economy. Not only would lightening that burden spur investment and growth, but providing tax incentives was a much more palatable way for government to do something about myriad societal problems than the alternative—namely, creating spending programs and government agencies. Democrats in Congress found their traditional demand for tax reform reduced to an ideal that competed poorly with the political attractiveness of giving out tax benefits to industries in their districts and with the prevailing judgment that business needed tax relief.

The coalition in support of tax reform was similarly broad, spanning the political spectrum. Elite opinion converged, cementing a broad alliance that cut across the branches of government, the two political parties, and ideological camps. It included such odd political bedfellows as the labor-funded Citizens for Tax Justice; most liberal Democrats like Bill

Bradley, Richard Gephardt, and Tip O'Neill; conservative Republicans Ronald Reagan and Jack Kemp; and corporations like General Motors and Procter and Gamble.

Once the fairness issue became salient in the 1980s, it made sense for the Democrats to return to their traditional support for tax reform. Doing so was especially attractive politically because the latest and largest out-pouring of tax breaks had been approved under a Republican president in 1981. As it turned out, many Democrats were spurred to move from mere rhetorical support for reform to actual legislative action when that same Republican chief executive and other key members of the GOP endorsed reform. Tax reform was no longer a lonely cause for liberals and some tax experts and Treasury bureaucrats.

The bipartisan alliance rested on a unique recombination and meshing of separate ideas in tax policy that had been circulating for years.[30] Henry Simons of the University of Chicago published a theory of public finance in the 1930s that advanced a comprehensive definition of income, includ-ing all gains received by a person, as the basis of income taxation. Si-mons's work inspired several tax reform proposals during the postwar years. His basic principles enjoyed widespread support from economists serving in both Democratic and Republican administrations. Among Si-mons's disciples were Joseph Pechman, an economist at the Brookings Institution, and Stanley Surrey, a Treasury official during the Kennedy administration, whose influence is still felt in that agency. Economists supported reform on the grounds of both horizontal equity and efficiency. If certain kinds of income were excluded from taxation or taxed at a lower rate, two individuals with the same earnings might pay different amounts of tax. Most economists also have an unshakable belief in the market mechanism as the most efficient allocator of resources. Tax ex-penditures were believed to create inefficiencies by distorting market decisions over resource allocation.

A newer group of tax reformers in Washington, whose economic the-ory was rooted in the nineteenth-century ideas of Jean Baptiste Say, favored supply-side economics. They urged significant cuts in marginal tax rates and helped to inspire the rate cuts effected under ERTA in 1981. Reacting to the apparent failure of Keynesian (demand-side) macroeconomic management in the 1970s, many conservatives embraced supply-side economics as an antidote to economic stagnation and low productivity. Reducing rates and social engineering through the tax code would stimulate production by providing workers and entrepreneurs with the incentive to increase work, savings, and investment.

These two ideas—a comprehensive income base and rate reductions—were not linked historically, but they were not logically incompatible, either. In fact, moving toward a broad-based definition of income by eliminating tax expenditures was gaining favor as a way to finance rate cuts that went beyond those of 1981. These two ideas were also compatible with another—the flat tax, whose main attractiveness is its simplicity. Although the flat tax had its greatest appeal among conservatives, a majority of the public favored eliminating almost all deductions and applying a 14 percent rate to everyone, because the notion that all citizens would be subject to the same tax rate apparently struck many people as fair.[31] One problem the flat tax encountered, however, was that rates for those with lower incomes would have to be raised to make up for the shortfall in revenue that would result from lowering rates for those with higher incomes. But this hurdle could be overcome by eliminating expensive tax expenditures instead of raising rates at the lower end.

Despite its rejection of progressivity, the flat tax is horizontally equitable because it imposes taxes of the same amount on those who earn the same income. Furthermore, even though tax reform as far back as Simons and Surrey had meant closing loopholes to enhance progressivity, all three ideas—base broadening, rate cuts, and the flat tax—were perfectly consistent with horizontal equity. And as a standard for tax policy, horizontal equity was far less politically divisive than progressivity because it avoided redistributing income among classes.

Although the Tax Reform Act of 1986 did not embody any of these ideas in their pure form, its contours did faithfully mirror them. The precursor to the 1986 act, the "Fair Tax" proposed by Senator Bill Bradley of New Jersey and Representative Richard Gephardt of Missouri, contained their essential principles. Bill Bradley was the chief author of the plan; he had spent much of his time talking to tax experts and reading widely about alternative tax proposals and the futile efforts of earlier tax reformers. When he ran for the Senate in 1978, he campaigned on the tax issue and then brought his ideas on reform with him to Washington. To help develop a reform proposal, he gathered a group of tax economists and lawyers who subscribed to the principle of base broadening. He was intrigued also by economist Milton Friedman's argument that a flat tax rate of 20 percent would raise as much revenue as the existing system.

The Bradley-Gephardt proposal contained both base broadening and rate cuts and moved closer to a flat tax than existing policy. The revenue gains from closing loopholes were to be converted into dramatic rate reductions, which was a powerful incentive for doing away with the loopholes. Previous attempts at reform had offered only the pain of taking away benefits without the pleasure of lowering rates. Coupling loophole closing with rate cuts created a sharp trade-off between specific and diffuse benefits, between benefits for the public and those for organized claimants. And, while the bill did not propose adopting a flat rate, it did call for reducing the existing rate schedule from fourteen brackets to three.

The rate cuts were the key to gaining conservative support for reform. The rise of the supply-side doctrine among conservatives like Representative Jack Kemp and President Reagan made possible the abandonment of tax incentives to spur capital formation, which had long been a tenet of conservative faith. As embodied in Bradley's plan, reform held out the opportunity for giving fresh impetus to the supply-side revolution. Doing away with tax incentives was the cost for reducing rates on corporations and individuals. Hence, for the first time a conservative, Republican president supported tax reform. With active presidential support, the issue stood a chance of getting on the agenda.[32]

Embracing supply-side rate cuts meant not only rejecting the idea of using tax incentives to spur capital formation but also abandoning use of the tax code to attain certain social objectives. For years Republicans had viewed tax incentives as a politically palatable way for government to address social needs. Allowing deductions for employer-provided health benefits, for example, avoided the need for higher government spending, increased regulation, and more bureaucracy. Tax incentives were more compatible with private control over economic resources than an enlarged public sector would be. Champions of using tax incentives for social welfare purposes, like Senator Robert Packwood, jettisoned that approach once it became clear that doing so would pave the way for large rate cuts.

Bradley's plan also attracted conservative support because it was distributionally neutral—that is, it left the distribution of the tax burden among income groups or between individuals and corporations unchanged for the most part. Bradley believed, correctly, that earlier reform efforts had failed partly because conservatives and moderates objected to redistributing income by raising taxes on higher-income taxpayers and business. He argued that the fight over income redistribution should be fought apart from the one on reform (except for providing some tax relief to the working poor).[33] Bradley sought fairness by redistributing the tax burden not among income classes but in favor of a large unorganized group (taxpayers in general) and against highly organized sectors of the economy. The plan was to enhance horizontal (not vertical) equity, a concept more in tune with the flat tax favored by many conservatives. A long-standing conservative objection to reform—that tax reform would mean "redistribution by Robin Hood"—was overcome because liberals were willing to abandon their own traditional approach to tax reform, that of progressivity across income groups.

Bradley established other key assumptions that distinguished his plan from previous tax reform initiatives and, in so doing, maximized political support. One of the most important assumptions was revenue neutrality—that is, the plan should raise neither more nor less revenue than the existing tax system. Previous efforts had foundered because they entailed either raising revenues or cutting them. Revenue neutrality avoided an ideological battle over higher taxes or bigger deficits, which had become a polarizing issue between Congress and the White House. Because tax reform was revenue neutral, it afforded conservatives a way to cut tax rates further without worsening the federal deficit.

Finally, Bradley decided to retain certain sacred cows—those tax provisions whose benefits were highly diffuse and too politically sensitive to touch. These included deductions for home mortgage interest payments, charitable contributions, and payments for state and local income and property taxes.

The pro-reform bipartisan coalition was not simply the product of intellectual convergence, however. The kind of policy changes favored by liberal and conservative tax reformers also meshed with each side's electoral strategy. Bradley, the so-called neo-liberal, wanted a return to an earlier time, when the Democratic party had taken the lead on economic growth and Democrats were not identified with high taxes and pandering to organized interests. Reform was an issue that he thought could recapture middle-class support. The Republican proposal Jack Kemp developed was similar to the Bradley-Gephardt one. As a self-described populist conservative, Kemp wanted the Republican party to shed its image as proponent of the rich and of big business and thereby become a majority party. Both Bradley and Kemp believed in the superiority of market incentives and rejected social engineering. Both had ambitions for the White House, and they saw tax reform as an issue with diffuse appeal. They framed the tax reform issue in populist terms, stressing that eliminating tax expenditures would make the tax code more intelligible, fair, and productive for the average citizen.

Furthermore, Bradley and others were able to construct a reform proposal with elements that appealed to such diverse ideological groups because earlier policy choices had prepared the way. The growth of tax expenditures, particularly the revenue losses from ERTA, made reform through large rate reductions both feasible and politically attractive. Those reductions could be financed by eliminating loopholes, which would draw support from conservative quarters and avoid exacerbating the budget deficit. The possibility for wholesale closing of loopholes, according to Senator Bradley's assistant, was the most important factor in bringing about reform: "There was just an awful amount of money slopping around for rate reduction. . . . The amount of revenue that had been expended in loopholes—that was available for rate reduction—was large enough that you had the ability to present a significant trade-off for the first time ever. Without that, tax reform never would have happened."[34] Hence tax expenditure growth bore the seeds of its own demise.

The Institutional Context: From Tax Expenditure Growth to Tax Reform

Institutions were also hospitable to tax reform in the mid-1980s. The three preconditions for challenging producer interests, discussed in chapter 1, were met: congressional committees that were not constituency oriented were disposed to act; an autonomous bureaucracy supported reform; and resourceful and committed leaders emerged in favor of reform.

CONGRESS. Congress's propensity to enact costly tax expenditures has varied with the Ways and Means Committee's capacity to act as an effective gatekeeper vis-à-vis such proposals. In the era preceding the congressional reforms of the 1970s, it performed its gatekeeping task much more effectively than after the reforms were adopted. In time, however, the committee recovered its institutional footing and was able to launch tax reform in Congress.

The importance of Ways and Means, standing as it does at the center of tax deliberations, and the respect it commanded made assignment to the committee desirable. The carefully recruited members of the committee all were experienced in the legislative process and exhibited a responsible legislative style. Because these seasoned legislators were not highly vulnerable to constituency pressures or electoral challenges, they were well equipped to balance particularistic demands with broader policy objectives. Under the leadership of the politically skilled and substantively knowledgeable Wilbur Mills, who aimed to "write a bill that would pass the House" (namely, one that would reflect the committee's responsiveness to the parent chamber and its influence within it), the committee was known for its hard work, consensual decisionmaking, and restrained partisanship.[35]

The committee's importance and prestige received special recognition from the rest of the House. Ways and Means could operate under a closed rule (that is, its legislation was exempt from amendment on the House floor); hold private markup sessions; exert extraordinary powers (it controlled all assignments to all committees of the House, for example); and expect and receive deference to its judgments on the House floor.[36] All of these arrangements constrained pressures to enact revenue-losing measures. As one researcher noted, "The assumption of liberal tax reformers was always that the powerful tax oligarchs . . . were restraining tax reform efforts. It now seems likely that whether or not they were restraining reform efforts, they were also restraining the flood of [tax expenditure] provisions constantly awaiting any major tax legislation."[37]

This institutional resistance to pressure for growth in tax expenditures eroded, however, once congressional reforms were adopted in the first half of the 1970s. The effort was spearheaded by a large influx of young, reform-minded legislators elected in the aftermath of Vietnam and Watergate. The common urge behind most of these reforms was to democratize the way Congress was run: to decentralize authority, to open up the process to wider scrutiny, and to make it easier for individual legislators to pursue their own agendas. The seniority system, which had protected the privileges and power of committee chairmen, was no longer inviolable in choosing committee chairs; committee power devolved (in varying degrees from committee to committee) to scores of subcommittees; and floor deliberations were made more open and participatory. In the late 1950s a loosening of party discipline (which always had been modest in Congress) and an erosion of legislative norms emphasizing deference to leadership, apprenticeship, and reciprocity had signaled a move toward a more individualistic, unregulated legislative arena; the reforms of the early 1970s accelerated the trend.

Particularly affected was Ways and Means, which drew much of the reformers' attention because it was one of the most powerful committees with one of the most powerful chairmen in the House. Reforms stripped the committee of its role as the "committee on committees" with the power to make committee assignments; forced it to create subcommittees; modified the closed rule under which Ways and Means bills could be considered on the House floor without amendment; mandated that committee chairs be selected by secret ballot, not by the seniority system; opened committee proceedings except when a majority of the committee agreed by a roll-call vote to close a meeting; and enlarged the committee by one-third. Another reform required roll calls on all critical floor votes. By decentralizing power, these changes made it no longer certain that the Ways and Means Committee chairman could contain and block demands for tax expenditures. It now was easier to offer revenue-losing amendments and more difficult for individual members to avoid casting votes that might offend particular constituencies. At the same time, the legendary Mills had begun to misjudge sentiment on the House floor and experienced a series of defeats. His power waned further when his alcoholism and a bizarre escapade with a stripper became public knowledge.[38]

After the reforms, Ways and Means operated in an unsettled environment. It was often buffeted by these changes, lost some of its prestige, and had a harder time developing a coherent direction on policy issues. Those who had pushed for the reforms in Congress had assumed that the more insulated and exclusive pre-reform process facilitated producer-group influence. Yet the strong committee leaders and "responsible" legislative style of the more closed system had actually insulated members from group pressures. While the more open procedures of the reformed Congress were advertised as "more democratic," they offered the best access to those interests with the greatest resources and highest stakes in the outcomes. Access to the process—by interest groups and the administration, as well as by members of the House and Senate in general—increased. Accountability was supposed to be enhanced by greater public exposure, increased voting on specific issues, and more decisions subject to floor votes. The result, however, was the loss of control over agenda setting and decisionmaking by the chairman, and thus a weakening of institutional restraints on tax expenditure growth. During this period President Carter's tax reform initiative was gutted and transformed into a vehicle for loophole creation.[39]

Yet in the longer run, the congressional reforms of the early 1970s did not permanently disable the Ways and Means Committee as an agent for tax reform. Even though committee assignment procedures were changed, the recruitment for Ways and Means positions was much the same as it had been before the reforms, and the committee chairman remained the most influential actor in the recruitment process. The 1980s saw a return to selecting electorally safe, more experienced members. As before, the committee is basically representative of the House as a whole in regional and ideological terms (although, as before, somewhat more partisan). The committee remains the most desirable assignment in the House and has retained much of its prestige. Members rank prestige and influence as the most important reasons for getting on the committee and constituency interests as the least important, as they did for the pre-reform committee. According to Randall Strahan, "Even with institutional changes that increased the importance of clientele groups in the committee's environment, patterns in members' goals suggest only a limited increase in responsiveness to clientele groups."[40]

Moreover, by the end of the 1970s many in Congress felt that the reforms had gone too far. The demands for openness, decentralization, and participation had spawned a lack of direction and chaos that was damaging to the institution, and particularly to the Democratic majority's ability to develop and legislate coherent policy positions.[41] In addition, the fiscal crisis from huge projected budget deficits in the 1980s and the need for high-level bargaining between Congress and the Reagan administration tended to foster greater centralization of decisionmaking and to constrain the influence of producer groups. Thus the atmosphere surrounding Ways and Means had become conducive to a return to the kind of stronger, more directive leadership that characterized the pre-reform era.

The leaders of the House Ways and Means and Senate Finance committees used several changes in the rules to further their goals; under the new rules, Ways and Means could, for instance, raise a point of order to prevent bills with revenue-losing provisions from coming to the floor without the committee's approval. They also closed committee markups, made frequent use of party caucuses to develop partisan majorities on the committees, molded legislation to take into account the concerns of committee members, used the rules to keep packages intact on the floor, and bargained and consulted widely on legislation. Reflecting on the performance of chairmen Daniel Rostenkowski, Robert Dole, and Robert Packwood, one observer commented that "their leadership is especially notable in light of the absence of formal coercive powers available to them and the great difficulty members of Congress, including members of tax committees, have saying 'no' to claimants."[42]

In contrast to the open, permissive approach of Al Ullman (Mills's successor), who chaired the committee from 1974 to 1980, Rostenkowski was assertive and effective. He strived to restore the committee's reputation as one that can win passage of its legislation on the floor, works hard, and takes its job seriously, and he largely succeeded. The committee's success rate on the floor in the 1980s under Rostenkowski's chairmanship was about 90 percent, virtually the same rate that marked the pre-reform committee.[43]

Considered an effective leader by most of his committee colleagues, Rostenkowski personally recruited for the committee, encouraged team solidarity and loyalty, and consulted early and then negotiated to win firm commitments; he was also capable of threatening dissidents and isolating defectors. He skillfully used constituency-oriented provisions of legislation and manipulated the organizational resources at his disposal to shape coalitions. Rostenkowski's Chicago-machine style, stressing deal making, compromise, and mutual loyalty, was the antithesis of the open, individualistic congressional politics that had predominated since the 1970s.[44]

BUREAUCRATIC AUTONOMY. Congress was the central arena for considering tax reform, as it is for all major revenue decisions. Bureaucratic support for reform was by no means trivial, however. The Treasury Department played a key role in getting the issue on the agenda. In 1984 the Reagan administration needed a major domestic policy initiative for its second term to divert attention from the problem of the budget deficit. Treasury stepped into the breach by proposing a radical tax overhaul plan called "Treasury I." Treasury I pushed the issue into the headlines and onto the president's lap. Eventually Treasury Secretary Donald Regan would persuade the president to support a reform plan that was less ambitious than Treasury's but still resembled it.

The Treasury Department's mission historically has been to "guard the revenue base."[45] That mission is consistent with reform, which is inherently base broadening, and the congruence of mission and reform was reinforced by pro-reform economists on the department's staff. Treasury thus had a strong incentive to act as a proponent of change. A close alliance among agency, congressional committees, and producer groups—an iron triangle that would have served as a formidable obstacle to reform—therefore never developed.

LEADERSHIP GOALS AND COMMITMENT. As already suggested in discussing committee chairs, those who held leadership positions played a key role in getting tax reform on the agenda.[46] Only when leaders backed reform was it elevated from a cause championed by a few committed advocates to an important item on the national agenda. Tax reform became the top priority of the president, committee chairmen, and the Treasury secretaries. Those leaders pushed and persuaded reluctant majorities in Congress to address the issue and to approve reform measures. They possessed greater incentives and capacities than nonleaders to champion diffuse interests over specific interests, and their support was an indispensable ingredient for the success of reform efforts.

Like other presidents before him, Reagan supported tax reform, as did would-be presidents like Bradley and Kemp. Leaders of both parties sought to claim credit for a reform intended to benefit a majority of voters; at the least, they wanted to avoid blame if the reforms were defeated. Voting against tax reform, in particular, was perceived as a vote against Democratic and Republican party positions. Republican leaders warned their members that the party would be weakened if the president's chief domestic initiative failed, and Democratic leaders warned theirs that a vote against reform would be held against their party at the next election.[47]

Reagan was first attracted to tax reform because he thought that Democratic candidate Walter Mondale would use the issue in the 1984 election, and Reagan wanted to preempt him. Mondale, as it turned out, avoided embracing tax reform and instead called for higher taxes, in part because his campaign was based on building a coalition of producer interests. Tax reform confuted that plan, threatening the interests of several groups the candidate was courting, including labor, real estate, and heavy industry. For Treasury Secretary (and White House chief of staff in the second Reagan term) Donald Regan, reform was a vehicle for regaining the spotlight in the administration's economic policy deliberations. For White House Chief of Staff (and Treasury secretary in the second term) James Baker, pushing reform was an expression of his loyalty to the president. As the administration's chief domestic priority in the second term, tax reform would be a major test of the leadership skills of Reagan, Regan, and Baker. Their reputations, they knew, hinged on their ability to get reform through Congress.

Bradley, the most important policy entrepreneur in the tax reform saga, took the lead by refashioning the ideas of tax experts into a proposal that would maximize political support for reform.[48] As already mentioned, his proposal contained the basic elements that would later become the Tax Reform Act of 1986.

For Bradley, tax reform was a matter of great personal interest and intellectual commitment. As a highly paid basketball player, he had developed a strong disdain for the tax system. His sizable salary put him into the uppermost income brackets, requiring him to grapple with the complexities of the tax code and undertake intricate tax-sheltering strategies. Bradley was one of the few senators who voted against ERTA in 1981, and afterward he launched the painstaking effort to devise a completely new tax system. On trips back to New Jersey he spoke and listened to any constituents he found who were interested in the issue. In the Senate, Bradley engaged in tireless advocacy and continually served as a "fixer" whenever the fate of reform was in jeopardy.

Rostenkowski got on board because Reagan had thrown down the gauntlet to him and his fellow Democrats. He knew that he could not let Reagan outflank him on a traditional Democratic issue, particularly when Reagan was accusing the Democrats of being wedded to the past and captives of special interests. The issue also held out the chance for him to be the chief legislative architect of the most important tax legislation in forty years. Rostenkowski, viewed more as a ward politician than as a leader on Capitol Hill, could make his own mark with such a significant legislative accomplishment. Finally, Senate Finance Committee Chairman Robert Packwood felt that he would be blamed for dropping the ball and yielding to interest-group pressure if he did not go along with Reagan and Rostenkowski.

Hence, leaders seized on tax reform as an opportunity to enhance their reputations. By fundamentally redirecting policy in a way that entailed defeating reputedly powerful interests, they could demonstrate their superior political skills. By the same token, because the leaders were compelled to meet one another's challenges, tax reform constituted a major test of their influence. Given the widespread discontent with taxes generally (and with perceived unfairness of the income tax in particular), a tax reform proposal that contained elements supported by both liberals and conservatives held out a reasonable chance of success. It also offered potentially major political payoffs for leaders. In such an atmosphere, credit could be gained (or at least blame avoided) even for putting up a good fight and losing. Leaders calculating the political rewards and risks apparently thought that undertaking reform was worthwhile.

LEADERSHIP STRATEGIES. The leaders' success depended on persistently pursuing strategies that steered reform over hurdles in Congress.[49] By artfully manipulating powerful symbols, specific elements of proposals, and rules and procedures, they built support for reform and thwarted the actions of opponents. When almost no Republicans voted for the House Ways and Means reform bill, the president conducted perhaps the most forceful lobbying campaign of his presidency, visiting the Capitol to plead personally with GOP lawmakers.

No one articulated the populist attack on the tax code better than Reagan, who described the system as "complicated, unfair, cluttered with gobbledygook and loopholes designed for those with the power and influence to hire high-priced legal and tax advisers."[50] Instead, the code ought to "reflect and support our deeper values and highest aspirations," as well as "our special commitment to fairness."[51] By tapping into public disillusionment with the income tax and evoking widely shared values, the president succeeded in framing reform as a "white hat issue" that was difficult to oppose openly.[52]

Furthermore, once the issue was defined this way, a symbiosis developed between the leaders and the mass media that kept decisions of the average member of Congress in the glare of publicity. Even though the public remained immobilized, tax reform aroused great interest among news reporters. It included all the ingredients of a good political story— a clash between idealistic reformers and crafty politicians, on one side, and Gucci-shod lobbyists and the powerful interests they represented, on the other. By heightening the salience of tax reform and casting it as a political morality play, the media served as a surrogate for a public that remained inactive and as a powerful counterweight to the organized opposition.

Rostenkowski's strategy included building a majority on his committee by working with only the Democrats. While this tactic required preserving the state and local tax deduction, it allowed him to eviscerate those provisions valued by Republicans, and particularly by their allies in business and investment. He also targeted concessions to key committee members that were critical to their districts but cost relatively little in terms of revenue forgone. For example, although the use of tax-exempt municipal bonds to aid private projects was mostly eliminated, committee member Wyche Fowler of Georgia rescued the exemption for certain port and airport projects located in his district, and Raymond McGrath of New York was given a similar break for solid-waste disposal facilities.[53] But the chairman "maintained his game plan" throughout the process, according to one committee member. "He gave only when he was forced to give. He was very, very tenacious."[54] By granting selective incentives, Rostenkowski circumvented incipient efforts by committee members who sought to kill reform by logrolling the preservation of each other's favorite tax breaks.

Unlike Rostenkowski, Packwood excluded no one from his dealings and permitted committee members to offer revenue-losing amendments with impunity. Packwood insisted on preserving provisions of special importance to his state; other committee members felt free to do the same. Soon it became obvious that the prevailing spirit of largesse would make it impossible to produce any meaningful reform, but rather than abandon the effort, Packwood started over. He adopted a radically different strategy based on what might be called reverse logrolling and assembled a core group of six committee members who pledged to sacrifice the tax benefits they had previously tried to protect in exchange for substantially reduced tax rates. Under the new strategy, no member or faction felt alone in bearing the brunt of reform. The result was a bill that included a top tax rate of only 25 percent. The large rate reductions, even more dramatic than the ones in the administration's proposal and in the House bill, mitigated the effect of taking away the tax expenditures.

Like his counterpart in the House, Packwood built support by targeting selective benefits. These included transition rules to ease the loss of a prized tax provision, private authorship provisions to grant exceptions or special favors to particular constituents, and other changes in the minutiae of the legislation.[55] The chairman's dominant role in conference committee deliberations is one key to this kind of coalition building. As one senator recounted,

> Packwood met with each one of us, and asked us, "What are the things that you really care about?" . . . You know that at the end of the tax bill the two chairmen are going to be meeting together, so you know that it's

very important to be on the chairman's side. . . . The chairman cares about
the bill, and you're trying to save something that is extremely important to
some of your constituents, or something that you believe in very deeply.
And the result is that you tend to be very agreeable. . . . When the chairman says, "Look, it's very important to vote against the Bentsen amendment on passive losses," your reaction is, "Mr. Chairman, now that you've
explained it to me. . . ." I'm confident that if that is applicable in the
Senate, it is more applicable in the House.[56]

The way tax reform was packaged and the structuring of legislative
choices facilitated a vote in favor of reform and helped shield legislators
from the threats of interest groups. When Treasury secretaries and committee chairmen set out to draft a version of the reform measure, they
deliberately put aside the existing tax code and started with a blank slate,
which allowed legislators to consider a single package of fundamental
reforms instead of a series of particular provisions in the existing law.
Legislators thus could appear to be voting for reform rather than against
specific provisions. And because a substantial number (though not all)
of those groups who received tax benefits were required to make some
simultaneous sacrifice, legislators could legitimately and persuasively defend their actions on the basis of fair treatment.

Legislative procedures used in the final passage of the bill had a similar
effect. The closed rule in the House precluded voting on or amending
parts of the tax bill; members could only vote the entire package up or
down. The Senate bill, for which there was no closed rule during floor
consideration, was open to unlimited amendment. To preclude a succes-
sion of anti-reform amendments from being approved, Packwood mandated that no changes made to the Finance Committee bill could violate
revenue neutrality. That is, any amendment intended to restore a tax
break would be required to contain a tax increase to make up for the
revenue loss. Most amendments offered were defeated because they
failed to muster a majority to raise a counterbalancing tax.

Anticompetitive Regulation

For many years it was taken for granted that important American
industries would be regulated by the visible hand of government rather
than by the invisible hand of the market. Much economic regulation was
established when there was a perceived economic need either to stabilize
markets, to nurture infant industries, or to address concerns about ser-

vice to small communities. Regulation was the American equivalent of European-style public ownership of industry. Regulation of this variety generated little public notice or concern, certainly less than the newer social regulation of the environment, consumer protection, and workplace safety, most of which emerged in the 1960s and 1970s. Nor did the president, the parties, or Congress take much interest once new regulatory authority had been established. Most specific policy decisions were delegated to the bureaucracy. Policy was made within a quiet, cozy triangle of industry representatives, regulatory commissions, and legislative committees who agreed more than they disagreed on fundamental issues. The agencies remained dominated by commissioners who were wedded to the idea that there were valid public interest arguments favoring regulation. Dissenting views existed, but they were confined mostly to dry academic journals. Deregulation made little headway into the political lexicon.

Appendix 2B-1 lists the major agencies involved in economic regulation and the years they were established. A few agencies, not shown in the appendix, were established after World War II, but the greatest number were created in the 1930s. Also, the powers of some of the agencies listed were expanded in subsequent decades as they were given new responsibilities. Not all of these agencies set prices and erected barriers to entry, nor did the regulated industries always welcome or prefer regulation over an unregulated market. But in several cases these agencies pursued anticompetitive regulation that benefited the industries rather than the public interest that they were ostensibly established to protect.[57]

Trucking shows how anticompetitive regulation worked. The Interstate Commerce Commission (ICC) approved the rates that trucking companies could charge, which were fixed collectively by rate bureaus around the country. The bureaus were made up of the trucking firms themselves. In effect, the rate bureaus acted as cartels. All rates had to be approved by the ICC, but in practice the commission simply rubber-stamped what the rate bureaus decided. The task of reviewing thousands of rates every day was overwhelming, and the ICC was extremely sympathetic to the industry and protective of it. In theory, any regulated firm could undercut the fixed rate, but few did because the other carriers could file protests with the commission. The ICC made price competition virtually impossible as well: it erected barriers to entry for new firms that sought to go into the trucking business. New firms had to prove that existing firms were not already providing a needed service and that those firms would not be damaged by the additional competition. A new firm's promise to offer its service at a lower cost to consumers was considered irrelevant. In addition, applications for entry were open to challenge by established firms, which often cost the would-be competitors hundreds of thousands of dollars in legal costs.[58]

The revolt against regulation began in the mid-1970s.[59] Suddenly industries and regulatory authorities were under attack. Deregulation became a fashionable policy prescription, and a range of industries were deregulated in varying degrees. Appendix 2C-1 shows some of the variety of deregulation efforts.[60] Among all the producer groups, the trucking, telecommunications, and air transportation industries put up the most resistance to change and therefore posed the greatest challenge to reform. And it was in deregulating these industries that reformers achieved their clearest and most far-reaching successes. The explanation for this outcome, as the following discussion shows, closely parallels the one offered for tax reform.

The Issue Context for Deregulation

Mirroring the trend in tax expenditures, regulation was a growth industry in the 1970s. This is clear whether one measures that growth in the number of agencies created, the number of rules and procedural requirements issued, expenditures on regulatory activities, the size of the agencies' staffs, or the enactment of laws regulating business activity.[61] The bulk of regulatory growth was in social regulation, not the older, anticompetitive economic regulation that was the object of the most serious and successful deregulation efforts. Ironically, the form of regulation that the business community complained about most (that is, the newer social regulation), and whose explosive growth in the 1970s made regulation a salient issue, remained relatively immune to deregulation. Instead, the kind of regulation that many businesses sought to preserve (anticompetitive) proved the most vulnerable to reform.[62]

The rise in regulatory activity might not have engendered all that much concern if not for the fact that it occurred just before and during a period when the economy ran into trouble. Until then few people were aware, much less cared, that certain industries were benefiting from regulations that made the economy less efficient and kept prices higher than they needed to be. For thirty years following World War II, inflation was down, productivity was up, foreign competition was meager, and no one had heard of an energy crisis. U.S. economic performance, energy costs, and supplies were not salient issues.

The situation changed in the 1970s as the American economy suffered double-digit inflation and energy shortages. Also, by the end of that decade economists and policymakers had begun to talk of a productivity crisis in the American economy. Growing numbers of businessmen, academics, and political figures complained that government action was intrusive, did not achieve its goals, and produced other negative, unintended consequences. They perceived excessive regulation as the culprit that raised prices, created inefficiencies, wasted fuel, and provoked unnecessary government interference. Aside from being an economic hindrance, regulation was increasingly unfair, the argument went. Consumers faced higher prices and inadequate services because the regulated industries had captured agencies that had been established to regulate in the public interest.

In their search for responses to these problems, policymakers were greatly influenced by the advice of experts in and out of government. As with tax reform, economists were virtually unanimous in the judgment that deregulation was a sound idea. For a long time they had argued that much regulation allowed industries to extract rents from consumers and created inefficiencies by distorting market decisions over the allocation of resources. A theoretical literature critical of regulation emerged in the 1950s and 1960s, and by the early 1970s economists started building a strong empirical case favoring deregulation.[63]

Once stagflation and energy became salient problems, in the mid-1970s, economists such as Alfred Kahn came forward with their solutions. A small community of these economists found their way into government. They marshaled substantial empirical evidence showing that (1) the existing system produced excessive and discriminatory prices and monopoly profits, wasted scarce resources (for example, fuel), limited consumer choice, and led to senseless restrictions; (2) deregulation would do away with such restrictions, allocate resources more efficiently, and increase competition, consequently lowering prices and increasing consumer choice; and (3) accomplishing these objectives would not lead to market chaos, monopoly, reduced safety, or service disruptions to small communities. A major barrier for proponents of these kinds of reforms is uncertainty—people prefer the devil they know to the devil they do not know. The substantial empirical evidence not only showed the efficiency gains that could accrue from deregulation but also credibly countered predictions by opponents that deregulation would have disruptive effects.[64] The actual impact that deregulation could have on slowing inflation, it was obvious, would be small. But no other solution to the problem seemed more plausible or could command such professional consensus at the time.

It was not simply the quantity and quality of the empirical evidence that deregulation advocates arrayed that impressed policymakers; it was also the politically strategic ways in which it was deployed. Research findings were disseminated widely in the policy community. Many of the economists who helped develop the solution were the same ones who engaged in campaigns to educate politicians and the public on the folly of regulation and the wisdom of deregulation. Sophisticated economic analyses were conveyed in ways that were understood by laymen, combining statistical evidence with dramatic anecdotal evidence. And there was effective coordination and communication between the analysts and the political operatives. The dissemination of analysis was well timed and tailored to the specific concerns of policymakers.[65]

The coalition favoring deregulation was broad and diverse, spreading over the political spectrum. As with tax reform, elite opinion converged, forging a broad alliance that cut across the branches of government and the two political parties. Deregulation attracted the support of Ted Kennedy, Ralph Nader, Jimmy Carter, Gerald Ford, the American Conservative Union, the National Association of Manufacturers, a variety of other business groups and industries, and many regulators themselves.[66]

Conservatives like President Ford were first drawn to deregulation because they were convinced that government was a chief cause of inflation. Deregulation was more than an element in Ford's anti-inflation program, however; it came to be viewed as an end in itself, consistent with conservative beliefs in the virtues of a competitive free enterprise system and the reduction of government growth.[67]

Just as tax reform gained unlikely allies among conservatives, the coalition favoring deregulation would not have been possible without liberals changing their views on regulation. The academic critique of regulation dovetailed with consumerism, which was a major vehicle for disseminating a liberal-populist critique of regulation. Liberals no longer saw economic regulation in all cases as a tool for safeguarding the public against monopoly profits and chaotic markets. Instead, they saw it as a way in which big business, with the help of a captured government agency, was able to charge unreasonably high prices, provide inadequate service, and engage in anticompetitive behavior. It was consumerism that attracted Senator Kennedy to the issue.[68] As chairman of the Subcommittee on Administrative Practice and Procedure, he launched hearings that were an outstanding dramatic success.[69] The emergence of the consumer movement in the 1960s and 1970s signaled the rise of organizations attentive to diffuse economic interests, making it possible for liberals and conservatives to join together to roll back regulation.

The Institutional Context for Deregulation

As in the case of tax reform, the bureaucracy served as an agent of change, but the bureaucracy's role was even more important in this case because much of the regulatory reform could be accomplished through administrative fiat. Congress acted only after the changes were well under way. Had deregulation depended solely on congressional action, it might never have occurred.[70]

The critique of regulation affected the regulatory commissions in different ways. Some commission chairs and members were persuaded directly by the intellectual arguments. In other cases, pressure from the president, the Congress, and the courts produced the conversion of the commissions. In still others, commission vacancies were filled by pro-reform appointees. Although they are formally independent, regulatory commissions are vulnerable to the president's appointive powers, Congress's ability to call them to account in public and embarrass them, and the courts' authority to reverse regulatory decisions.

Even though the leading role of the regulatory commissions in initiating deregulation (and in some cases accomplishing it) was partially attributable to their vulnerability to sanctions, it is also the case that the commissions have certain advantages over the elected branches in undertaking deregulation. The commissions' formal independent status and their "broad, flexible grants of statutory authority . . . emboldened reform-oriented chairmen to fundamentally reverse long-standing practices and presumably would have helped [them] to withstand court tests if congressional action had not made most of those tests moot."[71]

Leaders also played a key role in bringing about deregulation, which became the top priority of the president, the committee chairmen, and the leaders of the agencies involved.[72] Kennedy embraced deregulation in part because he lacked a significant record of achievement in 1974 as a subcommittee chairman in Congress. And because he was a potential presidential candidate and a highly visible political personality, he was in an excellent position to initiate reform.

Kennedy's well-publicized hearings in 1974 on airline deregulation launched the issue and helped capture President Ford's attention. In part because Ford had prepared the issue for action and in part because Kennedy's actions prodded him, President Carter seized on trucking deregulation as an issue in 1980. Both Kennedy and Carter, locked in bitter rivalry during the 1980 primaries, claimed credit for the reform movement; Kennedy even dubbed himself the "father of deregulation." Kennedy's initiatives also spurred Senator Howard Cannon, chairman of the Commerce Committee. Cannon was not initially a crusader for deregulation, but he wanted to defend his committee against encroachment on its jurisdiction and any resultant loss of prestige; he sought as well to build a record of legislative achievement, as his predecessor Warren Magnuson had done in the area of consumer safety. So he too got behind deregulation.[73] Similarly, competition developed between the chairmen of regulatory commissions and the subcommittee chairs in Congress. And commission chairs often followed the well-publicized example of Alfred Kahn, who, as chairman of the Civil Aeronautics Board, accomplished much of the airline deregulation through administrative means.

Prospects for Enduring Reform

No one can say whether tax reform and deregulation will be lasting. The reforms rested on a broad mobilization of political support that may be very difficult to sustain over a long period of time and on a particular combination of conditions and individuals that is unlikely to be repeated.[74] Moreover, neither deregulation nor tax reform was prompted or accompanied by institutional reforms that might permanently alter political incentives. Therefore one might plausibly argue that it will be only a matter of time before producer-group fortunes will rise again. Nevertheless, the deregulated industries have not been reregulated, despite proposals to do so for the airlines industry. Nor have tax incentives crept back into the tax code. Congress blocked the Bush administration's efforts to reinstate the capital gains preference, and the House and Senate tax-writing committees eliminated several provisions proposed by the Clinton administration in 1993, such as a new investment tax credit.

Certain reforms are more likely to endure than others. Deregulation has been in place for more than a decade, while the tax reforms of 1986 have been under more serious threat. Differences in the conditions that prompted the two initiatives may provide a key to understanding why some reforms may be more lasting than others.

Reformers in the tax arena capitalized in good measure on the atmosphere of scandal that surrounded the fallout from ERTA. When such events fade from memory, so does much of the political impetus for maintaining reformist fervor. And because of the salience of the fairness issue, tax reformers did not need to present a strong empirical argument demonstrating its beneficial impacts on the economy. The ferment for deregulation, on the other hand, was built to a greater degree through the slow accumulation of empirical evidence and analysis that unequivocally demonstrated the idea's economic merits.

Second, tax reform depended critically on lowering tax rates, which purchased conservative backing (especially Reagan's) and served as a powerful inducement for acquiescence from members of Congress generally. Even so, the bill was nearly defeated by House Republicans and saved only by Reagan's personal lobbying effort. Most Republicans were not converted to the economic rationale for tax reform (which is that efficiency and growth would be enhanced by removing tax incentives that distort market incentives) and continue to adhere to the old wisdom that tax incentives are needed to encourage capital formation. According to Catherine E. Rudder, "The confusion surrounding the application of economic theories has augmented this phenomenon of *ad hoc* policy making. . . . Partly as a result, tax policymakers have little to lean on when making important decisions affecting fiscal policy other than the prevailing arguments of the moment."[75] Deregulation efforts, by contrast, succeeded without a bargain between liberals and conservatives or any direct provision of diffuse benefits to constituents. They relied instead on a firm, broad intellectual conversion. Finally, recent proposals to reimpose regulations are compatible with the essential goal of deregulation—market competition—and do not signal a return to the protectionist status quo ante. Reinstitution of tax incentives for business, however, would be clearly detrimental to reform and would signal a rise in producer fortunes.

The fluidity and protean nature of the issue context make an unraveling of the reforms not unlikely. Periods in which policies benefiting producers culminate in a reformist backlash may be followed by a return to the very same policies that caused the need for the original reforms. Thus far, however, the issue context has supported the changes in the 1986 tax legislation. The fairness issue was sufficiently potent during the Bush years to mount effective opposition against the capital gains proposal, and the salience of the deficit issue in the first year of the Clinton administration kept many of the revenue-losing incentives proposed by the president out of the tax legislation passed by Congress.

Conclusion

What made politicians willing to challenge reputedly powerful producer groups in the tax and regulatory cases, and what allowed them to succeed for the most part? The answer begins with the salient issues of the 1970s and 1980s. Inflation, slower economic growth, high taxes, and a vague concern with big government are all problems that entail diffuse economic burdens. Because subsidies for producer groups have diffuse externalized costs, they can accumulate over long periods of time. And because these policies have few obvious diffuse benefits, they have little support among the public. As a result, they become enticing targets for elimination when the kinds of economic problems encountered in the past two decades become pronounced.

The distributive problems associated with business-oriented tax incentives, especially fairness and middle-class tax burdens, worsened over time and became salient in the wake of abuses publicized after the passage of ERTA in 1981. Similarly, regulation was linked in clear and plausible ways to inflation, anticonsumer behavior, slow growth, and the energy crisis. As these two cases show, a dialectical process is at work. As the benefits of these kinds of policies grow and proliferate, the visibility and the negative effects of the policies increase; in turn, a corrective response is more likely to be elicited from reformers.

An issue context favorable to change, however, does not guarantee that it will come about. Tax reform as a policy prescription had to be refashioned to maximize political viability and to build a broad-based, pro-reform coalition. Deregulation was supported by an unassailable body of analysis and evidence that not only showed the benefits to be gained from reform but also allayed fears and uncertainty that deregulation would produce unwanted consequences. Both prescriptions were congruent with the evolution of conservative as well as liberal thinking and policy goals. With the widespread perception that a decision on the merits of the case meant supporting these reforms, and with the glare of media attention focused on the issue (especially tax reform), the electoral calculations of the average member of Congress were tipped in the direction of supporting constituents' diffuse interests.

Still, for the pro-reform coalitions to be consolidated and to triumph over producer-group interests, certain institutional actors had to be committed to achieving reform. The Treasury Department acted at the critical time to get tax reform on the agenda, and the regulatory commissions launched much of the deregulation on their own. The missions of these agencies were or became congruent with reform. Also, leaders were able to bring to bear the resources and other advantages of their positions to push vigorously for the reforms. The opportunity to take credit for effecting major reforms over the opposition of reputedly powerful opponents influenced their calculations, as did competition with and imitation of one another. Such achievements would enhance their prestige and their prospects for exerting influence in the future.

Appendix 2A-1. *Major Provisions of the Tax Reform Act of 1986*

Repealed

Deductions for state and local sales taxes

Deductions for consumer interest (like credit card, auto, and student loans), with a
phaseout through 1990

"Marriage penalty" deduction for two-earner households

$50 tax credit for political contributions

Exclusion of $100 of dividend income

Income exemptions for many "private activity" municipal bonds

Provisions for income averaging

60 percent deduction for long-term capital gains, treating all capital gains (short- or long-
term) as ordinary income

Exclusion of income from unemployment compensation benefits

Deductions for expenses of adopting a child

Exclusion for most prizes and awards

Deductions for charitable contributions by nonitemizers

Deductions for educational travel

Extra personal exemptions for the elderly and blind

Deductions for land-clearing expenses of farmers

Lower rates on capital gains of corporations

Investment tax credit (ITC) for business expenditures on machinery, automobiles, and
other property placed into service after December 31, 1985

Limited or modified

Deductions for medical and dental care to expenses over a 7.5 percent income floor, up
from 5 percent under previous law

Deductions for contributions to individual retirement accounts (IRAs) and 401(k) plans

Deductions for business meals and entertainment to 80 percent of expenses

Deductions for mortgage interest to qualified first or second homes

Exclusion of scholarship and fellowship grants

Deductions for home office expenses

Personal exemptions, as well as the lower 15 percent tax rate, for upper-income taxpayers

Reporting requirements for municipal bonds

Deductibility of losses from "passive" activities, rather than salary or dividend income

Foreign tax credits

Many miscellaneous individual and employee business expense deductions (including
employment-related education, professional and union dues, work-related tools and
supplies, tax and investment counseling, and job-search costs) by imposing a
2 percent income floor

Deductions for business cruise travel

Credits for rehabilitation of historic buildings and provision of low-income housing

Credits for research and development

Depreciation rules for business property under the accelerated cost recovery system
(ACRS)

Appendix 2A-1 *(continued)*

Retained

Deductions for state and local income, real estate, and personal property taxes

Deductions for mortgage interest on a primary residence and a second or vacation home

Exemptions for income from "public activity" municipal bonds

Tax deferral on proceeds from sale of a personal residence

Credit for child and dependent care expenses

Credit for elderly and permanently and totally disabled

Deductions for alimony, business gifts, and gambling losses

Exclusion of employer-provided fringe benefits, life insurance proceeds, workers' compensation payments, and veterans' disability benefits

Tax incentives for natural resources (including oil and gas drilling, timber growing, and solar and geothermal energy)

Increased

Standard deduction (or old "zero bracket" amount) from $2,480 to $3,000 for single taxpayers and from $3,670 to $5,000 for married couples

Personal and dependency exemptions from $1,080 to $2,000 in 1989 and after

Liberalization of earned income tax credit for low-income families with children

Taxes on unearned income in excess of $1,000 by children under age 14 by applying the parents' top rate

Alternative individual minimum tax (AMT) by adding preference and adjustment items and raising the rate to 21 percent

Corporate minimum taxes by creating an alternative minimum tax of 20 percent, with a $40,000 exemption, to replace the previous add-on minimum tax penalties for tax negligence and fraud

Reduced

Number of individual tax rate brackets from fourteen to two

Individual tax rates from a maximum marginal rate of 50 percent to 28 percent

Corporate income taxes from 46 percent to a maximum rate of 34 percent, with lower brackets at 15 percent and 25 percent

Source: Timothy J. Conlan, Margaret T. Wrightson, and David R. Beam, *Taxing Choices: The Politics of Tax Reform* (CQ Press, 1990), adapted from table 1-1, pp. 4–5.

Appendix 2B-1. *Major Economic Regulation Agencies*

Year established	Agency	Activity
1887	Interstate Commerce Commission	Establishing price, entry and routes for railroads, trucking, buses, and inland and coastal waterways
1913	Federal Reserve Board	Providing financial system stability (that is, preventing bank panics by providing a flexible national monetary system); setting bank reserve requirements; ensuring macroeconomic stabilization (since 1935)
1920	Federal Power Commission[a]	Licensing hydroelectric dams and setting interstate electric and natural gas rates
1922	Commodity Futures Trading Commission	Protecting farmers and investors in commodity exchange activity
1932	Federal Home Loan Bank Board	Supervising and insuring savings and loan institutions
1933	Federal Deposit Insurance Corporation	Supervising nonmember state banks and insuring deposits
1934	Federal Trade Commission	Monitoring competitive practices, fraudulent advertising, and certain dimensions of antitrust policy; providing consumer information
1934	Securities and Exchange Commission	Providing information to consumers on new securities issued and regulating the securities market
1935	National Labor Relations Board	Overseeing procedural fairness of collective bargaining elections
1936	Federal Maritime Commission	Setting ocean shipping rates and subsidies for the U.S. shipping industry
1938	Civil Aeronautics Board	Managing airline prices, entry, and route allocations

Source: Adapted from Michael D. Reagan, *Regulation: The Politics of Policy* (Little, Brown, 1987), p. 46.
a. In 1977 the FPC became the Federal Energy Regulation Commission.

Appendix 2C-1. *Scope of Deregulation, 1976–82*

Year	Deregulation activity
1976	Railroad Revitalization and Reform Act
1977	Air Cargo Deregulation Act
1978	Airline Deregulation Act Natural Gas Policy Act
1980	Motor Carrier Reform Act Household Goods Transportation Act Staggers Rail Act Depository Institutions Deregulation and Monetary Control Act Federal Communications Commission deregulation of cable television
1981	Oil price decontrol completed by executive order
1982	Bus Regulatory Reform Act Garn-St Germain Depository Institution Act Settlement of American Telephone and Telegraph antitrust case

Source: Reagan, *Regulation*, p. 73.

CHAPTER THREE

Trade Protection

TRADE POLICY evolution followed a different, more complicated course than did tax and regulatory policy. Trade barriers had dropped steadily for four decades, but the 1970s and 1980s saw increases in the number and variety of industries seeking protection and of those able to get it. The ferment for enacting trade restraints reached its zenith in the 1980s.

Nevertheless, despite the upsurge in demands for protection and the erosion of resistance to them, a largely liberal trade regime remains intact. Not only has there been no return to the rampant legislative protectionism of an earlier era, but the retreat from openness and movement toward market closure has been much less than might have been expected, given the economic and political changes detailed in this chapter. Protectionist pressures have been contained.

From Declining Fortunes to Containment

International markets became relatively open in the decades following World War II. Free trade in its pure form did not exist, but the much greater openness signaled a distinct break from the past. Nothing exemplified the waning fortunes of producer groups in the trade area more dramatically than the steady decline of the tariff, the classic tool of protectionism. Trade negotiations conducted among nations over the past several decades have continued to lower tariff levels.[1] By 1980 tariffs were only about 20 percent of their average level in 1930 (see table 3-1). The

Table 3-1. *U.S. Duty Reductions, 1934–79*
Percent

GATT conference	Date	Proportion of dutiable imports subject to reductions	Average cut in reduced tariff	Average cut in all duties	Remaining duties as a proportion of 1930 tariff
Pre-GATT	1934–47	63.9	44.0	33.2	66.8
First round, Geneva	1947	53.6	35.0	21.1	52.7
Second round, Annecy	1949	5.6	35.1	1.9	51.7
Third round, Torquay	1950–51	11.7	26.0	3.0	50.1
Fourth round, Geneva	1955–56	16.0	15.6	3.5	48.9
Dillon round, Geneva	1961–62	20.0	12.0	2.4	47.7
Kennedy round, Geneva	1964–67	79.2	45.5	36.0	30.5
Tokyo round	1974–79	. . .	. . .	29.6	21.2

Source: Robert E. Baldwin, "The Changing Nature of U.S. Trade Policy since World War II," in Robert E. Baldwin and Anne O. Krueger, eds., *The Structure and Evolution of Recent U.S. Trade Policy* (University of Chicago Press, 1984), p. 6.

average tariff level on dutiable imports fell from about 60 percent in 1931 to about 10 percent in the early 1970s.[2]

Although the overall level of U.S. tariffs has remained low, nontariff trade barriers (NTBs) have increased sharply. It is NTBs, no longer tariffs, that are the principal mechanisms now used by developed nations to protect their markets. Most of the upsurge in NTBs in the United States during the 1980s was in the form of voluntary export restraints (VERs), the major ones covering steel and automobiles. NTBs also include a variety of other practices and policies: government subsidies for particular firms and industries to make them more competitive, procurement policies that restrict government purchase of goods and services from foreign firms, and product standard regulations and approval procedures that make it more difficult for foreign firms to compete.

Several experts argue that NTBs have constricted U.S. markets in recent years. Others disagree. Assessing the effects of NTBs is a difficult technical task,[3] yet the estimates that have been attempted indicate a substantial increase in U.S. protection in the 1980s.[4] By 1982 NTBs overtly protected 34 percent of the market for American manufacturers, when weighted by each sector's share of total consumption in manufacturing.[5] Nevertheless, despite their greater prevalence and coverage of the U.S. market, NTBs appear to have only a limited impact.[6] One observer characterizes their overall effect on U.S. market closure during the 1980s as "marginal."[7] World trade has continued to expand, not contract, as it did before when protectionism was on the march.[8] As one study concludes, "On average across the full spectrum of manufacturing, the NTBs studied here that limit or discourage imports do not appear to have grown to the same importance as tariffs."[9]

The increase in market closure in the 1980s is overwhelmingly attributable to a single voluntary export restraint on Japanese automobiles. Even this important barrier had lost much of its impact by late in the decade, although it remained in force technically. An increase in the quota negotiated with Japan, the weaker dollar, and the increased production of Japanese cars in the United States all made it difficult to fill the import quota. When Japan unilaterally withdrew from the restraint agreement in 1993, the United States decided that it would be better to pursue negotiations aimed at opening the Japanese market to American autos than to seek another restraint agreement.

Another threat to liberal trade is the number of industries granted relief through administrative remedies from presumably unfair foreign trade practices. Two mechanisms provide most of the relief: countervailing duty legislation (CVD) and antidumping legislation.

Until the late 1970s these avenues of administrative relief were used more to keep U.S. markets open than to grant protection. This picture changed drastically in the 1980s, however. The number of industries petitioning for CVD and antidumping relief exploded: 345 CVD investigations and 438 antidumping investigations were initiated from 1980 to 1989, and the petitioners were much more successful than they had been. More often than not, in stark contrast to earlier decades, they won relief. Fifty-two percent of the CVD petitioners obtained either imposition of duties or suspension of the offending foreign practice. Similarly, 53 percent of the antidumping cases resulted in duties or suspension agreements. Moreover, these forms of relief continue indefinitely. At the end of 1990 there were 72 CVDs still in effect and 202 antidumping duties, up from 56 and 137, respectively, in 1983.[10]

The actual imposition of administrative remedies probably has less effect on trade than does the threat of their imposition. The possibility that CVDs or antidumping legislation might be enacted pressures foreign governments to adopt voluntary restraints. The foremost example concerns the steel industry, which effectively exploited the unfair trade laws to get the Reagan and Bush administrations to negotiate a voluntary export restraint with foreign competitors.[11] "For decades," says I. M.

Destler, these remedies "had been a sideshow on an obscure bureaucratic stage; now they are prominently affecting—and impeding—trade
flows."[12]

Since the mid- to late 1980s, when the level of regulatory relief reached
its peak, the number of industries granted some form of protection has
declined, although not to prepeak levels. In addition, some of the provisions of the trade laws enacted in the 1980s that were labeled protectionist have turned out to provide little actual protection. Others, which
threatened retaliation against foreign competitors with closed markets,
have succeeded in opening markets abroad for U.S. producers.

In sum, after several decades in which trade barriers (primarily in the
form of tariffs) declined, protectionism rose, particularly in the 1980s.
On the other hand, the protectionism of recent years is unlike the widespread protectionism that characterized earlier periods of American history. The impact of NTBs has been limited, and the more than marginal
increase in administrative trade protection has still meant only a modest
increase in the overall level of protection.[13]

The rest of this chapter explores the historical decline and then recent
rise in protection. It also accounts for the containment—that is, why the
rise in protection since the 1980s has not been greater, given the economic
and political pressures to move in a protectionist direction.

The Issue Context before 1970

From World War II until the 1970s, the issue context overwhelmingly
favored keeping U.S. markets open and resisting demands for protection.
Solid support for more liberal trade prevailed at the elite level; the American public in general has never been enthralled with free trade. Even in
the 1950s—when the terms of trade for the United States were about as
favorable as they would ever be—opinion polls revealed mixed support
for free trade. While a plurality favored lower rather than higher tariffs,
a plurality also favored more restrictions on goods imported into the
United States over the availability of more imports.[14] Yet, as Destler
points out, "What really mattered . . . was that trade was not high on
the list of public concerns."[15] Low salience meant low conflict: trade did
not divide the public or those in government, and, with a few exceptions,
it did not give rise to clashes among organized interests. What the lack
of public concern did, then, was give those in government the freedom
to pursue trade liberalization.

It is true that free trade as a broad policy prescription fits well with American ideology. Standing as it does for market capitalism and minimal state interference on a global scale, free trade is fully consistent with the liberal tradition's stress on economic liberty, distrust of government power, and the social utility of consumer sovereignty. But opinion polls suggest that Americans' faith in markets, like their ostensible disdain for "big government," is ambivalent and qualified, particularly when practical considerations are at stake.[16] Moreover, the United States has not always been a bulwark of free trade. During the nineteenth century the United States was highly protectionist, using the tariff to nurture infant industries and to raise revenue for the federal government. The tariff issue was highly salient for decades, and it sparked considerable partisan debate among different economic and regional interests.

Given this history, it is difficult to credit ideology or culture for the strength of liberal trade as a policy idea after World War II. It was not unquestioned belief in the principles of laissez-faire capitalism that led American elites to embrace liberal trade. Rather, experience with protectionism and with the liberal trade alternative that supplanted it produced the enthusiasm. That experience includes the debacle engendered by a policy of high tariffs in the 1930s, the prosperity of the postwar decades, and the absence of significant competition from foreign economies after the war.

Before the 1930s the protectionist label carried a positive connotation for many people. It meant protecting American jobs and nurturing American industry, often to the extent of jingoism. But protectionism fell into disrepute in the 1930s, along with isolationism in foreign policy. The Smoot-Hawley act of 1930 raised U.S. tariff levels dramatically, setting off retaliation abroad; the ensuing contraction in trade is widely cited as a chief cause of the Great Depression, and the depression in turn contributed to the rise of fascism in Germany and World War II.[17] World trade stagnated; the value of U.S. imports declined from $4.4 billion in 1929 to $1.45 billion in 1933, and exports dropped even more drastically.[18] The lesson elites drew from this disaster was that policies that jeopardized open international markets also jeopardized peace and prosperity. As a result, free trade became an unambiguously "white hat" position supported almost universally by American political and business elites.

If the prewar protectionist debacle drove the United States in the direction of liberalization, it was the apparent postwar success of that effort that confirmed the wisdom of the new thinking. Liberalization fueled an expansion in world trade, with the United States in the forefront in selling abroad. With strong demand from nations recovering from the war and few threats to domestic markets, U.S. industry was secure. In helping to rebuild and strengthen the economies of Europe and Japan, liberal trade (along with the Marshall Plan) not only helped create a market for American goods but also ensured the kind of political stability that immunized those nations against communist expansion.

The ascendance of the liberal trade idea was reflected in changes in political coalitions. For almost a century after the Civil War, the Republican party favored high tariffs and the Democrats opposed them. The division reflected the former's strength in the industrial North and the latter's base in the rural South and Midwest. Democrats associated high tariffs with monopoly profits for rich industrialists and low tariffs with low prices for goods consumed by the average citizen.[19] In addition, they contended that low U.S. tariffs encouraged low foreign tariffs, which made U.S. exports, especially agricultural commodities, more attractive to foreign markets. Tariffs reached their zenith under the Republicans with Smoot-Hawley in 1930. That debacle chastened the GOP and helped boost the Democrats to power under Franklin D. Roosevelt, who, following the party's tradition of support for low tariffs, passed the Reciprocal Trade Agreements Act of 1934. That act permitted the president to negotiate tariff reductions with other nations, beginning the downward trend in tariffs that lasted throughout the postwar decades.

Table 3-2 shows the results of House and Senate roll-call votes on major trade legislation from 1934 through 1993. Most of the legislation authorizes the president to undertake trade negotiations and approves trade treaties already negotiated. In accord with the pattern since the Civil War, Democratic support for free trade was solid until the 1970s. What looks like an anomaly in 1948 is not. The Republicans controlled Congress that year, and they insisted on giving the president a one-year extension of negotiating authority rather than the three years the Democrats wanted. Democrats therefore voted against the legislation, but not because they had abandoned their position in favor of free trade. The legislation passed and President Harry Truman did not veto it. In 1953 the Democrats voted to recommit (that is, kill) the trade bill; in the end, however, they voted overwhelmingly for its passage. As for the Republicans, opposition to the free-trade position was strong until the 1950s, when Dwight Eisenhower took office. A majority of Republicans voted protectionist in all but two of the eight recorded votes between 1934 and

Table 3-2. *Major House and Senate Roll-Call Votes on Trade Legislation, by Party, 1934–93*

		Position on free trade							
		House				Senate			
		Democrats		Republi-cans		Democrats		Republi-cans	
Legislative action	Free trade position	Pro	Con	Pro	Con	Pro	Con	Pro	Con
Trade Agreements Act of 1934 (TAA)	Yea	269	11	2	99	51	5	5	28
Extension of TAA, 1937	Yea	278	11	3	81	56	9	0	14
Extension of TAA, 1940	Yea	212	20	5	146	41	15	0	20
Extension of TAA, 1943	Yea	195	11	145	52	41	8	18	14
Extension of TAA, 1945	Yea	205	12	33	140	38	5	15	16
Extension of TAA, 1948	Nay	142	16	5	218	17	23	1	47
Extension of TAA, 1949	Yea	234	6	84	63	47	1	15	18
Restoration of "peril points," 1951	Nay	163	42	4	183	No vote taken			
Extension of TAA, 1951	Yea	Voice vote				38	0	34	2
Motion to recommit extension of TAA, 1953	Nay	15	178	200	6	No vote taken			
Extension of TAA, 1953	Yea	184	9	179	25	Voice vote			
Extension of TAA, 1954	Yea	155	14	126	39	34	1	37	2
Extension of TAA, 1955	Yea	186	35	109	75	37	6	38	7
Motion to recommit extension of TAA, 1958	Nay	160	61	180	85	No vote taken			
Extension of TAA, 1958	Yea	184	39	133	59	36	6	36	10
Motion to recommit Trade Expansion Act, 1962	Nay	210	44	43	127	No vote taken			
Trade Expansion Act, 1962 (authorized Kennedy round)	Yea	218	35	80	90	56	1	22	7
Trade Act, 1974 (authorized Tokyo round)	Yea	112	121	160	19	45	3	32	1

Table 3-2 *(continued)*

		Position on free trade							
		House				*Senate*			
	Free trade	*Democrats*		*Republicans*		*Democrats*		*Republicans*	
Legislative action	*position*	*Pro*	*Con*	*Pro*	*Con*	*Pro*	*Con*	*Pro*	*Con*
Trade Agreements Act, 1979 (approval of Tokyo round negotiations)	Yea	395	7	148	2	52	3	38	1
Vote to remove Taiwan, Hong Kong, and South Korea from Generalized System of Preference, 1984	Nay	91	160	142	14	No vote taken			
Trade and Tariff Act, 1984	Yea	193	24	66	71	44	0	52	0
Vote to override Reagan veto of bill to restrict textile and apparel imports, 1986	Nay	43	205	106	71	No vote taken			
Gephardt amendment to retaliate against Japanese "unfair" trade practices, 1987	Nay	55	201	159	17	No vote taken			
Omnibus Trade Act, 1988 (authorized Uruguay round)	Yea	243	4	133	41	50	1	35	10
U.S.-Canada Free Trade Agreement, 1988	Yea	215	30	151	10	43	7	40	2
Resolution to terminate fast-track negotiation of free trade agreement with Mexico, 1991	Nay	91	170	140	21	23	31	36	5
Resolution to approve fast-track negotiation of free trade agreement with Mexico, 1991	Yea	173	80	156	4	No vote taken			
North American Free Trade Agreement, 1993	Yea	102	156	132	43	27	28	34	10

Sources: Robert A. Pastor, *Congress and the Politics of U.S. Foreign Economic Policy, 1929–1976* (University of California Press, 1980), p. 97; and author's tabulations, using data from Congressional Quarterly, *Congress and the Nation*, and *Congressional Quarterly Weekly Report* (Washington, various years).

1951. And many of the Republicans who did vote in favor of extending the president's negotiating authority did so only after protectionist provisions such as the peril point were included in the legislation.[20]

Many thought the Republicans' return to the White House in 1952 would mean a return to protectionism, but it did not. Eisenhower was, after all, an internationalist. The Eisenhower administration saw trade liberalization as an important foreign policy instrument for rebuilding U.S. allies and consequently staving off communist expansion. In 1953 a group of Republican business leaders assembled by Eisenhower issued the Randall report, which concluded that a liberal trading order was good from a commercial standpoint.[21] Democrats were not the only ones who had learned the lesson of Smoot-Hawley or had realized the economic and military usefulness of opening markets. Moreover, free trade was more consonant with the Republican party's ideological distaste for government intervention in the economy than their defense of protectionism had been.

Hence trade issues became largely (although not completely) bipartisan in the 1950s and 1960s. As table 3-2 shows, the Senate, which had been more bipartisan than the House in the 1940s, became solidly bipartisan in the 1950s and 1960s. With Eisenhower in the White House, most House Republicans too began voting for free trade. This consensus, which reflected a common belief in the economic and foreign policy benefits of freer trade, permitted the United States to remain a staunch defender of free trade throughout the post–World War II period. It encompassed business elites, congressional and executive branch leaders, and Democrats as well as Republicans.[22] Although presidential support for free trade was always stronger in principle than in practice, the thrust of every postwar president's policy has been toward liberalization.

The Institutional Context before 1970

The abandonment of protectionism in the 1930s was not simply a major policy reversal. It also led to a transformation of the trade policymaking process. To ensure that it would not again be subject to irresistible pressures to logroll tariff relief—as it had been under Smoot-Hawley—Congress delegated much of its constitutional power to regulate commerce with foreign nations to the executive branch. The result was a centralization and insulation of policymaking.

Congress delegated to the president authority to negotiate ambitious agreements with other nations for mutual reductions in trade barriers.[23] Once a trade agreement was struck, it could be implemented without further action by Congress. Starting with the Reciprocal Trade Agreements Act of 1934, Congress has periodically extended the president's authority to cut U.S. duties by some specified percentage and to negotiate similar reductions with other countries in exchange for such cuts. The 1934 act reduced duties by 50 percent in return for reductions by competitors. Congress routinely extended the 1934 act three times until 1945, which resulted in twenty-eight bilateral agreements. After 1945 Congress regularly authorized U.S. participation in multilateral negotiations under the General Agreement on Tariffs and Trade (GATT), including the first four GATT rounds of the 1950s, the Kennedy round of the 1960s, the Tokyo round of the 1970s, and the Uruguay round of the 1980s and 1990s.

Congress also refrained after 1945 from setting tariffs on a regular and comprehensive basis, shifting discretion for industry-specific trade remedies to the executive branch. It limited itself to establishing administrative procedures for determining whether particular industries had valid grievances against foreign competitors; specific demands for trade relief would then be processed and adjudicated through "depoliticized" institutional channels. The stated policy rationale for the new quasi-judicial process was that it offered recourse for industries whose demands were legitimate—ones that could show they had been injured by foreign competition—by applying "fair and objective" rules. The latent political rationale was quite different, however, and at least as important as the stated one. To wit, such a process would provide a safety valve to deflect protectionist pressures away from elected officials.

Three agencies—the U.S. International Trade Commission (ITC), the Department of Commerce, and the U.S. Trade Representative (USTR)—share responsibility for deciding whether to grant protection. The ITC, the most important of the three in the protection-granting process, adjudicates petitions brought by domestic producers for import relief. Relief can be granted through four mechanisms: escape clauses, antidumping legislation, countervailing duties, and section 301 of the amended Trade Act of 1974.

Escape clauses (section 201) are a form of insurance to workers injured by foreign competition. Trade treaties and legislation allow the president to impose duties or other restrictions (and withdraw or modify trade concessions) on any article that "causes or threatens serious injury to the domestic industry producing a like or directly competitive article."[24] Under escape-clause legislation, the ITC investigates the complaint, determines whether it is valid, and offers a recommendation to the president, who has final authority to grant or deny relief.

The second mechanism, antidumping legislation, is intended to offset allegedly unfair advantages of foreign firms. The purpose is to discourage dumping, which is the practice of selling goods in a foreign market at prices below those in the home market or below the cost of production. Firms seeking antidumping protection petition the Commerce Department, which investigates and determines whether a good is being sold at less than its fair market value. If the decision is affirmative, the ITC determines whether the dumping has produced a domestic injury.

Countervailing duties, the third remedy, are levied on foreign manufacturers to offset any unfair competitive advantage attained when foreign governments subsidize or otherwise promote their exporters. Countervailing duties are imposed when the secretary of commerce finds that a foreign government has extended subsidies to an exporter and caused injury to a U.S. industry.

Section 301 of the amended Trade Act of 1974 gives the president authority to provide aid that ailing American businesses may not have available under the injury requirements of the antidumping and countervailing duty statutes. The president may undertake action under section 301 on his own initiative or in response to a petition filed with the USTR by a producer.

In addition to these four relief mechanisms, trade adjustment assistance (TAA) can be granted to facilitate "adjustment" for American workers displaced by international competition. TAA comes in the form of retraining and extended unemployment insurance, to help move workers into growing, competitive industries.

As intended, for many years these mechanisms were used less to grant protection than they were to maintain open U.S. markets. Little relief was granted under them because of stringent eligibility criteria (for escape-clause and adjustment assistance) and lax enforcement (of the CVD). Under the escape clause, 143 claims were investigated from 1948 to 1974; relief was recommended in 45 instances and approved by the president in only 15 cases. Similarly, fewer than 45 CVDs were imposed between 1934 and 1974 out of about 200 investigations. Out of 371 antidumping cases processed from 1955 to 1968, only 12 resulted in findings of dumping. In trade adjustment, not a single petition was granted until 1969. Although the volume of petitions rose in the early 1970s, fewer than half of the 110,640 workers seeking benefits were awarded them.[25]

These new arrangements had several advantages for members of Congress, however, even if they offered little relief for business. They insulated Congress from trade-restrictive pressures and passed to the executive branch the authority to establish and maintain a free-trade regime. Individual legislators could voice dissatisfaction with trade policy when a politically potent constituency was injured by foreign imports or excluded from markets abroad, yet they knew that they would not be called upon to make specific protectionist decisions. Indeed, legislators were more free than ever before to expound in favor of one or another industry.

Congressional delegation to the executive was only part of the institutional arrangement that facilitated pursuit of liberal trade. Congress also protected itself internally by making it difficult for proponents of protection to mobilize within the legislature. "Open US trade policy," writes Destler, "had been founded, in part, on closed politics, on a variety of devices that shielded legislators from one-sided restrictive pressures. It had prospered under congressional barons . . . who had enough leverage to manipulate issues and to protect their colleagues from those up-or-down votes that forced a choice between conviction and constituency."[26] Because most protectionist legislation aimed at specific firms and industries never came to a vote on the House floor, legislators could support free trade without offending important business constituents.

The House Ways and Means Committee, under strong chairmen like Wilbur Mills, insulated those rank-and-file members who favored liberal trade in principle but who, in practice, often found the political appeal of restrictive measures irresistible. The impressive power and autonomy of the committee (see chapter 2) enabled it to restrain protectionist impulses, just as it had checked the growth of revenue-losing provisions in the tax laws.

The passage of the Trade Expansion Act of 1962 and the Kennedy round of negotiations that followed provide a good example of the process in action.[27] The bill that John F. Kennedy submitted to Congress was the centerpiece of his legislative effort in 1962. He supported it vigorously, centering his lobbying campaign in the White House.[28] President Kennedy managed to get the support of the textile industry and its powerful allies among southern Democrats, thus dividing the opposition. Opponents demanded the imposition of quotas, but Kennedy defused the challenge by offering a nonlegislative concession, namely, a promise to negotiate a voluntary export restraint with foreign nations. Congressional leadership also was strong, particularly in the hands of Mills. He skillfully moved the bill through his committee, defeating a series of protectionist amendments along the way. Because it went to the House floor with a closed rule, the bill was shielded from damaging amendments. The final legislation included no exemptions for particular products and no other provisions for specific interests.[29]

What followed was one of the most successful international trade negotiations in history. The tariff reductions achieved were wide and deep. Tariffs on 64 percent of all dutiable imports of the forty-six participating nations were reduced. The average tariff cut for industrial products—which made up 80 percent of all products that still carried tariffs—was about 35 percent.[30]

A New Issue Context: The Rise of "Unfair" Trade

The issue context changed only gradually, but beginning in the mid-1970s trade became a more salient issue than it had been previously.[31] To the extent that trade had been a problem before this time, it was defined in terms of maintaining momentum in the effort to reduce trade barriers and finding ways to keep shortsighted, parochial interests at bay. Now a new, competing definition of the problem emerged: American industries were being besieged by foreign competitors, and many of those competitors engaged in unfair trade practices. For *fair*-trade proponents, *free* trade had come to be an increasingly one-sided arrangement skewed in favor of foreign competitors. Only the United States, it seemed, was playing by the rules, and in the process it was losing to countries that targeted American markets while insulating their own from foreign competition.

Free-trade stalwarts argue that calls to take action against unfair trade are merely a rhetorical cloak for age-old protectionist sentiment, but this position too readily overlooks two developments that make the issue especially salient and powerful today. First, calls for protectionism are couched in terms of morals instead of raw commercial interest. Before World War II, when protection was granted as a matter of course, it was not necessary to buttress calls for protection with moral arguments. But in an era when protectionism remains discredited as an economic policy that smacks of crass promotionalism and bailouts, calls for protection must come accompanied by calls for equity.

Second, grievances about unfair trade practices are not wholly unfounded. As Pietro Nivola put it, "This has not been simply a ruse." Policymakers "have been trying to rectify some genuine injustices."[32] Such calls can be expected at least to receive a hearing in the political arena, especially if mistreatment of American firms can be established.[33] U.S. producers frequently report that they have been disadvantaged by other nations' variable levies, export subsidies, import equalization fees, border taxes, cartels, dumping, import quotas, government procurement practices, and licensing and product standards that discriminate against U.S. goods. In contrast, the U.S. market is clearly less restrictive than those of major competitors. The series of GATT negotiations had left the U.S. market more exposed than any other. Although other nations' tariffs and quotas had fallen, other barriers of the sort just mentioned were less visible, more difficult to eliminate, and more resistant to remediation through the GATT process.[34] "As long as the U.S. economy generally remained more open than others, restitutions [to U.S. producers] appealed to an intuitive sense of justice—and smacked less of special pleading or 'protectionism.' "[35]

Yet the problem was not so much that inequities and restrictiveness had grown. As Nivola observed, "For the most part the pressures and the [international trading] system were not less 'fair' [to American producers] than in the past."[36] Rather, now they were perceived as more salient and troublesome because other changes were taking place in the trade policymaking environment. What made trade pressures that were "not less 'fair' " come to be seen as increasingly "unfair"?

ECONOMIC CHANGE. The greater salience of the inequities in foreign trade was the result, first and foremost, of a range of economic challenges and ills that spelled the end of U.S. economic hegemony.[37] These included the greater exposure of U.S. firms and their workers to the global economy and, concomitantly, the relative decline of the United States as an economic power. From 1960 to 1990 U.S. trade with the rest of the world grew dramatically. Imports rose more than eightfold and exports rose more than sixfold in real terms. The growing importance of international trade to the U.S. economy can be seen in the degree of an economy's openness (measured as the total value of imports and exports as a proportion of total production). That figure was 13.5 percent in 1960; it had risen to 41.4 percent by 1990.[38]

The fortunes of American workers were affected as never before by trade flows. Many of those threatened by the competition were concentrated in particular sectors of the economy and in geographic areas marked by high rates of unionization, high wages, and stable employment. As long as the U.S. economy prospered and few domestic markets were penetrated by foreign firms, the costs of allowing American markets to be more open than those of its competitors were minimal. But once the economic environment changed, it appeared that the United States could no longer incur the disproportionate costs of maintaining an open trading system whose benefits were distributed diffusely around the world.

Along with greater openness to trade, the United States in the 1970s began experiencing both real and perceived economic difficulties. The gap in per capita income between the United States and Europe and Japan narrowed over this decade, and the U.S. share of world trade fell. These trends marked the so-called decline of the United States vis-à-vis its major competitors. Much of the decline was to be expected, of course, because other countries were merely playing catch-up to the United States, which, unlike other industrialized nations, had not been physically or economically devastated by World War II. Nevertheless, many people saw the changing numbers as a loss for the United States rather than simply a gain for other countries. Moreover, the U.S. economy, like that of all industrial nations, was beset by stagflation (an unusual combination of high inflation and unemployment), and the growth in real per capita income for Americans came to a halt in the early 1970s and has been at a standstill ever since.

One of the most visible indications of trouble was the start of regular, growing merchandise trade deficits; the deficits marked a reversal of a long-standing pattern of surpluses. From the late nineteenth century to 1970, the United States had always sold more abroad than it had imported. Every year from 1960 to 1976 the trade deficit remained below $10 billion; from 1977 to 1983 it never fell below $25 billion; and from 1984 to 1990, $108 billion was the lowest the deficit went.[39]

Although the growing trade deficit was not altogether unexpected or negative, politicians and the general public interpreted it as problematic.[40] Not only were a few old-line industries still hurting (for example, textiles, steel, and automobiles), but by the 1980s even high-tech "sunrise" industries such as semiconductors, telecommunications, and machine tools were being threatened; old-line and sunrise industries both began pressing for government intervention. If the U.S. economy was losing out in world commerce, as it appeared to be, specific industries seeking protection looked not so much like pleaders for special favors as victims of a systemic crisis. Complaints about unfair competition seemed more plausible in light of the trade deficits: "Once we equated negative trade balance figures with a decline of the United States," writes Destler, "it was more comfortable to blame this on foreign nefariousness than on domestic inadequacies."[41]

Japan led the upsurge in foreign competition, challenging the United States across a wide variety of industries. Assisting its phenomenal increase in economic growth and trade were a range of discriminatory barriers to imports and governmental efforts to promote exports. The pace of dismantling these barriers has not kept up with that of Japan's export success, and in trade negotiations Japan typically delays opening its markets until diplomatic pressure has mounted high. Moreover, Japan's culture and history are neither shared nor understood by most Westerners. Japan's tradition as a closed and clannish society, the memory of the Japanese attack on Pearl Harbor, and the perceptions of the country as an economic and military free-rider all contribute to many Americans' negative image of Japanese motivations and conduct. A 1990 poll found that 60 percent of the public saw the "economic power of Japan" as a "critical threat" to "the vital interest of the United States in the next 10 years." Seventy-one percent of the public agreed that Japan practiced "unfair trade with the United States."[42]

THE IMPACT OF POLICY. Even as the new economic environment raised questions about the adequacy and relevance of the liberal trade doctrine, the mechanisms through which liberalization was implemented, especially the General Agreement on Tariffs and Trade, were showing signs of wear and tear. One problem was that GATT, in an ironic twist, had become a victim of its own success. The dramatic reduction in tariff barriers impelled nations to look to nontariff barriers for trade advantages, and NTBs are much more resistant to negotiation than other barriers because they are harder to detect, define, and measure. Moreover, negotiating their elimination entails encroaching upon the domestic policy and national sovereignty of other countries. Agreements were struck in the Tokyo round of the 1970s on codes of conduct regarding subsidies, product standards, dumping, government procurement, and so on. Not all GATT members accepted these strictures, however, and achieving reductions has proved slow and cumbersome.

Other problems confronted GATT. For one, its bedrock principle of nondiscrimination—meaning that each nation would give equal treatment to the products of all others in the GATT club—was eroded by other, superseding multilateral and bilateral trade arrangements. The rise of the European Economic Community, for instance, was based on the idea that member nations would grant more favorable treatment to other EEC members than to nonmembers.[43] The U.S.-Canadian Free Trade Agreement and the North American Free Trade Agreement (NAFTA) are departures from the global multilateralism of GATT as well. Similarly, voluntary export restraints and "orderly marketing arrangements," negotiated bilaterally, are further evidence of an erosion of the U.S. commitment to an open, multilateral system. Finally, new competitors, many from Asia, joined GATT. Without the common history and cultural traditions that fostered agreement on what constituted fair trade practices, resolution of trade problems became more difficult.[44]

The weakening of GATT undermined the strategy that America's liberal traders had used so effectively to stave off domestic trade pressures. The idea of the "bargaining tariff" was that any protectionist action by the United States should be avoided because it would subvert U.S. efforts to negotiate open markets in other countries. But if the GATT system failed to keep markets open, the argument that U.S. compliance with GATT resulted in gains for this country would not be persuasive.

Changes in other policies also adversely affected an issue context that once had been hospitable to free trade. The shift to floating exchange rates in 1971 meant that the dollar's price relative to other currencies would be set and reset daily in foreign exchange markets. These fluctuations have powerful effects on the attractiveness of imports and exports. A weak dollar, other things being equal, benefits American exports by making them cheaper abroad and disadvantages imports by making them more expensive. The weakness of the dollar in the 1970s eased import competition and consequently helped to contain protectionist pressures. But circumstances changed dramatically in the 1980s. The value of the dollar rose sharply, with just the reverse effects: imports became more attractive to American consumers and U.S. exports became less attractive abroad.[45] The trade-weighted value of the dollar rose by 67 percent from 1980 to 1985, about 40 percent above the value that would have brought the U.S. current account into balance. American producers thus faced a cost disadvantage of 40 percent vis-à-vis their trading partners.[46]

The strong dollar was caused in large part by another policy, namely, persistent, large fiscal deficits. Financing the large deficits required borrowing from abroad. To attract the needed foreign capital, interest rates had to climb. Lenders, attracted by these rates, bid up the price of the dollar in international currency markets. The high demand for the dollar in turn increased its value on exchange markets, which severely damaged the competitive position of U.S. goods on the world market.[47]

The end of the cold war and the policy of containment, beginning in the late 1980s, altered the issue context as well by removing one of the most important postwar rationales for international cooperation on trade liberalization. Without the common ideological desire and security need to contain communism, the incentive for industrial democracies to maintain open trade was an exclusively economic one, an incentive that does not induce cooperation as readily as those in the security realm.

Finally, any explanation for the erosion of the consensus in favor of free trade would not be complete without a recognition of what did not happen. In other words, why did alternative issue definitions, which might have skirted the dispute between free trade and fair trade, not take hold? Much like the old prewar debate between free traders and protectionists, the dichotomy of free trade and fair trade frames issues in zero-sum terms. If industries are granted protection in retaliation for the unfair trade practices of foreign competitors, consumers and import-dependent industries lose. Yet if protection is denied, industries threatened by foreign competition lose. What is missing is any consensus on a non–zero-sum, ameliorative strategy that uses government intervention not to protect domestic industries but to speed and smooth adjustment to structural change in the world economy.[48]

Consensus on such a strategy has been blocked because both sides in the current debate have failed to discard certain basic assumptions about the operation of the international economy. Free-trade enthusiasts would have to adjust their notions that virtually all government intervention on behalf of domestic industries creates inefficiencies and that all American industry needs to compete well is open markets. Protectionists, for their part, would have to abandon the idea that the behavior of foreign competitors—not American industry and government—causes American trade problems. In addition, protectionists would do well to take seriously the dangers of setting off a trade war.

Predictably, the rise of the unfair trade issue affected political coalitions. Despite its bipartisanship, the coalition in favor of free trade showed fissures from almost the very beginning of the postwar period. First, a significant minority of House Republicans remained in the protectionist camp during the Eisenhower years (75 voted against the free-trade position in 1955, and 85 and 59 rejected free trade in the two votes of 1958; see table 3-2). They were able to block the president's attempts to cut tariffs until 1955, when Eisenhower obtained a 15 percent cut in duties; he obtained an additional 20 percent cut in 1958.[49] Eisenhower's success rested on Democratic support. The softness of GOP support for free trade was evident also in 1962 with the trade expansion act, which authorized the Kennedy round of tariff cuts. With a Democrat back in the White House, the Republicans were badly split and a majority of them returned to the protectionist position. Not until the 1970s did Republican support for free trade gel.

Just as the GOP began moving solidly toward the free-trade position, the Democrats began moving away from it. As early as the 1950s Democratic support for free trade showed signs of strain. Pressures mounted from the cotton textile, coal, and petroleum industries, whose employees tended to vote Democratic. The Eisenhower administration won southern Democratic support for its trade bills by pressuring the Japanese into agreeing to voluntary restrictions on their cotton exports to the United States. The administration got similar concessions for the petroleum industry. Again, in 1962, southern votes were bought (by President Kennedy, this time for the Trade Expansion Act) with an agreement to negotiate quantitative import restrictions on cotton textiles.[50] Yet the Democrats remained a mostly free-trade party. On the critical vote on the 1962 Trade Expansion Act, Democrats voted 210 to 44 in favor of the free-trade position, while Republicans opposed it by 127 to 43.[51]

By the 1970s, however, the switch in the two parties' positions was becoming evident. The House Republicans voted 160 to 19 in favor of authorizing legislation for a new round of trade negotiations in 1974. Meanwhile, House Democrats voted 121 to 112 against the legislation. Among northern Democrats the vote was 101 to 52 against authorizing legislation in 1974, compared with 141 to 7 in favor of it in 1962. The change in votes reflected the change in which party controlled the presidency, of course, but it also reflected a shift in the geographical bases of support for the two parties. Historically the Republicans' bastion was in the industrial North, but Democratic presidential and congressional candidates began winning in those states after the Great Depression, just as the South and West became increasingly Republican territories by the 1970s. Republicans were thus less dependent on that area of the country that was most hurt by rising international competition, while Democrats had become more so.

In the late 1960s the AFL-CIO, the Democrats' most important constituency group, broke with its historical commitment to liberal trade by supporting a quota bill. The shift in labor's position reflected the increasing importance of exports in many manufacturing sectors that were trade-union strongholds (textiles, automobiles, steel, and electronic goods, for example). It also reflected labor's disenchantment with the trade adjustment assistance program, which was established under the 1962 Trade Expansion Act to extend training and additional unemployment benefits to workers in industries hurt by foreign competition. It was not until November 1969 that any workers were granted such assistance, too little and too late to deter the AFL-CIO from testifying in favor of protectionist legislation in 1970.

The two parties shifted their positions, mirroring the change in labor's position. In 1970 Wilbur Mills, chairman of the House Ways and Means Committee and long-time champion of free trade, yielded to pressures from many of his committee members to sponsor a bill that established quotas for textiles and footwear and required the president under certain conditions to accept affirmative import relief decisions of the International Trade Commission. In the House, 137 Democrats voted in favor of the bill, with only 82 against it. Republicans opposed the bill 82 to 78. In voting on the Trade Act of 1974—which afforded the president authority to cut duties by an additional 60 percent—Democrats lined up against and Republicans in favor. The trade act probably would not have passed without the concessions made to particular industries and organized labor, concessions that relaxed the criteria for obtaining adjustment assistance, extended the multilateral arrangement on textiles to cover products manufactured from wool and manmade material (in addition to cotton), and extended voluntary export restraints Japanese and European steel producers had agreed to in 1968.

One analyst calculates that 60 percent of Ways and Means Committee votes on trade legislation from 1975 to 1986 were partisan.[52] Perceiving a potentially large electoral payoff, the Democrats made trade an increasingly partisan issue in the 1980s. As Representative Tony Coelho, chairman of the Democratic Congressional Campaign Committee, put it, trade had become "a Democratic macho issue,"[53] one that afforded the opportunity to couple the recurrent Democratic theme of "fairness" with toughness and patriotism.

In 1985 the Senate and House passed resolutions denouncing "unfair Japanese trade practices" and calling for retaliation unless Japan opened its markets enough to offset the ballooning trade imbalance. In the summer of 1985 three centrist Democrats on the trade committees, Senator Lloyd Bentsen and Representatives Dan Rostenkowski and Richard Gephardt, cosponsored a bill imposing a surcharge on countries running large trade surpluses with the United States. The same year the House passed a highly restrictive textile bill, and the Senate approved one that included provisions for shoes and copper. President Ronald Reagan vetoed the bill in December, but the veto was nearly overridden. Most important, bills for new omnibus trade legislation were introduced. In 1986 the House passed by 295 to 115 a bill that reversed U.S. trade laws to make it easier for firms to qualify for import relief and harder for the president to deny it to them; it also mandated retaliation when other nations refused to open their markets and provided for import quotas when countries ran large trade surpluses with the United States (the Gephardt amendment). The effort failed only because the Senate was preoccupied with other major legislation—tax reform—and did not have time to report the trade bill to the floor.

Restrictive pressures resurfaced in the next Congress, when Democrats made trade their top priority in 1987–88. In 1988 the Reagan administration sought extension of fast-track authority to commence the multilateral Uruguay round. The House passed a bill in April 1987, 290 to 137, that included the Gephardt amendment. Although the amendment was not supported in the Ways and Means Committee, it passed on the floor narrowly by a 218-to-214 vote. The bill also imposed new procedural conditions on fast-track authority for the Uruguay round, mandated retaliation against unfair foreign trade practices, and curbed presidential discretion in escape-clause cases. The Senate Finance Committee excluded the Gephardt amendment and passed instead on the Senate floor an alternative called "Super 301." This provision required the USTR to name, and target for trade sanctions, those countries that maintained patterns of import barriers and unfair, market-distorting practices. Also included was a ban on imports from the Toshiba Corporation.

A Strained Institutional Context

For the newly congenial issue context to prove beneficial to producer groups' fortunes, the institutional arrangements that were biased against protectionist policies had to change. They did. Although the arrangements established in the postwar decades have not collapsed, their weakening has been decisive in bringing about a rise in protectionist benefits.

Some of the weakening of institutional arrangements, of course, has been a direct result of the upsurge in demands for protection, which arose from the economic, political, and policy changes that combined to alter the issue context. Take the growing importance of NTBs, for instance. When tariffs were the focus of trade negotiations, free traders had a great advantage: they could secure advance authorization from Congress to negotiate tariff cuts, and once they had such authorization, no further approval from Capitol Hill was needed. This arrangement boosted the credibility of U.S. negotiators with their foreign counterparts, because commitments that negotiators made could not be undone. But once NTBs became the central focus of multilateral negotiations in the 1970s, prior authorization became unworkable. NTBs were less easy to identify and to quantify than tariffs, and they reached into subsidy, procurement, and regulatory policies. If Congress were required to approve NTB agreements after the negotiations, U.S. negotiators would be less able to make firm commitments, Congress would no longer be as insulated from political pressures, and opponents would have an opportunity to reject or amend the negotiators' handiwork.

Furthermore, any agreements affecting these policy areas required statutory changes that fell under the jurisdictions of legislative committees outside the trade policy arena. Responsibility for managing trade legislation thus was no longer monopolized by the House Ways and Means and Senate Finance committees. As trade measures moved beyond tariff reduction, over which the two committees had exclusive jurisdiction, and as the breadth and complexity of trade legislation necessitated multiple referrals, a plurality of committees and subcommitees became involved. Pieces of the action were acquired by the House Energy and Commerce Committee (domestic content, certification standards), the House Foreign Affairs and Senate Foreign Relations committees (foreign loans, export controls), the judiciary committees (antitrust reciprocity), the banking committees (financial services, foreign investment, the Export-

Import Bank), the agriculture committees (farm commodity trade), the armed services committees (procurement codes), and others.[54]

Yet the weakening of institutional restraints on protectionism also resulted from changes in the institutions themselves that were independent of trade issues. The change in the issue context that began in the 1970s could not have come at a worse time vis-à-vis the changes under way in Congress. The decentralizing reforms adopted in the 1970s made it uncertain whether a free trade–oriented chairman could control the agenda. Opening the process made it easier to offer trade-restrictive amendments and more difficult for individual members to take positions offensive to particular constituencies. At the same time, Wilbur Mills apparently began to lose his legendary ability to judge sentiment on the House floor as he became enmeshed in personal problems.[55]

Reformers had assumed that the more insulated and exclusive pre-reform process facilitated special-interest influence. In fact, the more closed system under the control of free trade–oriented committee leaders had insulated members from many of those pressures. Moreover, although the more open procedures of the reformed Congress were advertised as more democratic, they offered the best access to those interests with the greatest resources and highest stakes in the outcomes.[56]

There is another reason why it would be a mistake to believe that antiprotectionist institutional arrangements weakened only because the issue context became more conducive to protection. The nature and extent of institutional adjustments to the new issue context were under the control of institutional actors themselves, for the most part. That the institutions would accommodate the new issue environment was perhaps inevitable. How and how much they would accommodate was another matter, however. Two of the most important ways in which institutional actors have coped with the changing context of trade are by making special deals with particular industries and by fine-tuning administrative remedies for those producers seeking redress for alleged inequities.

SPECIAL DEALS. Special deals proliferated for particular industries that were too loud in their protests and too politically important to be ignored. Typically, an upsurge in imports and its attendant industry pressure have led to congressional bills to take restrictive action. The U.S. executive branch and the foreign government in question would then negotiate an agreement to limit exports to the United States. Voluntary export restraints were the usual vehicle: in response to the threat of U.S. import restrictions, exporters "voluntarily" agreed to limit their exports.

One of the first deals cut was for textiles and apparel products. The Multi-Fiber Arrangement (MFA) of 1973 succeeded the Long Term Arrangement struck by the Kennedy administration in 1962, which inaugurated export restraints for cotton textiles. Under the MFA those restraints were extended to manmade textiles. The arrangement also established a framework for negotiating bilateral orderly marketing arrangements (OMAs), whereby nations would limit their exports of textile and apparel products. If agreements could not be reached, importing nations could impose quantitative import restrictions.[57]

Other industries gained protection as well. In the late 1960s Japanese and European exporters of steel agreed to limit their volume of sales in the U.S. market. This arrangement was abandoned in the 1970s, but in 1977 the Carter administration responded to domestic pressure with the trigger-price mechanism: if the price of an imported steel product was below the production costs of the world's most efficient producer of the product, an antidumping investigation would be triggered. A third major special deal was cut for the automobile industry. In 1981 the United States concluded an agreement with Japan, whereby Japan committed itself to limit automobile exports for two to three years. The restraints were extended until 1993, when the Japanese withdrew from the agreement. Because the VERs had been ineffective from the start (the dollar was weak and the Japanese had shifted auto production to the United States), U.S. policymakers took a new tack: they are negotiating to get better access to the Japanese market for American auto manufacturers.

CHANGING THE RULES. Besides making special deals and rhetorical protests, legislators latched onto the maze of rules and regulations as a vehicle to address mounting grievances against unfair trade practices. After all, these mechanisms ostensibly existed to remedy unfair practices, and they could handle such complaints more indirectly and less obtrusively than heavy-handed legislative protectionism could.[58]

Once unfair trade became a salient issue, the contradiction between the stated policy rationale of administrative mechanisms (to provide remedies) and their latent political objectives (to deflect pressures for remedies) became more apparent. The stiff criteria required for demonstrating injury to a U.S. producer and the overwhelming number of decisions against petitioners discredited the policy rationale. Even if industries filed petitions when agency investigations had revealed that foreign firms were clearly guilty of dumping, for instance, years passed in administrative and legal wrangling before duties or other penalties were imposed.[59] By discouraging industries from filing petitions (the unstated intention of the regulatory regime), the credibility of administrative mechanisms was diminished. Put another way, the administrative apparatus could continue to shield Congress only if its remedies actually offered the credible chance for obtaining some relief.

Opportunities for making such changes were episodic throughout the 1970s and 1980s, but they were frequent enough. Pressures to modify regulatory procedures and standards to make it easier and faster for industries to secure relief arose whenever the president requested a renewal of negotiating authority or whenever a negotiated agreement had to be ratified.

The rule changes began with the Trade Act of 1974. In addition to making it clear that the trade practices of America's competitors should be the focus of the Tokyo round of negotiations, the statute significantly altered several administrative procedures. First, it mandated that action on countervailing duties be taken within a year of receipt of a petition and made judicial review possible for those denied relief in CVD and antidumping decisions. Second, the definition of dumping was changed. Under the legislation then in existence, sales of products to the United States were considered unfairly priced only when products were priced lower abroad than in the home market. The 1974 act allowed imports to be challenged if they were sold "below cost," even if domestic and foreign prices were the same. The result was a finding of dumping in the majority of complaints that trade officials investigated.[60] Third, the act granted the president new, sweeping authority under section 301 to take a broad range of retaliatory actions against countries that maintained "unjustified" tariffs or provided subsidies that hurt American sales of competing products. The 1974 act also made it easier to qualify for trade adjustment assistance, lowered the threshold for granting relief under the escape clause, increased the independence of the ITC from the president by lengthening the terms of its members from six to nine years, and required the president to grant relief within sixty days.

The outcome was that many more petitions were filed and the bureaucracy processed them more expeditiously. Little relief actually resulted, however. The ITC recommended relief for a higher proportion of escape-clause cases, but few of them were approved by the president.[61] Countervailing duties likewise offered little relief. The Treasury secretary could waive the imposition of CVDs for four years if foreign governments were taking steps to remedy the offending practice, the idea being that a waiver would be a useful bargaining chip in trade negotiations. Negotiators apparently put the bargaining chip on the table frequently. The number of CVD cases approved from 1976 to 1978 rose to thirty-five, and waivers were granted in nineteen cases.[62] The number of antidumping cases remained about the same, and in none of the petitions filed under section 301 between January 1975 and July 1979 was retaliatory action taken.

In 1979 Congress was afforded another opportunity to revise the administered-relief mechanisms in exchange for congressional approval of the recently concluded trade agreements. Again Congress refined the statutory remedies for petitioners claiming unfair competition from abroad. First, Congress stipulated, in great detail, the kinds of export subsidies that could be subject to countervailing duties. And in cases where subsidies (and dumping) could be demonstrated, penalties could be waived if the offending party agreed to enter into negotiations. Congress thus sanctioned a trend toward voluntary export restraints and orderly marketing arrangements, which were more politically palatable than retaliation.[63]

Second, each stage in the processing of CVD cases had a time limit (the Commerce Department had to initiate an investigation within twenty days after a firm filed a petition, for example). The overall timetable was reduced from a year to seven months, which meant that foreign governments and businesses had less time to develop the evidence needed to challenge the claims filed by U.S. firms. Other changes to open up the administrative process made it easier for petitioners' lawyers to make their case. Similar steps were taken for proceedings under section 301. One of the most important changes shifted administrative responsibility for unfair trade remedies from the Treasury Department to the Commerce Department. The latter—traditionally more sympathetic to U.S. firms' complaints of unfair competition—was given the task of enforcing the CVD and antidumping laws.[64]

This time the result was not only a sharp rise in the volume of petitions seeking relief but also a rise in the number of industries to which it was granted. "There was now, for the first time, a serious enforcement operation, a core group of professionals organized to give priority to their [the laws against unfair trade] implementation."[65] Use of the escape clause declined over the entire period, but in 1984 it rose as industries sought to take advantage of Reagan's presidential reelection campaign.[66] Relief was granted in two major cases, steel and copper. Antidumping cases rose gradually over the decade, but the number of CVD investigations exploded in the 1980s, going from 10 in 1980 to 146 in 1982. The increase in section 301 petitions increased modestly.[67] "For years," states Destler, these administrative remedies "were properly denounced as ineffective; by 1992 they were, with equal accuracy, attacked as tilted in favor of US producers."[68]

Despite greater access to administrative remedies after 1979, pressure to do even more continued into the 1980s. Several industries failed to recover in the wake of the 1981–82 recession, when the value of the dollar climbed. Thus in the Trade and Tariff Act of 1984, three principal provisions represented renewed efforts to aid specific industries ranging from fresh-cut flower growers and winemakers to the manufacturers of footwear and steel. First, an industry that could not show that it had been harmed by dumping or subsidies from a single nation could now seek redress if it could show that the cumulative impact of several foreign producers aided by such practices contributed to material injury. Second, the 1984 legislation made it more difficult for the ITC to reject petitions under the standards of section 201. Third, although Congress resisted pressures to enact legislation for stringent quotas on steel, it did direct the president to tighten existing voluntary restraint agreements with European producers.

In 1988 the Reagan administration sought authorization for new GATT negotiations, the Uruguay round. This time, as congressional Democrats sought to put the Republicans on the defensive and to please particular constituents, efforts centered on penalizing nations that enjoyed persistent merchandise trade deficits with the United States. The Gephardt amendment, proposed by a prominent member of the Ways and Means Committee, required nations with "excessive and unwarranted" trade surpluses with the United States to make specified reductions in those surpluses or face trade sanctions. The amendment was scuttled in the conference committee, but as a compromise new language was substituted for section 301. "Super 301" requires the U.S. Trade Representative to publicly identify countries exhibiting a "consistent pattern of import barriers and market distorting practices." If negotiations to reduce surpluses with offenders were to fail to rectify the problem, then sanctions would be in order, according to Super 301.

Other important changes in section 301 included making retaliation mandatory whenever negotiations did not "obtain the elimination" of unfair trade practices. Although the president could still waive this requirement in certain cases, it would no longer be easy to do so. There were other provisions buried deep within the 1988 law, many of which arose out of specific recommendations from companies that had yet to secure relief under the existing trade laws. In particular, Congress broadened the reach of antidumping regulations. When pork producers complained about the export of Canadian pork products to the United States, U.S. regulators were directed to look at the entire Canadian subsidy of agricultural inputs to determine whether prices for processed foods were fair. In response to complaints from outboard motorboat manufacturers, antidumping regulations were extended to U.S. products that were undersold not just in the United States but in third countries as well. Another provision mandated that the ITC evaluate not only actual material injury under antidumping and CVD laws but also the threat of such injury. The commission was to examine the behavior of a suspected foreign firm in the markets of other GATT members, which was supposed to indicate how that producer would behave in the United States. Finally, after hearing complaints from the Smith Corona Corporation that its foreign competitors were evading antidumping laws by making small changes in product design and by shipping parts and reassembling them in the United States (or in other ways circumventing the law), Congress established procedures to monitor downstream products and extended the antidumping law to remodeled and reassembled products.[69]

Many of these provisions were arcane and obscure, hardly noticeable except to those who were most familiar with the intricacies of trade regulation. Among the cognoscenti, of course, were American firms, which fastened onto these mechanisms as a way to make life difficult for foreign competitors and to force them into negotiated deals. While many of the petitions filed by U.S. firms have legitimately identified unfair trade practices, the objective has been to use litigation to disrupt foreign industries and to exert political pressure. The result has been a series of negotiated voluntary restraints and quotas, especially for the steel industry. According to critics, this amounts to legal protectionism, which turns administered relief mechanisms themselves into U.S. nontariff barriers.[70] "Designed (in part) to divert political pressures, the unfair trade laws were instead diverting—or deterring—trade," writes Destler. "They now offered seemingly endless possibilities for creative lawyers to generate innovative new approaches."[71] The objective rules have been used to return the system of trade dispute resolution to the overtly politicized deal making that they were intended to replace.

Containing Protectionist Pressures

Yet none of the changes chronicled above signaled a lurch into rampant protectionism or a return to a congressionally centered trade policy. Congressional threats to impose restrictive measures increased, as did demands that the executive branch be more aggressive in trade negotiations, and administrative mechanisms became more friendly to U.S. producers. On the other hand, Congress certainly was not willing to risk an economic conflagration by abandoning GATT principles and the liberalization achieved in earlier decades. After all, the aim of much of the legislative activity of the past two decades had been to liberalize markets abroad, not simply to keep open markets at home.

In the larger context of trade policy, it appears that the rise in protection has been little more than modest. Congress made only marginal changes in the trade bills submitted by presidents in 1974, 1979, 1984, 1988, 1991, and 1993. The creeping protection of the past twenty years has amounted to less than some might have feared. As Destler says, Congress "stepped back from the abyss."[72] And as Nivola recently concluded, with specific regard to administered trade relief:

> Just how self-limiting this regulatory regime has been in practice is a matter of debate. Technically, formal grievances about trade violations peaked in 1982, but our preference for open trade remained sturdy enough to keep the country more hospitable to imports than were various other industrial nations. Fears that the United States was resorting to extraordinary "export protectionism" also proved largely unfounded. Europe's direct agricultural export subsidies and Japan's mixed credit expenditures continued to outpace American efforts. So far the retaliatory provisions in recent U.S. laws have not caused the widespread trade diversion or rigged market allocations that critics had foreseen. American negotiators generally succeeded in steering these new legal devices in a constructive direction, not only winning a number of concessions for U.S. companies but sometimes advancing broader interests. . . . Unilateral U.S. pressure did not derail the latest attempt to reach multilateral accords, and may even have provided some stimulus.[73]

Many of the fears about provisions like Super 301—that the United States would goad and humiliate its trading partners into a trade war, for

instance—have proved exaggerated. The final legislation set a time limit
for the expiration of its most problematic element, the mandatory identification of offenders. And USTRs have not repeatedly indicted suspected offenders, such as Japan, under Super 301.[74] Critics predicted that
the provision would be used aggressively, and the Clinton administration
appears to be doing so. It is too early, however, to discern whether the
outcome will be harmful for trade relations.

The key question, then, is why the past two decades have not shown
more protectionism, given the changes that began in the 1970s: the erosion of the free-trade consensus and the rise of the fair-trade issue, as
well as a weakening of the institutional restraints that favored the free-
trade position. Looking more closely at the more recent issue and institutional contexts provides some answers.

ISSUES AND COALITIONS. Free trade remains a cherished (albeit tar-
nished) ideal among policy experts and top policymakers while protectionism remains discredited.[75] Contemporary critics of free trade have
continued to distance themselves from the protectionist label, insisting
that what they want is "fairness." More important, defenders of free
trade have adeptly defused protectionist pressures by redefining the
unfair-trade issue as an export-politics issue. That is, instead of seeing
unfair foreign practices as transgressions justifying retaliatory market
closure, they see them as opportunities for opening markets abroad.
Efforts to erect U.S. barriers are arrested or delayed with the promise
that new markets can be won.[76] Giving in to protectionism would undercut the chance to gain trade concessions from foreign governments, thus
hurting U.S. export industries and inviting retaliation. The effect is to
change the political equation by focusing on the interests of U.S. exporters rather than on those of domestic industries.

Second, despite the erosion of Democratic support for free trade,
protectionism lacks a reliable majority in Congress. This may be because
political parties themselves are less important than they used to be in
structuring the congressional vote on trade issues. According to Robert
E. Baldwin, "The vote of an individual member of Congress on trade
policy is now more influenced by economic conditions in his district or
state and by the pressures on him by the president rather than by his
party affiliation."[77]

Clearly though, enough of the bipartisan consensus on free trade
remains intact to stem protectionist pressures. This is especially so in the

Senate, where a majority of Democrats has continued to join a majority of Republicans on virtually all major trade votes (see table 3-2). Democratically inspired protectionist legislation has been confined to the House, and there it has been kept largely outside major trade legislation. Protectionist efforts either have failed in the House, like the attempts to remove the General System of Preferences in 1984 and to override President Reagan's veto of the textile bill in 1986, or they were stopped in the Senate, like the Gephardt amendment in 1987. Neither authorizations of new negotiations nor approval of major trade agreements have been blocked. With the exception of the 1993 NAFTA legislation, on which House Democrats were split, the Democrats have voted overwhelmingly for every trade act since 1974, including the acts of 1979, 1984, and 1988, the U.S.-Canada Free Trade Agreement, and the granting of fast-track authority for NAFTA.

Although the erosion of bipartisanship in the House means that free-trade proponents now have to work harder to get trade bills through Congress, they have done so and they have succeeded. Those with protectionist impulses lack the numerical strength and intellectual appeal to push through their most stringent initiatives.

INSTITUTIONAL INNOVATION AND CONGRESSIONAL RESTRAINT. A key part of the answer to the question "why not more protection?" is institutional innovation. The solution to the problem of approving trade agreements involving NTBs was found in the adoption of the fast-track procedure. Ninety days before entering into any agreement to reduce NTBs, the president consults with the trade committees and notifies Congress of his intent. Congress must act within sixty days of the agreement's submission, and no committee or floor amendments are permitted. Since this arrangement requires congressional approval after reaching agreement with foreign governments, it is not as attractive from the president's perspective as advance authorization, but it does ensure expeditious legislative approval with no opportunity to modify or amend trade treaties on the floor. In addition to facilitating negotiations abroad, it turns out that the fast track reconstitutes the closed nature of the process that existed before the congressional reforms of the 1970s. Because of the time limitations, the Ways and Means and Finance committees have been the key actors in the process, just as they had been before the fast-track procedure was introduced. As long as the president worked to get the support of the members of these committees, the pitfalls of the reformed, open Congress could be avoided. Congress has authorized negotiations under the fast track in every bilateral and multilateral negotiation since 1974, including the Uruguay round of GATT and the NAFTA.

When protectionist pressures could not be ignored or defeated, concessions have been made in a manner that has contained the damage. One of these escape valves works by extending special deals to selected, usually major industries, as discussed earlier. (For smaller industries, the escape valve has been the relaxation of the criteria for gaining administered relief, as was discussed above.) It is true that these special deals have circumvented both U.S. trade laws and international agreements.[78] Yet, as Destler observes, they also

> reinforced the protection for Congress that was the system's political foundation. They kept industry-specific protection out of our trade statutes. They gave executive officials significant leeway to cooperate with exporting countries in working out the form that protection would take, thus limiting the risk of retaliation. They let congressmen play the role they preferred: that of making noise, lobbying the executive branch for action, but refraining from final action themselves.[79]

Throughout the 1980s Congress took great interest in trade policy and turned up the volume of rhetoric insisting that the United States get tougher with its competitors. Rather than legislate protection, Congress strengthened the USTR's hand in negotiations with other nations and modified administrative criteria for securing relief. Such concern with trade tends to be episodic, however, reflecting highly changeable economic trends. Pressure on the executive branch to take action often intensifies when recessions occur, imports surge, and the value of the dollar in international exchange increases. By the time Congress gains sufficient momentum to take action, however, conditions usually will have changed. For example, the voluntary export restraint for automobiles that the United States and Japan agreed to in 1981 provided modest protection for the U.S. industry. But the deepening recession a couple of years later hurt the auto industry, and the Japanese share of the U.S. market expanded despite the VER. The United Auto Workers, disappointed at the dilatory pace of Japanese auto companies in investing in the United States, pushed for domestic-content legislation. Under this law, the greater the number of cars that a company sold in the United States, the higher the proportion of the cars' total value (that is, the greater the number of parts) that would have to be made in this country.

The law would have sharply reduced imports. The bill passed the House but never made it to the Senate floor; once the economy recovered and auto sales rebounded, the issue faded.

The more important point is that Congress's basic orientation after Smoot-Hawley—to refrain from both legislating protection and directly controlling trade policy—has not changed. The core of the trade policy-making process is in the executive branch, which remains characterized by a free-trade bias. For all of the concern about the cumulative effect of the patchwork of unfair trade regulations and restraint agreements with various nations, the process is still more cumbersome for producers seeking relief than the old process of legislated protection. Congress stays once-removed from granting benefits to specific constituencies; it relies instead upon pressuring the executive branch or setting the parameters for the regulatory process to satisfy constituent complaints. It has re-frained from granting benefits, opting instead to keep the arena centered in the executive branch, under whose procedures each battle to aid a specific industry must be mounted separately and in isolation from other battles, thus precluding the kind of logrolling that was the hallmark of legislated protection.

Abdicating much of its role for making trade policy decisions benefits Congress in several ways. It can appease the wrath of specific industries injured by competition and avoid the blame for starting a trade war, a risk always inherent in taking restrictive action.[80] Individual legislators can still act as visible trade policy activists—they can undertake a range of activities (making speeches and press releases, proposing legislation, holding hearings, traveling to foreign countries) that have no policy im-pact, but from which they nevertheless gain political benefits. Such activ-ities are part of the position taking and credit claiming that electorally minded members engage in.[81] "An overall system in which Congress eschews direct responsibility can be attractive to legislators because it gives them greater flexibility and initiative in preserving and advancing their careers as politicians while avoiding blame for mistakes."[82] The executive branch serves as a convenient and acquiescent scapegoat in such a process, a small price to pay for the ability to actually shape policy outcomes without meaningful congressional interference.

Also important is the fact that the congressional reforms of the early 1970s did not permanently disable the Ways and Means Committee as a buffer against protectionist pressures. As chapter 2 points out, much of the committee's strength, autonomy, and prestige was restored in the

1980s. There was little discernible increase in its responsiveness to clientele groups.[83] In addition, by the end of the 1970s many in Congress felt that the reforms had gone too far, creating a lack of direction and chaos that was damaging to the institution and the Democrats' ability to develop and legislate coherent policy positions.[84] The budget deficits of the 1980s and the need for high-level bargaining between Congress and the Reagan administration tended to foster greater centralization, making Ways and Means conducive to a return to the stronger, more directive leadership that characterized the pre-reform era.

LEADERSHIP. Leadership commitment may be the most important institutional reason for the containment of protectionist pressures despite an issue context less hospitable to freer trade. The leadership of the Ways and Means and Senate Finance committees in the 1980s took advantage of several changes in the rules, such as allowing Ways and Means to raise a point of order to prevent bills with trade restrictions from coming to the floor without the committee's approval. They also closed committee markups, made frequent use of party caucuses to develop partisan majorities on the committees, molded legislation to take into account the concerns of members of the committees, used rules to keep packages intact on the floor, and bargained and consulted widely on legislation. Most important, chairmen Rostenkowski, Dole, and Packwood provided strong and effective leadership.[85]

Every postwar president has supported free trade, although the intensity of that support has varied somewhat.[86] Presidents might be expected to support freer trade and oppose protectionism for the same reasons that presidents can be expected to oppose other policies that impose diffuse costs on society. The president appeals for votes nationwide and represents the citizenry as a whole, his electoral fortunes rising and falling with the performance of the nation's economy. Policies that impose costs on society (for example, trade barriers that raise prices for goods and services, risk setting off a trade war, or create inefficiencies in the allocation of resources) are counterproductive, even if they satisfy myriad producer groups. And in large constituencies, the influence of particular groups is likely to be diluted or balanced by other interests. Finally, the president may define trade issues, as Bill Clinton did with NAFTA, as foreign policy issues. The special constitutional powers given to the president for conducting foreign affairs, the practical considerations of prudent statecraft, and the long-standing expectation of presidential leadership in foreign policy give him a potential advantage over his domestic political rivals in trade policy.

Although the president is an important actor in trade policy, those he appoints to represent his administration on trade are probably even more so. Until 1962 the State Department had principal responsibility for trade policy. In the trade act of that year, however, Congress created a special trade representative (STR) because it felt that the State Department was too willing to sacrifice or ignore domestic interests in favor of accommodating interests of foreign governments. The idea was to create an institution at the very top echelon of the executive establishment that could balance international and domestic interests. Congress placed the STR at first in the White House. In an effort to strengthen the STR, Congress made it a statutory office in 1974, moved it from the White House to the executive office of the president, and gave it cabinet rank and salary. In 1979 Congress strengthened and enlarged the office again, renaming it the Office of the United States Trade Representative.

The USTR has two major tasks: representing the United States abroad in bilateral and multilateral trade negotiations and getting major trade bills enacted by Congress (which it has done approximately every five years since 1974). It plays the role of broker, mediating between Washington and foreign governments, between the executive and legislative branches, and between domestic and international interests. But the USTR has been a broker with a very definite, abiding commitment to freer trade.

In playing the brokering role, one of the most crucial and effective strategies employed by the USTR has been export politics. In pushing trade expansion as a way to contain and deflect pressures for trade restriction, the political equation is reformulated so that the interests of U.S. exporters, not those of producers for the domestic market, become the preoccupation of policymakers. Lowering U.S. trade barriers (as well as preventing their imposition in the first place) is defended on the basis that new markets for U.S. products are being won abroad.[87] This strategy was the logic behind the "bargaining tariff" employed so effectively in multilateral negotiations when tariff levels were high in the first decades after World War II. It was used by USTR Robert Strauss during the 1970s when he pressured Japan to gradually expand its markets to U.S. agricultural products and to eliminate nontariff barriers related to government procurement.[88] It was used again, aggressively, from 1985 to 1988 by the Reagan administration under section 301 of the trade laws. That provision gave the president sweeping authority to take retaliatory actions against nations that engaged in unfair trade practices. The president ordered the USTR to recommend retaliation against several nations as a way to get them to open their markets to U.S. products kept out by practices deemed unfair.[89]

The importance and influence of the trade representative have varied over time, depending on the pace of trade negotiations; bureaucratic politics; the closeness of the political or personal relationship of the USTR and the president; and the reputation, skill, and ambition of the occupant of the office. From the early to mid-1970s, for instance, the USTR was in eclipse. There was a lull in trade negotiations, and the Nixon administration's Council for International Economic Policy, headed by an assistant to the president for international economic affairs, subsumed the USTR.

The USTR was at its height of influence during the Carter administration, when it was headed by Robert Strauss. Strauss was a gifted negotiator, skilled at political persuasion and maneuvering. He revitalized the multilateral trade negotiations abroad and sold them to Congress. Strauss pursued export politics, and he deserves much of the credit for the successful completion of the 1979 trade act. Strauss also cultivated close ties to President Jimmy Carter, attaining the status of a top presidential adviser. This was a great advantage for the Texan, as it lent his efforts credibility on Capitol Hill and with foreign governments.[90]

Ronald Reagan's trade representative, William Brock, had a comparable reputation as a negotiator. Brock did not, however, develop as close a relationship with President Reagan as Strauss had with Carter, and he faced bureaucratic competition from an equally capable and ambitious administration official, Commerce Secretary Malcolm Baldrige. Baldrige sought a predominant role in trade, and he nearly succeeded. The struggle between Brock and Baldrige accounts for much of the ambivalence and tentativeness of Reagan's trade policy in the early 1980s.[91]

The USTR for the second Reagan administration, Clayton Yeutter, also shared responsibility for trade with Baldrige, but Baldrige had lost much of his clout because of his defeat on the issue of establishing a department of trade and the departure of his chief ally in the White House, Edwin Meese. The result was less conflict and more maneuverability for Yeutter than for his predecessor. Although Yeutter did not have Brock's ties with Congress or his political skills, he did have prior trade experience in the Agriculture Department and he was energetic in his pursuit of "aggressive unilateralism"—that is, negotiations aimed at opening specific foreign markets with the threat that, if they were not opened, U.S. markets would be closed.[92] He also chaired the U.S. delegation to the Uruguay round and got agricultural issues to the top of the GATT agenda, which was important for the United States as a leading exporter of farm products.

Carla Hills, George Bush's appointee to the USTR post, was an experienced Washington lawyer and earned a reputation for being "competent, tough and credible" in her role.[93]

In an era when bipartisanship on trade policy was precarious and pressures for trade restrictions were rising in Congress, the premium placed on leadership skills and commitment had to be extended to actors other than the USTR. It was. In 1984 the Reagan administration sought enactment of a trade bill that authorized the negotiation of a bilateral free-trade agreement with Israel and extended the General System of Preferences, which granted developing countries duty-free access to the U.S. market. While the former issue was noncontroversial, the latter provoked resistance from a range of economic interests, particularly organized labor, which complained about cheap imports from Taiwan, Hong Kong, and South Korea. In addition, several industries petitioned the Senate to impose restrictive measures. The final legislation, however, contained only one important restriction—for steel—for which the Reagan administration decided to negotiate a voluntary export restraint. Protectionist provisions were either kept off the floor or they were eliminated in the House and Senate conference committee. Destler attributes this outcome to "a confluence of particular personalities: [U.S. Trade Representative] Brock, [Senate sponsor John] Danforth and [Ways and Means Chairman] Rostenkowski. Each, in a different way, wanted the omnibus bill to pass, and each was skilled in moving it forward. Each was willing to limit rewards to special interests, and each proved indispensable to its success."[94]

For the next few years protectionist resolutions and proposals, Democrat inspired, made their way through Congress. That some of them, such as the Gephardt amendment, might find their way into the 1988 trade act dominated the entire trade policy debate. The stock market crash of October 1987, the start of the decline in the value of the dollar, and the desire of committee chairmen Bentsen and Rostenkowski to pass a bill that Reagan would sign led them to drop from the final legislation all provisions that directly restricted trade. The Gephardt amendment was replaced by Super 301, which contained ambiguous language as to when and against whom the United States would retaliate. The ban against Toshiba was narrowed to apply to only one of its subsidiaries. Several special-interest amendments were deleted and fast-track authority was extended.[95]

If passage of the 1988 trade act and the Canada-U.S. Free Trade Agreement of the same year had to be attributed to a single leader, it would be Rostenkowski, who was then in his eighth year as committee chairman. With the confidence and comfort of a seasoned leader, Rostenkowski effectively engaged his colleagues in the House, his counterpart in the Senate, leaders in the administration, and a variety of private interests. The House's acceptance of his leadership on the substance of policy and in political bargaining signified the continuation of the central role of Ways and Means in trade policy.[96]

Major trade bills of the 1980s bring to mind the proverbial glass of water that is either half full or half empty. The legislation of both 1984 and 1988 included (either directly or indirectly) concessions to protectionist forces, and the bills would not have passed without them. On the other hand, these outcomes could have been much worse. Both started out brimming with extreme protectionist provisions; the versions that finally passed were less protection filled. Vigorous leadership was indispensable in reaching that outcome.

Strong leadership was even more decisive in the fight over NAFTA in 1993. With NAFTA challenged more than any other trade legislation since the 1930s, with key Democratic leaders in the House opposed to the pact, and with committee chairman Rostenkowski hobbled by allegations that he had misused his office, resolute presidential involvement was vital for the agreement's passage. This Bill Clinton provided. He lobbied Congress heavily, rallied business and political elites to the cause, and publicized pro-NAFTA arguments in risky, high-profile events such as the televised debate between Vice President Albert Gore and Ross Perot. The effort was not wasted. Although just weeks before the House vote NAFTA had looked certain to fail, Clinton triumphed.[97]

Conclusion

The decline in protectionist policies in the post–World War II years was the result, first of all, of experience with Smoot-Hawley; policymakers believed that that act had contributed to depression and war, and they shunned similar legislation. The pursuit of freer trade coincided with a period of growing global economic prosperity. U.S. producers faced little foreign competition, and the more open world economy helped advance the goal of containing communist expansion. Because the issue context was favorable to liberalization, the political pressures for trade protection were relatively modest and it was possible to muster a solid, bipartisan elite consensus for free trade. Finally, the refashioning of institutional arrangements further dampened and deflected protectionist demands. A return to rampant legislated protectionism became a remote prospect. Congress refrained from industry-specific protectionism and delegated to the executive branch broad authority to negotiate tariff reductions with other countries. Congress did make special deals with industries too powerful to ignore, but these were kept out of the trade laws. Executive officials were given the leeway to find the specific form of protection that would minimize potential retaliation, and other, less compelling pressures were diverted to a depoliticized administrative process that was unfriendly to granting relief. Strong, committed leadership on legislative committees kept protectionist initiatives from coming to a vote. Meanwhile, similarly committed trade officials in the executive branch wielded bargaining tariffs to forestall protectionist actions and used administrative channels more to deflect pressures for relief than to satisfy them.

Since the 1970s the issue context has become much more hospitable for a rise in the fortunes of producer groups seeking trade protection. The United States has faced greater economic challenges, including slower growth, lower productivity, a strong dollar in the 1980s that was fueled by large budget deficits, and more vigorous international competition. Moreover, much of that competition has been perceived to be unfair. The success of GATT led to greater reliance on NTBs, which are more difficult than tariffs to eliminate through international negotiations. As more industries have been adversely affected, producer groups have mobilized for protection. At the same time, bipartisan support for free trade and institutional resistance to demands for protection have eroded. Not only did reforms in Congress weaken the Ways and Means Committee, thus opening the process to group pressures, but the administrative mechanisms that had been used to deny most pressure have increasingly become mechanisms for gaining relief and coercing competitors.

Yet protectionism's advance has been contained. Enough bipartisan support for free trade remains in Congress, particularly in the Senate, to defeat protectionist measures. Another reason for containment is that several antiprotectionist institutional arrangements, as well as an intellectual commitment to liberal trade among elites, remain in place. Trade policy is still largely the province of the executive branch, and institutional innovations like the fast-track procedure have facilitated the passage of trade bills in Congress. Protectionist initiatives supported in the House have been blocked, and major trade legislation continues to gain passage. Support for liberalization among executive branch officials, businessmen, and academics is still strong, and protectionism remains a discredited policy alternative for most elites (other than labor leaders, whose organizational strength has declined).[98] Vigorous leadership from the chairmen of the trade committees (along with the adoption of the fast track and other procedures) has restored much of the insulation of the legislative process from group pressures. Similarly, continued presidential support for trade agreements and the skills of special trade representatives have been effective in building coalitions in Congress in favor of free trade. In addition, most members of Congress remain comfortable with an arrangement that allows them to take positions sympathetic to the plight of distressed constituents yet simultaneously frees them from responsibility for the distress itself and from the risks of actions that could gravely injure trade relations abroad.

CHAPTER FOUR

Agricultural Subsidies

PERHAPS FEW sectors of the economy have been as regularly and generously subsidized by the federal government as agriculture. Although spending on farm subsidies has fluctuated over the years, the basic structure of a strongly interventionist policy—price and income supports—has remained in place. (See appendix 4A for a description of farm subsidy programs.) One finds here nothing like the reversals in fortunes experienced by producers in the other policy areas examined in this study. Changes in agricultural policy have been neither as fundamental and dramatic as tax reform or deregulation, nor as one-directional as the steady decline in protectionist trade barriers in the decades following the Great Depression.

Spending on agricultural subsidies, relatively modest in the 1970s, rose significantly in the 1980s and then late in the decade dropped somewhat. Spending has been stable in the 1990s, but it has not returned to its pre-1980s level. In short, for the years examined here, the pattern has been one of rising fortunes, followed by a period of maintenance. The source of these fluctuations in subsidy levels is no great mystery. They are mostly a combination of the state of the farm economy (when economic conditions deteriorate, spending rises, and when they improve, spending declines) and the open-ended entitlement features of subsidy programs, which lead to budgetary expansion when economic conditions automatically produce a larger pool of eligible recipients.

The more important question, and the focus of this chapter, is why farm interests have as yet escaped the misfortunes experienced by the producer groups in other policy areas. This question is all the more

107

interesting because a confluence of developments in the 1980s, reminiscent of what happened in the tax and regulatory arenas, opened the possibility of reversing a half-century of government intervention in agriculture. The opportunity for fundamental change passed unseized, however, and most of this chapter details the reasons why.

Reform Failures, 1981–90

Some of the proposals put forward since 1981 to eliminate or reduce farm subsidies have been quite ambitious and radical; others have been more modest. All of them have been market-oriented, in the sense that they would have reduced government manipulation of commodity markets and support of farmers' incomes, but only the first two listed below would have eliminated any of the principal instruments of farm policy. The proposals include (1) the Reagan administration's plan for comprehensive reform, which would have virtually ended farm subsidies; (2) elimination of specific commodity programs; (3) limitations on the total amount of subsidy payments each farm operator is eligible to collect and denial of subsidies to affluent farmers through means-testing; (4) control of overall farm spending through the budget process; and (5) adjustment of price supports below market prices. Comprehensive reform, elimination of specific programs, and means-testing failed to gain adoption. Payment limitations and budgetary control did not produce the intended result—that is, reduced government costs. Only price support reduction, the most incremental policy change of all, has met with a measure of success in terms of reducing government involvement in commodity markets and moderating subsidy costs. Even this success has been partially offset, because alternative ways—ones that do not show up in large budgetary outlays—have been found to deliver benefits to farm producers.

Comprehensive Reform

Farm groups were initially unconcerned with the Reagan administration plan for comprehensive reform because they assumed it sought only marginal reductions in the budget. In exchange, Ronald Reagan would lift the grain embargo to the Soviet Union, as he had pledged during his campaign. Their complaisance ended when the administration unveiled its budget and farm proposals in the spring of 1981. Target prices and the deficiency payments that went with them would be eliminated, and the secretary of agriculture would be given broad discretion to set price supports (or loan rates, as they are called). If the secretary chose to set price support levels below market prices, farmers would be forced to get what they could for their crops in the market. The two linchpins of agricultural policy—income and price supports—would be effectively jettisoned.[1]

The 1985 Reagan farm proposal, the Agricultural Adjustment Act, carried the same title as the depression-era Agricultural Adjustment Act of 1933 that it was intended to repeal. Using the same name underscored the administration's aim to write new, permanent legislation, not just to reauthorize existing law. Like the 1981 proposal, the act called for eliminating deficiency payments, this time by phasing them out over five years. The amount of the subsidy each farmer could receive would be capped at $20,000 in 1986 and decline to $10,000 by 1988. The proposal also set the price support level below the average free-market price—effectively getting the government out of setting prices and having farmers fetch what they could for their commodities in the free market.

Both of Reagan's proposals were dead on arrival in Congress. Members of the House and Senate Agriculture committees, who would have to approve the proposals, were not about to overhaul farm programs so radically. They marked up their bills in the traditional manner—that is, committee members sought to enhance the subsidy programs for the principal farm interests in their states or districts. The administration abandoned its efforts at comprehensive reform and entered into extended negotiations with Congress that centered more on where to set price and income supports and overall budget levels than on basic policy changes.

Eliminating Specific Commodity Programs

Efforts to eliminate or place major restrictions on commodity programs have been directed mostly at the sugar, peanut, and tobacco components of the farm bills, because the high visibility of these commodities (along with dairy products) has generated the most objections from consumer groups. Objections to support for these products arise also for a variety of other reasons peculiar to the manner in which they are subsidized. Archaic, complex systems of federal acreage allotments (which permit only those growers who had historically owned or rented allotments to produce for the market), as well as domestic sales quotas (which raise prices by limiting supply), governed the production of peanuts and tobacco. A system of import quotas and duties, which raises domestic market prices, kept sugar prices above market levels.

Attempts to change these systems have been almost complete failures. In 1981 the House voted to do away with peanut acreage allotments and quotas, while keeping price supports, and to end sugar price supports. But in conference with the Senate only the allotments were abolished; peanut quotas and sugar price supports were restored. Import duties and quotas for sugar also remain in place. In 1985, in the House, amendments to eliminate or phase out subsidies for sugar, dairy, tobacco, honey, and peanut production all failed to win adoption. In addition, in 1990 Congress added a new support program for soybeans, traditionally the most market-oriented commodity. In 1993 Congress abolished the honey, wool, and mohair subsidy programs, but given those commodities' minuscule portion of the subsidy budget (the smallest of all the commodity programs), that victory was more symbolic than real.

Means-Testing and Payment Limitations

The proven capacity of farm interests to resist comprehensive and specific commodity reforms has led to efforts to deny benefits to affluent farmers by applying a means-test or by capping the amount of subsidy any single farmer can receive, or both. Reformers have tried to expose subsidies as simple welfare programs and destroy the myth that most benefits go to struggling family farmers. In 1987, for instance, 30 percent of the $22.4 billion spent in subsidies went to the 4 percent of farm operators with net cash income of more than $100,000 a year and net worth of nearly $850,000. In some cases corporations and individual investors earning more than three times the annual income of the average American family have received subsidies.[2]

This strategy was laid out in the 1987 *Economic Report of the President*,[3] which criticized farm programs for providing little assistance to the most financially strapped farmers. It called for converting farm subsidies into direct welfare payments for poor farmers. In 1986, under pressure from urban members of Congress, deficiency payments were capped at $50,000 per farmer, but this restriction was skirted routinely in ways that made a mockery of the law.[4] In 1990 a bipartisan coalition of urban liberals and suburban conservatives in the House pushed means-testing, but they were defeated.

Farm interests in general view means-testing as a threat because it would turn perceptions of farm subsidies as welfare into a reality, which in turn would make the programs more politically vulnerable. One of the traditional purposes of subsidies has been to stabilize commodity markets, which is possible, some argue, only if the largest and richest farmers are kept in the program. More than other sectors of the economy, agriculture is a textbook example of a competitive market and one that is uniquely affected by the weather and natural disasters. Consumers benefit by having an assured, adequate food supply at stable prices. The government therefore asks farmers to idle portions of their acreage to control supply (and consequently prices) in exchange for subsidizing farmers' incomes. If large producers were not allowed in the program and made eligible for subsidies, stabilization would be impossible during times of drought or overproduction. If subsidies were rendered ineffective in stabilizing the farm economy and were provided only for needy farmers, welfare would be their sole purpose.[5]

Critics contend that farm producers should be treated like other sectors of the economy, which do not receive the kind of subsidization farmers get. The risks posed by weather and natural disasters are unique to agriculture, but these risks can be dealt with through more limited policies (crop insurance, for example) that would be less intrusive and costly than subsidies.

Reformers hoped that their means-testing plan would divide the farm lobby between midwestern populists and southerners. Means-testing was most threatening to southern commodities because crops like rice and cotton need to be grown on large farms to be profitable, unlike midwestern grains. Because the amount of subsidy received by a farmer is tied directly to the amount of crop produced, large producers would quickly reach the means-test limit. If forced to choose between cutting subsidies across the board or denying them to wealthy farmers, midwestern farmers would choose the latter, reformers hoped.[6] But nothing forced the farm lobby to make this choice. Means-testing, the producers thought, was a Trojan horse designed to weaken political support for subsidies per se and to enable their eventual elimination.

Because little progress could be made toward substantive reform, policymaking became a struggle over incremental adjustments to the status quo—that is, over raising or lowering support levels for prices and incomes and manipulating elements of the farm program to fit within budget constraints. This process involved protracted and sometimes bit-

ter conflict during the Reagan years, particularly between congressional
Democrats and the administration.

Budgetary Control

The budget process and persistently high deficits have been two of the
most important new features of farm politics in recent years. The specter
of farm commodities pitted against one another for limited resources has
strained, though not broken, the farm coalition. It is certain that without
the salience of the federal deficit issue, the congressional budget process,
and the administration's opposition to more spending, more would have
been spent on subsidies in the 1980s and 1990s. The agriculture committees consistently found themselves wedged between the pressures of their
constituents and those of the budget authorities. The levels of price and
income supports written into law were lower than what farm groups
demanded, and the committees were forced to pare down their original
authorizations time and again.

Nevertheless, it proved impossible to fully contain farm spending
through the budget process. The Reagan administration's major budget
victory came in 1981, when it got most of the cuts that it asked for through
the budget reconciliation process. After 1981, however, reconciliation
came under attack from the authorization and appropriations committees, which claimed that its use eroded their power. The administration
was forced to negotiate on programs directly with the committees with
relevant jurisdiction. Partial victories were the best that it could accomplish: it forced the agriculture committees to cut back their authorizations, but not by as much as the president would have liked.[7]

The greatest constraint on use of the budget to reduce subsidies has
been the combination of a deteriorating farm economy and the fact that
farm programs are designed as open-ended entitlements. These factors
are discussed at length later in the chapter, but let it suffice now to say
that without structural reform of farm policy (that is, changes in the
authorizing legislation), spending ultimately will be driven more by economic conditions than by budgetary decisions. Unless price and income
supports are eliminated or are restricted to needy farmers, or loan rates
and target prices are set at sufficiently low levels, then a revisit of the
economic conditions of the 1980s is bound to drive up the cost of the
programs.

Price Support Adjustment

The 1981 farm law, passed when inflation was still high, supported farmers' incomes with higher prices than farmers could get in the market. The agricultural surpluses that resulted were bought by the government in order to boost market prices, but that action also helped to price U.S. commodities out of international markets. The 1985 act steered a different course in the midst of a farm depression. The heart of the compromise between Congress and Reagan was that in exchange for lower government-supported prices (price supports), farmers would receive higher income supports. In effect, Congress approved the part of the 1981 Reagan proposal that would adjust price support levels downward so that they would stay below market prices. But Congress also maintained farmers' incomes with deficiency payments, which were based on target prices that fell more gradually than the price support levels.

The strategy turned out to be fairly successful. Farm policy became more market-oriented and subsidy costs dropped. With the help of a weakening dollar, American farmers were able to capture a larger share of the international market. Compared to the cost of farm subsidies in the mid-1980s, the $10 billion–$12 billion price tag for the current program seems to be a bargain.

There are two problems, however, with reform through price adjustment. First, farmers are more dependent than ever before on income support payments.[8] Many farmers who once looked askance at government assistance feel they can no longer refuse it.[9] Nearly $90 billion was spent on farm programs during 1986–90, more than $60 billion of it on income supports. In 1989, 82 percent of all growers of major crops such as wheat, corn, and rice collected subsidies. Government payments as a proportion of annual farm family budgets jumped from 8.1 percent in 1980 to 31.7 percent in 1988.[10] Second, whether price supports will continue to remain lower than market prices is uncertain. In 1990 Congress decided that price supports had fallen enough, making them irrelevant and thus reducing payments to farmers. In reauthorizing farm programs, Congress raised support levels, but no higher than the market price projected for the next five years. The Bush administration objected, contending that the price support increases departed from the market-oriented thrust of the 1985 act, which had reduced them each year; nonetheless, without enough votes in favor of lower supports, the administration ultimately acceded to the higher supports. If market conditions deteriorate, price supports could end up higher than the world market price, and subsidy costs could again soar.

Although heightened budgetary constraints and price support adjustment have led to some modest success in controlling the costs of commodity programs since the late 1980s, policymakers have found other mechanisms for serving farm clients. Trade protection and export promotion programs, whose impacts on the budget are either insignificant or less visible than commodity programs, have been enlarged in response to the budgetary pinch. Major beneficiaries of this approach are sugar producers. In 1981 Congress required the secretary of agriculture to support the price of sugar through the purchase of surpluses whenever the market price fell below the price support level. However, to avoid a negative impact on the budget, Congress also directed the president to use his authority under section 22 of the Agricultural Adjustment Act of 1933 to impose import fees on foreign farm products. The Reagan administration did so, and as world sugar prices fell, the administration ordered higher duties and eventually reinstated country-specific quotas that had not been used since 1974.[11]

Other assistance has been provided through programs intended to boost U.S. farm exports. A variety of creative financing arrangements (loan guarantees, for example) that require little in the way of appropriations have been afforded producers through the Export-Import Bank, the Overseas Private Investment Corporation, and the Commodity Credit Corporation of the Agriculture Department. These programs hardly show up in budgetary outlays, especially when compared with the expensive commodity supports. The indirect and almost invisible nature of these subsidies is politically advantageous for farm producers and their congressional allies.[12]

From Rising Fortunes to Maintenance

Using the framework employed to analyze the cases in the preceding chapters, the remainder of this chapter presents an explanation for why the policy fortunes of farm producers have taken a distinctive course.

The Issue Context: Cost and Inequity

As with tax expenditures and anticompetitive regulations, the diffuse burdens of farm subsidies became a salient issue in the 1980s, setting the

Table 4-1. *Costs of Farm Income Stabilization Programs, 1970–94*
Billions of current dollars unless otherwise specified

Year	Amount of subsidy	Percentage change from previous year	Consumer Price Index	Inflation-adjusted subsidy	Percentage change from previous year
1970	4.6	−12	5.7	4.3	−12
1971	3.7	−20	4.4	3.5	−18
1972	4.6	24	3.2	4.5	26
1973	4.1	−11	6.2	3.9	−13
1974	1.5	−63	11.0	1.3	−65
1975	0.8	−47	9.1	0.7	−45
1976	1.6	100	5.8	1.5	101
1977	4.5	181	6.5	4.2	179
1978	6.6	47	7.6	6.5	55
1979	4.9	−26	11.3	4.4	−33
Average for 1970s	3.7	17	7.1	3.5	17
1980	7.4	51	13.5	6.4	47
1981	9.8	32	10.3	8.8	37
1982	14.3	46	6.2	13.4	53
1983	21.3	49	3.2	20.6	54
1984	11.9	−44	4.3	11.4	−45
1985	23.8	100	3.6	22.9	101
1986	29.6	24	1.9	29.0	27
1987	24.7	−17	3.6	23.8	−18
1988	15.2	−38	4.1	14.6	−38
1989	14.8	−3	4.8	14.1	−7
Average for 1980s	17.3	23	5.6	16.5	21
1990	9.8	−34	5.4	9.3	−34
1991	12.9	32	4.2	12.4	33
1992	12.7	−2	3.0	12.3	1
1993	17.8	40	3.0	17.2	28
1994	12.0[a]	−33	2.8[a]	11.7	−32
Average for 1990s	13.0	1	3.7	12.6	−4

Source: *Budget of the United States Government*, various years.
a. Estimated.

stage for launching a major attack on existing policy. The criticism that
farm programs distort market incentives, thereby creating inefficiency,
had been heard for a long time.[13] The dramatic jump in the cost of
subsidies reinforced the perception of a wasteful and defective policy. At
the same time the federal deficit climbed to unprecedented levels, making
these high costs all the more salient. Table 4-1 shows the pattern of
growth of federal outlays for farm subsidies. Even when adjusted for
annual rates of inflation, subsidies in the 1980s averaged almost five times
as much as they did in the 1970s, going from $3.5 billion to $16.5 billion.

Thus far in the 1990s, the inflation-adjusted subsidy levels have been about three to four times the 1970s level, although they are lower than they averaged in the 1980s. Especially striking is the rise from the mid-1970s to the mid-1980s. In 1975 subsidies were less than $1 billion, but by 1986 they had reached almost $30 billion. The table also shows sharp volatility in the level of subsidies from year to year, departing from the familiar incremental pattern noted in studies of budgeting.[14]

Table 4-2 reveals that rises and declines in spending on farm subsidies roughly track fluctuations in the federal deficit, especially for the 1980s. The years of massive budget deficits in that decade were matched by large increases in farm subsidies, especially when compared with deficit and subsidy levels in the 1970s. The large deficits persisted into the 1990s, but farm subsidy levels dropped from their average in the 1980s (although, as stated above, they remained higher than they had been in the 1970s).

As a proportion of the federal budget, the level of subsidies appears fairly modest, averaging less than 2 percent of total federal spending and just over 2 percent of nondefense spending from 1970–89. Subsidies have never exceeded 3 percent of total federal spending, and only once did they exceed 4 percent of nondefense spending. Despite the substantial overall increase in farm subsidies from the 1970s to the 1980s, they have grown only somewhat faster than the total budget and nondefense spending as a whole. Still, annual farm subsidies in the 1980s averaged 54 percent higher as a proportion of the budget (and 44 percent higher as a proportion of nondefense spending) than in the previous decade.[15]

What was behind the sharp rise in farm benefits? The answer: the performance of the farm economy, the design of subsidy programs as mandatory spending in the budget, and the interaction between the two. As economic conditions in agriculture declined in the 1980s, more and more farmers became eligible for benefits and, as with many social insurance and income transfer programs, all eligible producers are entitled to government subsidies. For such open-ended entitlements, budgetary actions alone cannot determine the level of spending. If appropriations are insufficient to cover required costs, Congress must approve supplemental funds to cover the entire cost. Furthermore, unlike calculating future costs for social security, which relies on more or less predictable trends in demographics and contributions, estimating annual budget commitments for farm programs is fraught with uncertainty.[16] Congress specifies per-bushel loan rates and target prices, but the amount actually

Table 4-2. *Agricultural Subsidies and the Federal Budget, 1970–94*

Year	Amount of federal budget deficit (billions of current dollars)	Amount spent for agricultural subsidies	
		As percentage of total federal budget	As percentage of non-defense spending
1970	2.8	2.3	4.0
1971	23.0	1.8	2.8
1972	23.4	2.0	3.0
1973	14.9	1.7	2.4
1974	6.1	0.6	0.8
1975	53.2	0.2	0.3
1976	73.7	0.4	0.5
1977	53.7	1.1	1.4
1978	59.2	1.5	1.9
1979	40.2	1.0	1.3
Average for 1970s	30.2	1.3	1.8
1980	73.8	1.3	1.6
1981	79.0	1.5	1.9
1982	128.0	2.0	2.6
1983	207.8	2.6	3.6
1984	185.4	1.4	1.9
1985	212.3	2.5	3.4
1986	221.2	3.0	4.1
1987	149.8	2.5	3.4
1988	155.2	1.4	2.0
1989	152.5	1.3	1.8
Average for 1980s	151.3	2.0	2.6
1990	221.4	0.8	1.0
1991	269.5	1.0	1.2
1992	290.4	1.0	1.2
1993	254.7	1.3	1.6
1994	203.4	1.0	1.1
Average for 1990s	247.9	1.0	1.2

Source: *Budget of the United States Government*, various years; and *Economic Report of the President*, February 1994, p. 359.

spent is driven by forces that can fluctuate wildly and are difficult to control (the weather and economic conditions, for example).

This problem has worsened as U.S. agriculture has become more dependent on foreign markets and actions of foreign governments. And because farm subsidies interact closely with the market, unlike other entitlement programs, the programs themselves stimulate participation. Subsidies lower risk, which attracts resources into farming; more resources mean increased production, and more production reduces prices. As prices go down, government spending on subsidies to bolster prices and incomes rises, which stimulates further participation in the programs.[17]

The price support levels of the 1981 farm bill, which made prices artificially high, and a deteriorating farm economy forced the government to purchase huge amounts of surplus commodities and to support farmers' incomes. Spending on subsidies rose sharply until the late 1980s. The lower price supports legislated in 1985 directly contributed to the somewhat lower spending, and as the dollar weakened late in the decade, the farm economy revived because export markets rebounded. Spending on subsidies decreased substantially, although the amount remained higher than it had been in the 1970s.

Not only were the cost and inefficiency of farm programs becoming more apparent, but the programs seemed increasingly unjustified because of the dwindling number of farmers in the population and the inequitable distribution of the programs' benefits. Fewer eligible recipients of federal farm largesse exist, and benefits are skewed in favor of the largest farms.

In 1900 the farm population numbered almost 30 million, or 42 percent of the U.S. population; by 1980 the group was down to just over 6 million, or 2.7 percent of the population. Total farm employment declined from 9.9 million workers in 1950 to 3.5 million in 1982. The number of farms fell from about 5.3 million in 1950 to about 2.2 million in 1982. Average farm size in 1982 was 440 acres, three times larger than the average farm size in 1910. Also, by 1982 just 13.5 percent of all farms accounted for about 72.6 percent of total agricultural sales.[18]

As for the distribution of benefits, because the amount of the subsidy farmers receive depends on how much is produced (as opposed to other criteria, such as need), larger operators get a disproportionate share of the subsidy budget. One study estimated that, for 1978, the top 10 percent of farms, by size, received 55.5 percent of all net benefits; the smallest 70 percent received just 8 percent of the benefits.[19] In 1983, when direct payments to farmers were $9.4 billion, $4.1 billion (44 percent) went to the 12 percent of farms with sales of $100,000 or more and net farming income (before inventory adjustment) of $97,000. Off-farm income averaged $14,000 for each of these farms;[20] the average government subsidy for each was $14,000 as well. In contrast, the 72 percent of the farmers with the lowest level of sales received only 22 percent of the direct payments. Moreover, a significant fraction of all benefits has gone not to farm operators themselves but to landlords. Clearly, large farms have held a privileged position vis-à-vis family farms in receipt of federal assistance.

A coalition resembling the broad bipartisan ones that emerged during tax reform and deregulation developed in the agricultural arena during the 1980s. The Reagan administration came out in favor of reform, proposing the most radical market-oriented policy changes since farm programs began under the New Deal. In the House of Representatives (where rural districts are in the minority), a bipartisan group of urban, liberal Democrats and suburban, conservative Republicans mobilized for reform.

By 1990 this coalition had gained considerable strength under the leadership of Charles Schumer, Democrat of New York, and Richard Armey, Republican of Texas. Liberals reasoned that, because spending on programs for the poor and the cities was being cut or was not growing, rural interests should share the pain. In the Senate, "prairie populists" such as Thomas Daschle of South Dakota and Robert Kerrey of Nebraska, both Democrats, favored targeting more benefits to small family farmers. They were allied with Indiana's Senator Richard Lugar, whose interest was in restraining the cost of the farm program.[21] The appeal of reform for conservatives was rooted in the principles of free markets and less government. Those in both camps thought reform would benefit consumers and taxpayers and help reduce the deficit.

In sum, a strong case could be made—and was in fact made—that farm subsidies, like tax expenditures and anticompetitive regulations, contributed to diffuse economic burdens and inequity. The cost, inefficiency, and inequity of farm programs worsened over time and became highly salient in the 1980s, particularly in the context of high budget deficits and the resultant pressures to reduce spending. An emergent bipartisan group of officials in the administration and in Congress began to call for reform.

A Competing Issue: The Farmer as Victim

In one important respect, however, agriculture differed from the tax and regulatory cases: the problems associated with the diffuse costs of farm subsidies were overshadowed and displaced by the greater salience of another issue, namely, the economic distress of the farm economy itself.[22] Hence what hampered reform efforts was not the absence of subsidy-related problems—those were present in the agriculture area, as in the tax and regulatory cases—but rather the simultaneous emergence of a more salient issue. Instead of being painted as greedy claimants on the public purse, farmers were sympathetically portrayed as victims valiantly fighting for survival.

Farm distress blunted arguments against subsidies and deflected attention from their costs. Reagan's 1981 proposal came on the heels of the third consecutive year in which farmers' incomes declined from the level of the previous year. Net farm income, the most widely used measure of the financial state of farming, fell by about 41 percent in 1980 to its lowest point since 1964. Income rose by 26 percent in 1981, but it did not reach the levels of most of the 1970s.

By the time the administration put forward its 1985 proposal, the farm economy had deteriorated. Land values had plummeted, beginning in 1981 as inflation receded. In addition, farm production exceeded demand. Farm productivity peaked in 1982 and 1983 with bumper crops, just as export markets contracted. In 1982, for the first time in a decade, exports declined to $36.6 billion, from a record level of $43.3 billion in the previous year.[23] As a result, net farm income fell considerably in 1982 and 1983, to its lowest level since the 1950s.[24] Caught between falling land values, declining crop prices, and rising real interest rates, farmers found it difficult to repay loans they had taken out during the boom years of the 1970s when production and exports were rising.

Not only were farmers perceived as fighting for their economic survival, but it could be argued plausibly that they were not exclusively or even primarily to blame for their situation. Policymakers in the 1970s, such as Nixon's Secretary of Agriculture Earl Butz, had urged farmers to plant "fencerow to fencerow." Bankers had made low-interest loans available to expand production, and many farmers had gone into debt buying land and equipment in anticipation of growing world demand. The assumptions in the agriculture community as a whole were that the world would continue to buy as much as American farmers produced, and that inflation would continue making it financially feasible to accrue large debts.

With U.S. agricultural productivity outpacing growth in the domestic population, export markets loomed increasingly important; table 4-3 shows the growing dependence of American farmers on exports. Exports accounted for about a quarter of the gross farm product (GFP) at the start of the 1970s, for 40 percent by the end of the decade. The dollar

Table 4-3. *Growth of U.S. Agricultural Exports, 1970–91*
Billions of current dollars unless otherwise specified

Year	Gross farm product	Exports	Exports as percentage of gross farm product
1970	26.2	7.3	28
1971	30.4	7.7	25
1972	31.9	9.4	29
1973	49.9	17.7	35
1974	47.7	21.9	46
1975	50.3	21.9	44
1976	48.5	23.0	47
1977	50.4	23.6	47
1978	60.3	29.4	49
1979	71.8	34.7	49
Average for 1970s	46.7	19.7	40
1980	56.1	41.2	73
1981	79.8	43.3	54
1982	65.1	36.6	56
1983	49.2	36.1	73
1984	68.5	37.8	55
1985	67.1	29.0	43
1986	62.9	26.2	42
1987	66.0	28.7	43
1988	67.6	37.1	55
1989	81.1	39.9	49
Average for 1980s	66.3	35.6	54
1990	85.0	39.4	46
1991	79.1	39.2	50

Source: Bureau of the Census, *Statistical Abstract of the United States* (Department of Commerce, various years).

value of farm exports increased over the same period by more than 150 percent.[25] After shooting up to a record high of 73 percent of GFP in 1980, exports waned and waxed for several years, averaging about 54 percent of GFP over the decade.

As inflation became intolerable in the late 1970s, the Federal Reserve Board tightened monetary policy, boosting real interest rates and thus slowing economic activity in the United States and abroad. The global recession dampened demand in developing countries, which had gone heavily into debt to fuel domestic expansion and to finance imports. Now these countries were financially strapped and had trouble meeting their loan payments. Aggravated by unprecedented U.S. budget deficits, high interest rates attracted foreign capital, which drove up the value of the dollar in currency markets and made U.S. exports less attractive. Even though prices of American farm products had been pushed down considerably, they still translated into high, uncompetitive levels in foreign currencies.

The drop in world demand for American products was exacerbated by the grain embargo President Jimmy Carter imposed in retaliation for the invasion of Afghanistan by the Soviet Union. Moreover, competition from highly subsidized European Market countries and the emergence of Australia and Argentina as major grain exporters made it more difficult to expand exports when the embargo was lifted.

The farm crisis, salient throughout most of the decade, was never more so than in 1985 when Reagan put forward his second radical proposal. With many farmers in fact desperate and needy, it was difficult, if not incongruous, to depict them as privileged and powerful feeders at the public trough. Although Reagan's budget director, David Stockman, argued that the government had no responsibility to relieve farmers of their debt problem because it "was willingly incurred by consenting adults,"[26] many believed that government, banking, and impersonal national and international economic forces had promoted overproduction and shrinking demand for U.S. farm products.

Once the farm crisis seized Congress's attention, calls for eliminating subsidies seemed callously indifferent to the farmers' plight. Considerable media attention accompanied the crisis, including Hollywood movies such as *Country*, *Places in the Heart*, and *The River*, which depicted valiant struggles waged by family farmers in the face of economic exploitation and natural disasters. According to a congressional representative from South Dakota, the films "shed the stigma" of economic failure for farmers.[27] Television talk show host Phil Donahue featured farmers in a two-day telecast from Iowa, and CBS news anchor Dan Rather toured the farm belt for a series of broadcasts.

Not surprisingly, the public salience of the farmers' plight was exceptionally high. A poll taken in January 1985 revealed that 65 percent of the American public agreed that it was a "bad idea" to spend less on farm aid in order to reduce the budget deficit.[28] In February 1986, a *New York Times*/CBS News poll reported that 83 percent of respondents nationally thought that at least half of all farmers were experiencing financial difficulty, with 50 percent feeling that additional federal financial support of farmers was needed; only 12 percent favored a decrease in spending. Fifty-five percent said that they were willing to pay more taxes if an increase would help troubled farmers save their land. When asked whether farmers should be specially favored or whether the government should "treat farmers the way it treats other small businessmen," 52 percent of respondents said farmers should be given special treatment.[29]

"There was a shift," said one lobbyist, "from having the primary objective be movement toward the market to how do we maintain the income of the farmer."[30] Calls for market-oriented reforms that would deprive farmers of government help lost whatever appeal they had, and the reform issue evaporated from public discourse. Broad public support for increasing farm spending persisted into 1988, despite the fact that the debt crisis had bottomed out, the political activism of farmers had subsided, and the public wanted government to cut spending for many defense and domestic programs.[31]

The sympathy from politicians and the public that farmers evoked in the 1980s was based on more than objective economic circumstances, however. The reason that the farmers' situation had such resonance with Americans is because of the persistence of the agrarian myth, or agricultural creed. Ideas that emerge and take hold in one historical period, under one set of social and economic conditions, often persist for generations after the conditions that gave rise to them have passed. The agrarian myth, a hangover from America's rural past, conjures an image of farmers as a yeomanry devoted to tilling the land, as rugged individuals safeguarding Jeffersonian democracy, and as a populist mass exploited by greedy Eastern economic interests. The films and news broadcasts about the travails of farm life tapped widely shared, deeply embedded perceptions of farmers and of farming as "a way of life." As a result, farmers are not perceived in the same negative light as many other special interests. Most are viewed as wholesome family farmers, not affluent, powerful enterprises.

In a 1987 poll, 82 percent of the public agreed with the statement that "the family farm must be preserved because it is a vital part of our heritage." And 80 percent agreed that "agriculture is the most basic occupation in our society, and almost all other occupations depend upon it." These levels of agreement varied little with the age, income, education, race, partisan identification, or ideological orientation of the respondents.[32] A 1986 poll found that 58 percent agreed that "farm life is more honest and moral than life in the rest of the country," 64 percent felt that "farmers are more hard-working than most other Americans," and 67 percent said that "farmers have closer ties to their families than most other Americans do."[33]

The importance of this mythology in sustaining farm interests politically is hard to underestimate. According to two observers,

> Today, with a farm-based political majority long gone, this agrarian myth persists. It persists precisely because most people have limited experience with agriculture and its economic issues and because those in agriculture have an important stake in romanticizing its social role and seeking widespread public support. . . . The broadcast and print media are the prime purveyors of images. Messages are transmitted that reinforce a type of simple . . . learning. These features of modern communication make it possible for an active minority to proselytize and keep an agrarian myth vital and supportable even when its basic tenets are disputable and under constant intellectual attack.[34]

The myth is strengthened by the fact that it rests upon more than emotional appeals to a romanticized past. Most of today's farmers are indeed hard-working folks. The average farmer's income is fairly close to the median income of most American families, and most farms are not large corporate entities. Despite the decline in the number of farms and an increase in their average size, farming is still carried out by thousands of independent producers. Weather and natural disasters, over which producers have no direct control, make agriculture a uniquely risky and unstable endeavor. The biological character of agriculture makes it more difficult to manage than industrial sectors of the economy. Most inputs are fully committed at the beginning of a growing season, growth requires a lengthy period of time, and the output becomes available to the market all at once. And no commodity is more critical to any nation than its food supply. "All of these considerations," according to one observer, "endow agriculture with a large stock of public good will, the dimensions of which have been estimated with considerable skill by those who propose farm programs. This is the reason we would develop a parity program for farmers but not for barbers or hardware merchants."[35] Yet none of these circumstances necessarily justifies existing subsidies, especially since most of their benefits accrue to large, often affluent, growers rather than to the small family farmers who need help the most.[36]

While farm subsidies enjoy support from members of both parties, Democrats are clearly the farmers' stronger allies. Appendix tables 4B-1 through 4B-4 present the results of roll-call votes on farm program reauthorizations from 1977 to 1990. On votes affecting subsidy levels and eligibility (tables 4B-1, 4B-2, and 4B-3), the proportion of Democrats voting to support more generous provisions was higher than that of Republicans on twenty-two of the twenty-seven amendments. On average, a majority of Republicans (60 percent) voted to reduce (or not increase) benefits and eligibility, compared with a minority of Democrats (43 percent). These partisan differences hold even when results are controlled for the rural versus nonrural variation across congressional districts.

As discussed in appendix 4B, the roll-call analysis suggests that Democrats' support for farm producers rests on more than the benefits from urban-rural logrolling alliances involving the food stamp program and legislation of interest to organized labor. There is an ideological component to the Democrats' support, rooted in New Deal politics, which considers farmers to be an exploited group. If support for farm subsidies rested exclusively on an exchange of material benefits, urban Republicans might be expected to join urban Democrats in vote trading. Yet partisan differences in voting patterns remain even after controlling for the degree to which congressional districts are urban or rural. That is, urban Democrats are significantly more likely than their urban Republican counterparts to support farm subsidies.[37]

It is in this context that the coalition politics of the 1980s developed. The farm crisis of that decade breathed new life into the populist appeal of subsidies, undercutting any possibility of a strong bipartisan, liberal-conservative alliance in favor of reform. Almost daily during the deliberations over the 1985 farm bill, members of Congress made speeches and issued press releases and proposals about the crisis. The House Agriculture Committee staged well-attended public hearings, where famous actresses who starred in the farm-genre films testified as witnesses with special insights into the crisis. Republicans criticized these as mere public relations tactics, a crass bid for electoral advantage by the Democrats. By the end of the summer, however, many Republicans themselves had joined the Democrats in another media event, the Farm Aid concert held as a fund-raiser for farmers in trouble. Country-music recording artists featured at the concert visited Capitol Hill ostensibly to seek advice on how to spend the money; their conferrals with members of Congress occasioned much media attention. According to *Congressional Quarterly*, "Members of both parties were being drawn into a political cyclone of having to prove their commitment to farmers."[38]

Senate Democrats found the issue enticing because it put the Republicans on the defensive. Party competition to secure the votes of rural interests is particularly intense in the Senate for three reasons. First, rural interests are overrepresented in the Senate, where relatively underpopulated states such as the Dakotas are given equal representation with states that have much larger populations. Second, unlike in the House, party competition for control of the Senate has been sharp for the past several elections, with shifts of a few seats between the parties determining which party is in the majority. Finally, virtually every state has some agricultural component to its economy. In the House, farm interests are geographically concentrated in no more than eighty congressional districts; in the Senate, they are more diffuse. As a result, farm interests are able to exert greater and more direct pressure on electoral outcomes in the Senate.

In 1984 two Republican senators from the farm belt, Roger Jepsen of Iowa and Charles Percy of Illinois, were defeated. Republicans, who held a tenuous 53–47 majority in the Senate in 1985, were torn between the Reagan administration and fiscal responsibility, on the one hand, and the pressures to at least maintain existing levels of farm benefits, on the other. In the spring Republicans from farm states defected from party ranks by approving an emergency credit measure designed to help debt-ridden farmers through another planting season. Reagan, claiming that the credit bill was an unwarranted bailout for bankers who had made unwise loans to farmers, vetoed the bill. But the entire, predominantly Republican South Dakota legislature, joined by large groups from Nebraska, Kansas, and North Dakota, came to Washington to lobby for the legislation in a well-publicized media event. The administration subsequently suffered substantial Republican defections in the House and in the Senate on major votes on the 1985 farm bill.[39]

Twenty-two GOP senators were up for reelection in 1986, seven of them from farm states. As the economic slump persisted into the fall campaign, their Democratic opponents accused them of being tied to Reagan's reform efforts. The tactic seemed to pay off at the ballot box. The GOP suffered a net loss of eight seats, including those in North Dakota, South Dakota, Georgia, Nevada, and North Carolina. These losses provided the margin needed for the Democrats to reclaim control of the chamber. Three of the successful Democratic challengers took seats on the Agriculture Committee.

An issue context favorable to farm groups effectively kept reform off the agenda in the 1980s. The salience of the farm crisis, the dramatization of the farmer-as-victim, and the persistence of the agrarian myth have been the most immediate and important obstacles to launching effective attacks on farm producers, but they are not the only ones. With an issue context more hospitable to change in 1990, Congress seriously considered means-testing farm benefits. By that time, the farm economy had recovered, exports had risen, and commodity prices were healthy. Net farm income reached $40 billion in 1988, land values revived, and foreclosures slowed substantially.[40] With the crisis over, one major impediment to reform was gone: the plight of family farmers could no longer be used to fend off the challenges of reform advocates. With the budget deficit far more salient than farm issues, and with the pro-reform, conservative-liberal alliance gaining strength in Congress, some observers opined that farm programs were highly vulnerable.

Means-testing represented incremental rather than radical change; just as important, it was aimed at affluent farmers and investors who bore little resemblance to the family farmers extolled in the agrarian myth.[41] At the very least, such a proposal might have been expected to neutralize the populist sentiment supporting subsidies; at best, it might have aroused such sentiment in favor of reform. Yet even under these conditions—in particular, after economic conditions had improved—reform still failed.

It is true that even though the farm crisis was over, its political impact was still being felt in 1990. There was considerable trepidation among Republicans who had been chastened by their experience in the 1980s. They believed that Democrats had made Reagan's radical proposals and tough bargaining with farm interests a campaign issue, to good effect. Also, several farm states again emerged as key battlegrounds for the GOP's efforts to retake the Senate in 1990. But this cannot explain the defeat of means-testing in the House. Electoral pressure from farm interests was not as intense in the House as it was in the Senate. Proponents of reform were highly mobilized in the House, and rural interests do not enjoy the overrepresentation there that they do in the Senate.

It is also true that the end of the crisis removed the urgency for change. After years of record expenditures, subsidies had fallen from about $30 billion in 1986 to roughly $12 billion in the early 1990s. Moreover, lower price supports in the 1985 law and a weakening dollar fueled export expansion. By 1990, an election year, Congress as a whole was apparently not in the mood to substantially alter a policy that farm interests liked and that was cheaper than it used to be. Yet Congress did not feel any urgency to adopt tax reform or deregulation, either; those changes it had adopted only when it had been compelled to do so. Why was Congress not similarly compelled in the case of agricultural reform? If an issue context that was reasonably favorable to change did not produce reform in 1990, what were the obstacles?

The Institutional Context

In short, reform was unattainable in the absence of an institutional context conducive to it.

BUREAUCRATS AND LEGISLATORS. There appears to be little bureaucratic support for advancing bold policy changes in agriculture. The Department of Agriculture historically has been a constituency-oriented agency whose *raison d'être*, to advance the economic interests of farm producers,[42] contrasts with the internally driven mission of the Treasury Department, which took the lead on tax reform, and with the flexibly vague public-interest mandates under which the regulatory agencies operate. There has been little push for reform from the department's professional staff, as evidenced by its absence from the reform battles of the 1980s. Similarly, the agriculture committees are among the most constituency-oriented bodies in Congress. Legislators seek membership on the committees primarily to serve their farmer constituents, which enhances their reelection prospects. In their comparative study of committees, Steven S. Smith and Christopher J. Deering found that very few surveyed members of the Agriculture Committee expressed any other reason—such as prestige, influence with colleagues, or making good policy—for seeking to get on the committee.[43] The agriculture committees therefore cannot be counted on to be institutional sites for launching far-reaching reforms. By contrast, those in Congress who spearheaded tax reform and deregulation for the most part sat on committees that attract members whose primary motivation is making good policy or who seek prestige (Commerce, Judiciary, and Finance in the Senate, and Ways and Means in the House).

LEADERSHIP CAPACITY AND COMMITMENT. The most critical institutional ingredient for challenging producer groups successfully is leadership. Without the push from committed officials at strategic locations in government, reform of farm policy could never have come about even if other conditions had been conducive to reform, as they were in 1990. Those in leadership positions played a key role in getting tax reform and deregulation on the agenda and adopted.[44] It was only when key leaders made reform their top priority that the tax and deregulation issues were elevated from causes championed by a few to priorities on the legislative agenda. It was leaders who pushed and persuaded reluctant majorities in Congress to address the issues and approve the measures. It was they who put the producer groups under stress and on the defensive, breaking down their internal cohesion. Some of the leaders—the president, committee chairs, and the heads of the executive agencies involved—held formal positions within the government; others were legislative entrepreneurs who aspired to leadership positions and adopted reform out of personal commitment.

In the case of agriculture, leadership has been in short supply. Weak presidential leadership has been a feature of farm policy for decades. Presidents have ordinarily left it up to Congress to write farm legislation, only occasionally seeking to check congressional excesses in appropriations through veto threats.[45] The Reagan administration's commitment to reform was ambivalent. Its top priorities in 1981 were the budget and tax packages, and in 1985 it was tax reform. Reagan quickly signaled his willingness to sacrifice his farm proposal to achieve these other goals. To avoid antagonizing the southern "boll weevils," whose votes were vital for passage of the economic program, the administration reversed its opposition to the peanut and sugar programs.[46] David Stockman paints a picture of leaders in the White House and Department of Agriculture who would readily abandon market principles in the name of political expedience. Stockman blamed, in particular, presidential adviser Edwin Meese and Undersecretary of Agriculture Richard Lyng for engineering deals with conservatives like Senator Jesse Helms, whose state had important farming interests, and with California agricultural interests friendly to the administration.[47] Hence, rather than challenge key members of Congress to join reform efforts, as occurred in the tax and regulatory cases, the president abandoned agricultural reform when he met with resistance.

The Bush administration not only neglected to send Congress a reform proposal but, in a pattern that marked much of George Bush's domestic presidency, it remained disengaged from the policy debate until the very end. The administration wanted to avoid taking a rigid position early on that it might have to abandon, as had happened under Reagan. When the 1990 farm bill was under consideration in the Senate, Senator Lugar, who led Republican resistance to Democratic efforts to increase spending, expressed the problem this way: "Modestly, I am a counterweight [against the Democrats, but my stature] is not the same as the Secretary of Agriculture or the president. . . . At some point, there has to be something to play off of [the Democrats' proposals]."[48] Similarly, when all signs pointed to success in reducing the sugar price supports in 1990, *Congressional Quarterly* noted that "Republicans defected in droves from the administration, whose lobbying in behalf of the cut was only 'luke-warm.'"[49]

Turning to Congress, the two legislators most committed to reform have been House members Richard Armey and Charles Schumer. No champion like Bill Bradley or Ted Kennedy, whose personal and institutional stature helped get tax reform and deregulation on the agenda, has emerged in the Senate for agricultural reform. Nor have secretaries of agriculture taken bold initiatives to spearhead reform efforts, preferring instead to act as brokers between the White House and Congress in negotiations over farm bills. As William P. Browne described the deliberations over the 1985 farm bill, "USDA officials sat idly by, useful as legislative analysts but largely inconsequential as policy leaders."[50]

Several reasons account for the lack of leadership commitment to reform. As noted in chapter 1, in choosing among issues in which to invest their energies and resources, leaders and policy entrepreneurs must determine which ones offer the greatest chances for successful reform and which ones are likely to offer the greatest payoff in terms of political goals (that is, reelection, recognition among colleagues, and making desired policy changes, among others). Leaders may decide to avoid some issues that might contribute to goal achievement because they are deemed politically infeasible. Other issues may hold out reasonable chances for achieving reform, but those may not contribute substantially or at all to political goals.

One of the main reasons for the lack of reform leadership in agriculture is the issue context, that is, the salience of the prolonged farm crisis and the sympathy that was evoked for the plight of farmers. These circumstances almost certainly deterred potential reform leaders, who surmised that the chances of achieving reform would be slim and the risks of a political backlash great. This is particularly so in the Senate, where the combination of rural overrepresentation and precarious party majorities means that farm interests can influence elections in enough states to shift party control of the chamber. Even though the farm economy was recovering by the time of the debate on the 1990 farm bill, the memory of the Republican electoral setback associated with the 1981 and 1985 Reagan proposals was fresh in the minds of the Bush administration, which helps to explain its trepidation in advancing bold reform.[51]

Features of farm policy itself also constrain leadership initiative. Farm policy has a built-in disadvantage for reform leaders: the economic and budgetary costs of subsidies increase as the farm economy deteriorates. Hence, as the issue that reformers want to focus on becomes more salient, so too does the pain experienced by farmers. When the farm economy improves, farmers' need for assistance diminishes, as does the salience of the costs of subsidies. With the improvement in the farm economy by 1990 and the concomitant decrease in outlays for subsidies, the pressure to do something waned. Reformers faced no such constraint in the tax and regulatory arenas.

Moreover, because farm policy is sectoral rather than functional, it tends to be isolated from the central concerns of the president, congressional leaders, and Congress as a whole. An ambitious legislative entrepreneur in the Senate is unlikely to view farm policy as the kind of issue that will appeal to a broad national audience. By contrast, other reform efforts entailed change in two of the major functions of government, namely, taxation and regulation. These are policy instruments that affect the performance of the entire economy and have huge effects on the distribution of national income. Those reforms were focused not on a single sector of the economy but across several. Deregulation had to be sector-specific, but it was part of a broad shift in policy thinking that traversed several sectors. Also, deregulation turned out to be contagious: deregulation in one sector stimulated reform efforts in others.

Another distinctive feature of farm policy is its international economic component. American farmers are increasingly dependent on export markets, a fact that both provides an incentive for greater presidential involvement in farm policy and hamstrings presidential efforts to reduce subsidies. American farmers have refused to give up their subsidies without comparable concessions from producers abroad. Therefore, to gain leverage over domestic farm policy, the president must first persuade foreign governments to remove subsidies and restrictions.

Both the Reagan and the Bush administrations sought to buy political support for a market-oriented policy with the promise that U.S. farm products could find markets abroad. The farmers' loss of subsidies would be offset by a higher volume of sales in exports. But this plan depended on, among other things, the ability of the United States to negotiate liberal trade arrangements and maintain favorable and stable exchange rates.[52] The Bush administration's detachment from farm policy deliberations in 1990 owed in part to the GATT (General Agreement on Tariffs and Trade) negotiations, at which the administration was seeking to eliminate trade-distorting agricultural subsidies around the world, especially in Europe and Japan. If it had proposed simply cutting American subsidies, it would have been open to the same accusation of "unilateral disarmament" that farmers had leveled at Reagan.[53] The administration hoped to conclude an agreement under GATT that would have given it leverage over the farm bill, but it was unable to do so.

Conclusion

This chapter has traced an explanation for the rise in farm subsidies and the failure of reform efforts to eliminate or reduce them in the 1980s and 1990s. Fueled principally by a deterioration in economic conditions in agriculture and by the open-ended entitlement programs, which led to automatic increases in outlays, spending rose sharply in the decade. The subsequent decline in subsidy levels from their highest levels in the mid-1980s is due more to improved economic conditions (to which spending is tied) than to policy changes.

Just as important, farm producers have been able to defend their programs against efforts to reduce or eliminate them. Although elements of a pro-reform coalition have emerged in the agricultural arena, they have been too weak and narrowly based to successfully challenge the farm groups and their allies. Building the kind of strong, broad-based coalitions that emerged in the tax and regulatory arenas has not been possible for three reasons.

First, while the cost, waste, and inequitable distribution of farm subsidies became salient issues in the 1980s, they were overshadowed and displaced by the severe economic problems experienced by many farmers during these years. The problem came to be defined as one of struggling farmers who were victims of economic forces and events largely out of their control. The poor economy on the farm was joined with a symbolically powerful agrarian myth, embedded in American history and culture and transmitted through the mass media. The portrayal of farmers and of farming as embodying widely shared American values amplified public concern and sympathy for this producer group. The greatest political asset for the farm interests is the widespread perception among the public and policymakers that farmers need and deserve help from the government.

The Reagan administration's lack of recognition of this fundamental fact when it put forward its radical proposals fueled a highly partisan debate. With support from farm interests, which had been forged over decades of logrolling with urban-labor interests, and with a long-lived ideological affinity for the farmers' cause, the Democrats used the farm crisis of the 1980s as a populist rallying issue. Republicans were put on the defensive. This electoral strategy proved effective in the Senate, where rural interests have greater institutional leverage and where party majorities are precarious. In the tax and regulatory cases, by contrast, reformers did not have to contend with competing issues in which the producer groups could be portrayed as victims. Nor could the industries in those cases draw upon symbols and myths that would cast them in a sympathetic light. Instead, they were portrayed as selfish interests whose policy demands increasingly disadvantaged the public.

Differences in the kinds of issues that became salient and in how they were defined provide only part of the explanation for the outcome, however. Economic conditions and the agrarian myth were not so constraining as to prevent reform from reaching the agenda in 1990. By that time the economy had improved and reform (means-testing, in this instance) was targeted at affluent agricultural producers who do not fit the mythical mold of struggling family farmers. Looking only at the issue context in 1990, reform might reasonably have been expected to succeed, but it did not. The institutional context explains the failure.

There was little push from leaders for reform in agriculture, as there had been for the tax, trade, and deregulation cases. Presidential commitment was either ambivalent (as under Reagan) or tepid (as under Bush). Nor have bold initiatives come from the bureaucracy or from Congress, where both the Agriculture Department and the agriculture committees are constituency-oriented. Leadership has been particularly absent in the Senate; no legislative entrepreneur has stepped forward to champion agricultural reform, as happened in the other cases. For leaders and potential policy entrepreneurs who must choose where to invest their political resources, the salience of the farm crisis and public sympathy for farmers apparently made reducing farm subsidies a less attractive

cause than other issues. And because subsidy programs are tied to economic conditions, costs fall automatically when conditions improve,
which reduces the salience of the programs' cost and hence the urgency
to take action. Agriculture also is perceived to be less central to the
national economy than tax policy or regulation, removed from the concerns of broad national audiences to whom leaders like to appeal. In
addition, the growing internationalization of U.S. agriculture places constraints on presidential initiative, because building a consensus for cutting
U.S. subsidies is predicated upon getting other nations to lift their restrictions on imports of U.S. products.

Nevertheless, some recent developments may have brightened the
prospects for achieving market-oriented reforms in agriculture when farm
legislation is reauthorized in 1995. One harbinger of things to come may
be that price and income supports for producers of wool, mohair, and
honey were terminated in 1993. The cost of these programs was minuscule compared with the major commodities, but the elimination of the
supports at the very least seems to have emboldened the odd alliance
between urban Democrats and suburban Republicans that emerged (but
was defeated) in 1990. Another change has been the conclusion of the
GATT treaty, which, if ratified by Congress, will help to open markets
in Europe that have long been closed to American producers. That event
would both justify reducing government subsidies and make the reduction
more palatable for producers.

Finally, a growing chorus of farmers in some states has begun to
organize for reform. They are dissatisfied with programs that dispropor-
tionately benefit the largest producers and that impose onerous regulations as a condition for participation. The emergence of this group is a
pragmatic response, many believe, from farmers who view their political
influence as increasingly shaky in an era when pressures to reduce the
federal deficit are growing and the number of people dependent on farming for their living is dwindling. They want instead a program that would
help only those farmers who suffer significant revenue losses from
droughts, floods, or collapses in prices; even then the program would
restore only up to 70 percent of the yearly average of revenue earned
over the preceding five years. This plan, the Department of Agriculture
calculates, would cost less than half the amount that current programs
cost.[54] Most national farm lobbies and some farm-state lawmakers oppose
the idea, which may be reason enough for caution in predicting significant
change in agricultural policy over the next few years.

Appendix 4A
Farm Programs as Policy Instruments

Farm programs are intended to benefit farmers either by increasing the prices they receive for their products in the market (price supports) or by supplementing income (income supports). The chief price-setting mechanism is *non-recourse loans*, which farmers obtain from the Commodity Credit Corporation (CCC). A farmer obtains a loan at a level specified by the government on the amount of the commodity (for example, $4.50 per bushel of wheat). In return for the loan, the farmer pledges the commodity as collateral, placing it in a storage facility. The loan period is less than one year. When the loan becomes due, the farmer has the option of paying off the loan, with interest, and recovering the security (the commodity pledged) or of delivering the farm product to the CCC and having the loan canceled. If the market price remains higher than the loan rate, the farmer sells the crop, repays the loan, and keeps the profit. He chooses the second alternative when the market price is below the loan rate. In that case the farmer turns over the crop; in effect, the CCC purchases the product. Hence the loan rate sets the minimum price in the market and, in the case of grains, significantly influences the level of minimum world market prices. Note also that although the government makes what is called a loan, it incurs a cost, just as it does under any spending program, when farmers choose to give their crops to the government rather than to repay government loans. (As mentioned, farmers make that choice when market prices fall below prices specified in the loan agreement. The government, then, ends up with a commodity that will fetch less on the market than what was paid to the farmer.)

Deficiency payments, which are intended to support incomes rather than prices, supplement loans. Farmers are entitled to collect deficiency payments when market prices fail to reach target prices set by Congress. Target prices are set higher than the price used in calculating loans; they reflect the national average cost of producing a crop. The deficiency payment represents the difference between the target price and the market price, or between the target price and the loan price, whichever is lower.

Production limits (or acreage reductions) may be announced at the discretion of the secretary of agriculture. As a condition for getting loans and deficiency payments, farmers agree to idle a portion of their land. The government may pay farmers to idle still more land if market prices get too low. When market prices fall, government spending on loans and deficiency payments rise. Production limits are intended to depress supplies, which boosts prices and reduces spending on farm programs. The result is that some of the costs are shifted from taxpayers to consumers.[55]

Appendix 4B
Roll-Call Analysis of House Votes on
Farm and Food Stamp Programs

Tables 4B-1 through 4B-4 present the results of roll-call votes on the farm bills of 1977, 1981, 1985, and 1990, including roll calls on all amendments pertaining to the setting of subsidy levels, the repeal of specific commodity programs, the imposition of payment limitations, means-testing, and food stamps.[56] Two similar measures were used to categorize Democrats and Republicans according to the importance of agriculture in their districts. The first divides districts into three categories, from those with the least number of farm workers (as a proportion of the district's total work force) to those with the most farm workers ("least agricultural" to "most agricultural" in the table). The second measure is the proportion of the district's population classified by the Census Bureau as residing in rural areas. Here districts were divided into four categories ranging from the "least rural" to the "most rural."

What do these tables show? First, as one would expect, regardless of party affiliation, members of Congress representing more agricultural-rural districts favored more generous subsidy levels and eligibility requirements for receiving benefits (tables 4B-1, 4B-2, and 4B-3). Generally speaking, more legislators from more agricultural and rural districts voted for more generous provisions than did those from less agricultural and rural districts. Second, Democrats tended to give greater support to the farm program than Republicans. On votes affecting subsidy levels and eligibility, the proportion of Democrats voting to support more generous provisions was higher than that of Republicans on twenty-two of the twenty-seven amendments. On average, a majority of Republicans (60 percent) voted to reduce (or not increase) benefits and eligibility, compared to a minority of Democrats (43 percent). On amendments to the food stamp program (table 4B-4), party polarization is more pronounced. On every roll call a majority of Republicans favored reduced benefits or stricter requirements for recipients, while large majorities of Democrats opposed them.

There is also evidence of the logrolling relationship among urban and rural Democrats. In nineteen of twenty-seven roll calls (70 percent) a majority of urban Democrats (that is, those from the least agricultural districts) voted in favor of more generous subsidy provisions, and in fourteen of twenty-seven (52 percent) a majority of them from the least rural districts voted the same. Democratic districts falling in the middle categories (categories between the most and least agricultural and most and least rural) also substantially supported subsidies. Similarly, Democrats from predominantly agricultural areas strongly supported the food stamp program (table 4B-4). On every vote a majority of Democrats from the most agricultural districts voted against reducing benefits or eligibility; a majority of the most rural Democrats did the same, except on one vote.

The extent and nature of the partisan dimension of farm politics is further evidenced by comparing the voting behavior of Republicans and Democrats from the most agricultural and least agricultural districts. In effect, controlling for the importance of agriculture in congressional districts isolates the impact of partisanship. On twenty-three of the twenty-seven subsidy votes, higher proportions of Democrats than Republicans from the least agricultural districts voted to support more generous subsidy provisions. On average, 51 percent of the least agricultural Democrats voted in favor of reductions in benefits and eligibility, compared with 66 percent of the least agricultural Republicans. The figures for the least rural Democrats and Republicans were 53 percent and 70 percent, respectively. Comparing Republicans and Democrats from the most agricultural districts shows that on twenty-three of the twenty-seven subsidy votes, Republicans were less supportive of the farm coalition than were Democrats. On average, 19 percent of the most agricultural Democrats voted in favor of reduced benefits and tighter eligibility, compared with double that proportion among Republicans (38 percent). The figures for the most rural Democrats and Republicans were 29 percent and 46 percent, respectively.

On several votes, although not a majority of them, higher proportions of Democrats from the *least* agricultural districts were in favor of more generous subsidy provisions than Republicans from the *most* agricultural districts. This occurred in four of the twenty-seven votes using the least-to-most agricultural division and in nine of the votes using the least-to-most rural division.

Note that the votes on means-testing in 1990 depart from the partisan pattern. Considering the results of other subsidy votes, more Republicans than Democrats might have been expected to support means-testing. Instead, almost all of the variation is explained by the rural-agricultural variable rather than by partisanship. Republicans seem no more willing to support means-testing than Democrats, and for both parties means-testing was popular only among legislators from the least rural districts. The lack of partisan variation holds when comparing all Republicans and Democrats as well as when the comparison is broken down into rural and agricultural categories. Virtually identical proportions of Republicans and Democrats (less than half) supported means-testing. On the key vote to prohibit payments to farmers with incomes over $100,000 (see table 4B-3), only with the least-to-most rural measure is there some tendency for Republicans to vote more heavily than Democrats in corresponding categories for means-testing.

Still, overall it has been Democrats rather than Republicans, and liberals rather than conservatives, who have traditionally favored subsidies for agriculture. This difference reflects in part the logrolling relationship between legislators from farm districts, on the one hand, and urban liberal Democrats, on the other. Most urban Democrats support farm programs because they know that they can depend on farm legislators to support food stamps and issues of interest to labor. The results suggest that the differences between Democratic and Republican support for farm programs, however, are based on more than vote-trading among Democrats representing different material interests. If protecting the material benefits of their constituents were the sole basis for legislators' decisions, rural Republicans would be expected to be solidly behind farm subsidies and food stamps. Instead, this group's support for subsidies is mixed and considerably less than the support from their rural Democratic counterparts. As reported earlier, 38 percent of the most agricultural Republicans, on average, voted against their farm constituents, and almost half (46 percent) of the most rural Republicans did the same; both proportions were considerably higher than for rural Democrats. Likewise, farm Republicans, like their suburban and urban GOP brethren, voted overwhelmingly against food stamps. On average, 83 percent of the most agricultural Republicans favored reduced benefits and eligibility, compared with 22 percent for the most agricultural Democrats. The figures for the most rural Republicans and Democrats were 81 percent and 23 percent, respectively.

These results suggest that Democratic party support for farmers is based upon more than an expedient way to deliver material benefits; it includes an important ideological commitment as well. Since at least the New Deal, debate over farm bills has raised fundamental issues of principle for Republicans and Democrats.[57] The former have viewed subsidies and market controls as fostering inefficiency, creating dependency, and contributing to high taxes and bloated government; the latter regard them as necessary to stabilize farm incomes and prices against the volatility and harsh effects of the free market. Particularly in the postwar era, when big business and labor unions were able to protect their incomes, Democrats have thought farmers deserved similar protection. Thus farm benefits draw political support from the notion, rooted in the populist agrarian revolt of the late nineteenth century, that farmers represent a dispossessed and exploited segment of the population deserving of assistance.

The lesson for reformers is that a majority of Democrats would have to abandon farm producers before any reversal of producer-group politics could take place. In this sense agriculture bears more resemblance to the pre-reform regulatory arena than to the pre-reform tax arena. That is, the emergence of a pro-reform coalition in the agricultural arena would require that Democrats, particularly moderates and liberals, abandon their traditional support of farmers, and that Republicans maintain their opposition to subsidies. Just as Democrats like Kennedy embraced deregulation as a pro-consumer issue, so might consumerism be the basis for a Democratic attack on farm subsidies.

The problem with this scenario is that it is easier for liberal Democrats to have turned against anticompetitive regulation than it would be to oppose subsidies. Differences between the two producer groups and in Democrats' rationales for supporting government intervention in the first place explain why. Democrats are more likely to perceive policies to aid big business as less legitimate (especially if they perceive them as bad for consumers) than programs to aid farmers. Support for regulation was premised, in part, on the notion that industrial power needed to be restrained and order needed to be brought to chaotic markets. When the perception grew that regulatory authority had in fact been captured by the industries in many instances, abandoning regulation for the cause of consumerism was not a particularly difficult political leap. Agricultural subsidies, by contrast, were intended from the beginning to benefit producers rather than to restrain or discipline them.

Table 4B-1. *Recorded Votes in Favor of Reducing or Increasing Support Prices by Party and Type of District, 1977–90*

Percent

Party and type of district[a]	Reduce peanut price support (1977)	Establish sugar price support (1977)	Reduce sugar and dairy price support (1981)	Increase dairy price support (1981)	Reduce dairy price support (1981)	Reduce dairy price support (1981)	Reduce sugar price support (1985)	Reduce dairy price support (1985)	Increase wheat price support (1985)	Reduce wheat target price (1985)	Reduce sugar price support (1990)	Reduce wheat and feed grain price support (1990)
All Republicans	73	60	92	21	41	47	41	57	44	35	39	85
All Democrats	35	56	93	34	32	26	31	28	49	12	32	26
Republican												
Least agricultural	80	48	94	13	55	65	60	71	43	46	52	93
Some agricultural	64	69	93	37	22	24	29	53	32	27	24	91
Most agricultural	64	88	87	31	18	21	3	24	62	12	16	48
Democrat												
Least agricultural	46	46	93	17	46	37	41	34	52	17	40	32
Some agricultural	21	60	100	59	8	8	10	20	39	2	16	16
Most agricultural	11	88	86	77	2	2	0	0	50	0	0	0
Republican												
Least rural	88	54	90	11	60	67	60	86	40	63	54	90
Less rural	77	23	93	0	50	71	44	63	39	42	42	92
Some rural	56	61	93	32	39	39	31	40	41	15	28	80
Most rural	64	74	95	33	19	25	28	40	52	18	29	77
Democrat												
Least rural	49	47	94	15	51	35	44	37	57	18	43	32
Less rural	60	47	79	14	43	71	40	32	41	19	33	26
Some rural	20	63	94	55	6	10	12	12	43	6	19	16
Most rural	16	70	93	62	8	8	15	19	41	2	15	18

Sources: Congressional Quarterly, *Congressional Districts in the 1970s*; and Congressional Quarterly, *Congressional Districts in the 1980s*.

a. Agricultural measure reflects percentage of farm workers in each congressional district. Least agricultural = 0–3.0 percent; some agricultural = 3.1–6.0 percent; and most agricultural = more than 6.0 percent. Rural measure reflects percentage of population classified as "nonmetropolitan" in the 1970 census and "rural" in the 1980 census. Least rural = 0–15.0 percent; less rural = 15.1–30.0 percent; some rural = 30.1–45.0 percent; and most rural = more than 45 percent.

Table 4B-2. *Recorded Votes in Favor of Eliminating Support Programs, by Party and Type of District, 1981–90*

Percent

Party and type of district[a]	Repeal peanut quota and allotment (1981)	Repeal sugar price support (1981)	Repeal tobacco allotment and price support (1981)	Repeal tobacco price support (1985)	Phase out peanut quota and price support (1985)	Phase out honey price support (1990)
All Republicans	70	68	71	65	79	69
All Democrats	55	49	33	38	30	33
Republican						
Least agricultural	70	68	71	65	79	69
Some agricultural	66	51	43	53	71	41
Most agricultural	44	15	46	38	32	19
Democrat						
Least agricultural	73	65	47	49	38	42
Some agricultural	24	27	14	13	17	16
Most agricultural	12	9	7	5	0	0
Republican						
Least rural	77	66	80	75	87	85
Less rural	79	79	64	56	76	50
Some rural	57	64	36	54	60	38
Most rural	49	32	47	42	49	35
Democrat						
Least rural	75	66	43	54	40	43
Less rural	79	71	69	30	37	26
Some rural	39	26	29	34	22	22
Most rural	21	25	26	10	13	22

Sources: Congressional Quarterly, *Congressional Districts in the 1970s*; and Congressional Quarterly, *Congressional Districts in the 1980s*.

a. See table 4B-1 for explanation.

Table 4B-3. *Recorded Votes in Favor of Payment Limitations and Means-Testing, by Party and Type of District, 1977–90*

Percent

Party and type of district[a]	$20,000 cap per producer (1977)	Prohibit payments to corporations (1977)	$50,000 cap on sugar producers (1977)	$30,000 cap per producer (1977)	Cap honey price support loans (1985)	Tighten regulations on limits (1990)	Tighten regulations on limits (1990)	Prohibit payments to those with incomes over $1 million (1990)	Prohibit payments to those with incomes over $100,000 (1990)
All Republicans	50	33	55	66	90	45	84	41	37
All Democrats	39	54	31	39	80	35	86	40	37
Republican									
Least agricultural	58	29	58	80	95	59	80	43	50
Some agricultural	44	25	50	50	98	33	89	43	22
Most agricultural	32	60	52	40	68	16	90	32	16
Democrat									
Least agricultural	48	65	35	49	88	45	83	39	49
Some agricultural	29	43	38	24	64	12	92	43	6
Most agricultural	16	25	14	14	55	13	100	38	8
Republican									
Least rural	55	27	57	80	98	75	73	37	63
Less rural	54	38	54	69	91	37	82	50	29
Some rural	50	33	50	67	90	30	90	45	23
Most rural	45	38	43	50	81	31	94	35	25
Democrat									
Least rural	51	69	38	52	90	46	83	38	55
Less rural	47	73	47	33	68	33	70	41	33
Some rural	24	37	22	22	71	22	92	30	14
Most rural	24	33	23	24	71	22	98	48	14

Sources: Congressional Quarterly, *Congressional Districts in the 1970s*; and Congressional Quarterly, *Congressional Districts in the 1980s*.
a. See table 4B-1 for an explanation.

Table 4B-4. *Recorded Votes in Favor of Food Stamp Limitations, by Party and Type of District, 1977–85*

Percent

Party and type of district[a]	Prohibit purchase of non-nutritional foods (1977)	Reduce spending (1977)	Reduce spending (1977)	Prohibit strikers as recipients (1977)	Require recipients to pay for part of stamps (1977)	Restrict eligibility (1977)	Require recipients to pay for part of stamps (1981)	Reduce benefits and eligibility (1985)	Require recipients to work (1985)
All Republicans	86	86	89	77	57	79	73	87	87
All Democrats	22	16	40	21	8	13	5	7	13
Republican									
Least agricultural	87	81	88	70	51	69	70	83	91
Some agricultural	83	92	92	89	64	97	78	88	90
Most agricultural	88	92	88	84	64	88	79	97	71
Democrat									
Least agricultural	20	11	30	11	4	10	4	4	10
Some agricultural	38	36	74	40	19	26	8	12	22
Most agricultural	16	18	49	39	11	16	7	24	14
Republican									
Least rural	84	82	88	79	66	70	74	90	96
Less rural	85	85	100	62	38	69	71	86	91
Some rural	78	89	94	83	39	83	71	85	83
Most rural	91	88	86	78	57	90	74	86	78
Democrat									
Least rural	19	9	27	7	3	11	4	3	5
Less rural	27	20	40	13	7	13	14	8	8
Some rural	27	22	51	34	12	22	3	14	34
Most rural	22	24	57	40	13	13	7	13	16

Sources: Congressional Quarterly, *Congressional Districts in the 1970s*; and Congressional Quarterly, *Congressional Districts in the 1980s*.
a. See table 4B-1 for an explanation.

CHAPTER FIVE

An Alternative Explanation?

IT STANDS to reason that producer groups themselves may account for variations in their own policy fortunes. Groups may differ along at least four politically relevant dimensions: levels of mobilization and resources; group size and membership composition; the level of organized opposition they face; and their effectiveness at coalition building. This chapter explores the likelihood that these different aspects of groups produce different policy fortunes.

Mobilization refers to the level of activity and visibility of producer groups in the policymaking process and the groups' financial and organizational resources—for example, campaign contributions, membership size, and lobbying presence in Washington. Higher levels of mobilization and resources might be expected to produce rising group fortunes and prevent declines in them. As groups demand more benefits, policies should move in that direction, just as greater mobilization should make it harder to reduce groups' benefits. Likewise, groups that possess greater resources should be more successful at securing (and retaining) policy benefits than those with fewer.

Second, the larger the group or, alternatively, the more exclusive its membership, the better its policy fortunes. Larger groups would presumably have a greater impact on the economy and thus greater political leverage than smaller groups. On the other hand, smaller groups tend to be more exclusive and homogeneous, thus making it easier for them to overcome "obstacles to collective action."[1] Since these groups are better able to come to agreement on their interests, policy aims, and political strategy, they should have greater policy success. These two factors, then—largeness and exclusivity—would seem to be in conflict. Larger groups are less likely to be able to overcome the problems of collective action, yet more exclusive groups, which should be relatively small, are less likely to have economic clout.

The third differential, level of opposition, simply indicates the degree to which other organized interests have mobilized to oppose producer groups. Finally, coalition-building effectiveness refers to the degree of cohesion and cooperation among producer groups and to the ability to forge alliances with other interest groups. Greater cohesion, coalition-building capacity, and the absence of opposition should be associated with rising group fortunes and a greater likelihood that efforts to reduce benefits will fail.

For an explanation based in producer groups to be persuasive, policy fortunes should correlate with differences among these four dimensions in the ways predicted above. Beyond that, however, groups must be shown to be more important than the issue and institutional contexts discussed in preceding chapters in explaining policy outcomes. Do the predictions in fact hold, and are the correlations decisive? In other words, do producer groups determine their own policy fortunes?

Levels of Mobilization and Resources

It is clear that periods of heightened producer-group mobilization coincide with rising fortunes. The pressures exerted by organizations representing various interests are often credited with the rise in tax expenditures in the late 1970s and early 1980s.[2] Lobbying by interest groups in general surged during this period, especially in the business community. New organizations representing business proliferated while established ones were revitalized. The rise in general business organizations, trade associations, lobbying firms hired by individual companies and industries, and corporate political action committees was part of what one observer called an "advocacy explosion" in Washington.[3] There was no lack of mobilization among farm producers in this period, either.

It is also telling that as more industries claimed injury or threatened injury by foreign competition and increased their mobilization in the 1970s and 1980s, the level of protectionist relief granted to them increased as well. No longer were just a few industries lobbying for protection. Joining textiles-apparel in gaining significant protection were other major industries such as steel and automobile manufacturing, followed later by newer, high-technology industries such as semiconductors, electronics, and telecommunications. Reflecting concern over unfair trade practices, these industries demanded protective action if foreign nations refused to open their markets or to establish a level playing field for American products. Because many of the most threatened import-sensitive industries are unionized, with workers enjoying high wages and employment security, most of organized labor has favored trade restrictions since the 1970s.[4] In 1990, 75 percent of labor leaders believed tariffs to be necessary.[5]

Yet the link between mobilization and policy outcomes is partial and tenuous, at best. First, changes in the level of mobilization are related to changes in the issue context. As issues of salience to groups rise and fall, so does group activity. Mobilization is not so much a predictor of policy outcomes as it is a measure of a group's perception that its interests are at stake in deliberations over policy. That is, mobilization rises and falls as group-relevant proposals for policy change move on and off the agenda. Businesses affected by changes in the tax laws, for instance, were highly mobilized in both 1981 and 1986 because major changes in tax policy were contemplated at those times. Yet the policy outcomes of those two years, and thus the fortunes of producers, differed greatly.

Second, although periods of rising benefits seem to coincide with heightened mobilization, mobilization appears less consequential when groups are on the defensive and are seriously threatened with a decline in benefits. The upsurge in business lobbying that began in the mid-1970s, which apparently contributed to the rise in tax benefits, did nothing to prevent deregulation of industries in the same period—and without doubt the industries threatened with deregulation were as highly mobilized as those seeking tax benefits. Far from being determinative, lobbying efforts against deregulation may not have even ameliorated the outcomes.[6]

These points suggest that other factors in the political environment are critical to determining whether mobilization will be effective; prime candidates are the issue and institutional contexts. Mobilization matters more in raising benefits than in warding off declines for the simple reason that policymakers are more likely to accede to producers' wishes when the issue context favors producers' interests than when it does not. When the issue context was running against producers, the success of those interests that nevertheless mobilized and countered attacks on their benefits depended on their being perceived as exceptions. For example, oil and gas producers' retention of tax benefits depended on showing that their industry was already in dire economic straits and thus should be spared the fate that befell other sectors of the economy.

Similarly, for each of the cases examined in this book, mobilization usually succeeded when institutional resistance to group pressures was low and usually failed when it was high. There were, however, cases in which high mobilization succeeded despite an adverse institutional context. But in these instances, as when state and local governments preserved deductibility for most of their taxes, it was these groups' superior access to key institutional actors that enabled success. The fact that several members of the Ways and Means Committee represented high-tax states like New York and California, coupled with Chairman Dan Rostenkowski's coalition-building strategy (which centered on Democrats from such states), meant that the mobilization efforts of those interests could be translated into a policy impact. Judith Goldstein makes a similar observation in her study of trade policy from 1945 to 1984. As the United States became more open to foreign trade during those years, domestic industries mobilized. But the increased mobilization did not automatically ensure receipt of assistance under the trade laws. Whether an industry received aid depended on the fit between the strategy employed by the industry and the relevant state structures (that is, the specific trade laws and procedures for considering petitions).[7]

In short, the impact of mobilization was *contingent* on other conditions. The effects of group activity are not automatic—they depend on what is extant in the issue and institutional contexts.

Third, farm groups, which staved off most attempts to reduce their benefits in the 1980s and 1990s, were not more mobilized than the groups in the tax and regulatory areas, which lost. Groups in all three cases fought vigorously and adamantly against reform. There is no evidence that the producer groups involved in the tax and regulatory cases favored reform, were indifferent to it, or had failed to mobilize after resigning themselves to defeat.[8] More important, it is difficult to see how the mobilization of farm groups accounts for either the rise in farm subsidies in the 1980s or the failure of Reagan's proposals to scrap farm subsidies altogether. Because outlays for subsidies increase automatically with higher production levels (and thus lower commodity prices) and a deteriorating farm economy, it was not necessary for farm interests to mobilize to achieve that result. Nor was mobilization essential for farmers to escape the defeats visited upon producers in the tax and regulatory cases, because an issue context hospitable to agricultural interests effectively kept Ronald Reagan's proposals from reaching serious consideration in Congress. Only in 1990—when means-testing reached the agenda and was voted upon in Congress—did mobilization arguably make a difference.

As for trade policy, the growth of protectionism in the 1970s and 1980s, which was only incremental, did not match the stepped-up producer demands. Indeed, according to I. M. Destler, "The net increase over the decade was less than one might have expected *given the pressures at play*."[9]

The link between levels of financial and organizational resources and policy outcomes is even more tenuous than for mobilization. If resources predicted policy success or failure, farm groups—not industries in the tax and regulatory arenas—might have been expected to be defeated. The farm groups represent only about 3 percent of the U.S. population, a figure that has been declining over time. In terms of sheer numbers and economic clout, organizations representing the owners, managers, and workers in the tax, regulatory, and trade areas were at least as formidable as the farm groups. The period from the mid-1970s to the mid-1980s was, after all, an era of resurgence in the level of resources corporations devoted to political activity.[10] Indeed, business won a bounty of particularized tax benefits in 1978 and 1981, just a few years before they lost many of the same benefits under tax reform.

In one examination of the relationship between key floor votes on the Finance Committee's tax reform bill of 1986, House Ways and Means Committee votes during markup, and PAC (political action committee) contributions, researchers found no significant connections between votes and contributions (while controlling for important political and regional variables).[11] Many other studies have likewise found no strong or consistent relationship between PAC contributions and legislative voting behavior.[12]

Some evidence suggests that groups that spend significant sums of money may actually hurt their cause. Lavish spending can be perceived as a sign of political vulnerability rather than strength, and it may imply that the groups' policy positions are unsustainable on their merits. As one high-ranking congressional staff member who was involved in the 1986 tax reform deliberations put it:

> I've seen the people who throw a lot of money around Capitol Hill and how well they've done. Generally they either do worse or no better than others. If you're throwing money around, the immediate suspicion is that

you've got a case that really stinks. And the same thing is true of hiring high-visibility lobbyists. The suspicion is that you've got a case you couldn't hope of selling on your own. The members know that.[13]

Size and Exclusivity of Membership

Examination of size and exclusivity of group membership also yields little evidence to support the idea that producer groups determine their own policy fortunes. On the one hand, the larger the industry, the more likely it is to secure protectionist trade policies.[14] The textile, automobile, steel, and semiconductor industries are among the largest in the country, and they are also among the most successful in getting relief from foreign competition. On the other hand, many of these same industries fought against tax reform and lost. The steel industry, for instance, steadfastly defended the investment tax credit, to no avail.

With regard to exclusivity, agriculture offers the strongest support for the producer-group explanation of policy outcomes. Farm producers are organized along commodity lines for food and fiber; group memberships are therefore very narrow and homogeneous. Decades ago broad farm organizations were the most important representatives of farming interests. Their problem was that they were intensely divided on basic principles. The American Farm Bureau Federation was conservative and adamantly opposed most forms of government involvement; others, like the National Farmers Union, took the opposite view. To overcome stalemate and combat, specialized commodity organizations formed and eventually eclipsed the general organizations. Organizations such as the National Wheat Growers Association, the National Cotton Council, and others emerged in the 1950s; by the 1970s they "spoke more accurately for most producers of price supported commodities."[15] "Concerned narrowly with the status of a single crop, the commodity lobbies shied away from great ideological debates . . . to focus on the concerns of a single class of farmers."[16]

But do the farm groups really have more homogeneous memberships and narrowly focused aims than producers in other policy areas? Several groups active in the tax and regulatory cases are as homogeneous and focused in their aims as the farm commodity groups. Are American Airlines and American Telephone and Telegraph, two typical producer groups that were active in the fight against deregulation, any less exclusive and homogeneous than the farm commodity organizations? Similarly, not only large, diverse business organizations such as the Chamber of Commerce and National Association of Manufacturers lobby for tax policies they believe favorable to business; so too do organizations representing particular industries and even firms. The National Association of Home Builders, the American Bankers Association, the American Horse Council, the Weyerhaeuser Company, the Aluminum Company of America, American Express, and many others tried to defeat tax reform.[17] And lobbying in favor of trade protection is undertaken largely by particular industries and firms.[18] Any relationship between policy fortunes and group size and degree of exclusivity appears to be weak.

Organized Opposition to Producer Groups

There is somewhat more support for the proposition that producer groups facing mobilized opposition from other groups are more likely to suffer declines in their fortunes, or that policymakers will find it easier to contain the growth of producers' benefits. Conversely, if they do not face such opposition, their fortunes are more likely to rise or be maintained.

Tax reform was supported by a broad array of businesses joined together in the Tax Reform Action Committee (TRAC) and the CEO Tax Group, which were drawn from a coalition of about 250 companies that included such heavyweights as General Motors, IBM, and Procter and Gamble. By the mid-1980s many businesses that had supported tax expenditures in the past realized that other businesses, and not their own, were the main beneficiaries. They had tired of paying higher tax rates so that other industries could enjoy their tax breaks. If the repeal of generous tax breaks were combined with corporate rate cuts (as they were under the Tax Reform Act of 1986), these businesses calculated, they would come out ahead. They would also benefit from a more level playing field created by the removal of provisions in the tax code that skewed incentives for investment. These pro-reform industries tended to be in growing sectors of the economy, such as high-tech, service, and retail sales industries. Businesses opposed to reform tended to be in manufacturing and heavy industry, because these sectors invested heavily in plant and equipment and were able to take the greatest advantage of such lucrative incentives as the investment tax credit and accelerated depreciation allowances.[19] Not only did the pro-reform businesses help to counteract the arguments and pressure from the anti-reform businesses, but tax reform proponents gained greater respectability because reform could hardly be portrayed as a purely liberal, antibusiness initiative since it had support from several important industries.

Similar to the split that developed among producer groups in tax reform was the division among groups affected by trucking regulation. The economic climate of the 1970s and early 1980s—persistent inflation, energy shortages, and declining productivity—made arguments for deregulation particularly compelling for the shippers that relied upon the trucking companies. In addition to shippers, farm groups, the National Federation of Independent Businesses, the National Association of Manufacturers, and others joined liberal-oriented consumer groups, conservative public-interest organizations, and other particularistic organizations in an ad hoc coalition to fight for trucking deregulation.[20] "The breadth and diversity of the coalition," states Dorothy L. Robyn, "were the ultimate evidence . . . that trucking deregulation was in the public interest."[21]

An organized opposition might also help to explain why there has not been more trade protection since the 1970s; that is, why the fortunes of producers seeking protection have been contained. In her study of trade politics, Helen V. Milner compared the 1920s and the 1970s, two decades in which American industry was beset by rising import competition. She explains the relative absence of protectionism in the 1970s compared with the earlier era, when protectionist policies surged, by pointing to changes in the level of integration of the domestic and international economies. Greater international economic interdependence in the post–World War II era put the brakes on protectionist impulses in the 1970s. The growth of export-dependent and multinational businesses in the decades after the war altered the policy preferences of many firms: the number of industries tempted to ask for protection fell and the number with a stake in greater openness rose, resulting in fewer protectionist policies.[22] For many more industries than in the past, in other words, the political and economic costs of protectionism outweighed potential benefits. "The growth of international ties meant that by the 1970s many more firms were more willing to resist protectionist pressures."[23]

While industries sensitive to import competition may prefer protection, others, such as agriculture, financial services, chemicals, pharmaceuticals, energy, agriculture, aerospace, and biotechnology industries, have reaped great gains from the upsurge in world trade and from the open markets that make that trade possible. These groups have not initiated liberal trade legislation, but they have been called upon to endorse it when it is on the agenda. For instance, the Emergency Committee for American Trade, which represents major multinational firms, was founded in 1967; although it has not been very visible, its members have been well connected to policymakers and have supplied them with valuable arguments and information. General business organizations like the Chamber of Commerce, National Association of Manufacturers, and Business Roundtable have been active supporters of open trade. Their support waned in the mid-1980s, but they backed the 1988 trade act and the 1991 fast-track authority.[24] Business support for eliminating tariffs rose from 71 percent to 78 percent between 1986 and 1990.[25]

Also active in the 1980s were a number of producer groups reliant upon exports or imports, who willingly—and often successfully—fought against producers seeking protection. Battles fought and won, frequently in alliance with foreign firms and their governments, include organizations, retailers, and importers in opposition to textile restraints; fabricators of wire and other copper products versus the U.S. copper industry; and steel users against the renewal of negotiated steel quotas in 1990.

Conversely, farm policy lends some support for the notion that the absence of strong organized opposition is politically advantageous for producers. While agribusiness organizations have favored a more market-oriented farm policy, and restaurant chains (for example, Pizza Hut and Burger King) and food processors oppose subsidies because of their effect on food prices, the most visible and potent organized opposition to farm interests seems to manifest itself not on subsidy issues but on such issues as pesticide use, soil and water conservation, hunger, and nutrition.[26] Public-interest and other groups representing these concerns demanded access and gained it both in Congress and in the Agriculture Department. The major concern of these groups is not with subsidies, however. Although they have had an impact on such matters as food quality, conservation, and nutrition, "for those programs providing direct financial assistance to farmers, [they] have been a negligible force."[27]

Hence, some of the evidence in the preceding paragraphs suggests that whether organized opposition exists can affect producer group fortunes, but just how decisive is it for explaining policy outcomes? First, it is clearly possible for producers' fortunes to decline even without such opponents. Opposition groups figured little, if at all, in the deregulation cases, except perhaps in trucking.[28] Neither other kinds of industries nor public-interest groups played much of a role in the deregulation of airlines and telecommunications.

What of cases where producer-group fortunes declined and there is clear and hard evidence that a broad coalition of economic interests backed the policy change, as they did under tax reform? To assign the economic interests that favored tax reform a decisive role in the outcome is not persuasive for several reasons. First, those interests were motivated by their calculation that they would pay less in taxes under a reformed system (reductions in the corporate tax rate would be financed by eliminating incentive provisions that primarily benefited the businesses fighting against reform). But the issue context for tax reform was dominated by the fairness argument, which maintained that taxpayers in general were paying higher taxes and corporations were escaping paying their "fair share." In the midst of an economic boom, the economic growth issue that pro-reform businesses championed—that a reformed tax code would be better for newer, "sunrise" industries—was a subsidiary argument for getting reform on the agenda. Had there been no perception of rampant tax evasion among corporations and the wealthy, which spread in the wake of the passage of the 1981 tax law, tax reform would not have occurred. The 1981 act not only created the sense of scandal; in addition, had there not been revenue losses from the loopholes that it legislated, a reform package could not have been developed centering around a diffuse benefit—large, politically irresistible rate cuts for taxpayers generally. One Senate aide involved in tax reform described the role of the pro-reform businesses as helpful but not decisive: "I think that the TRAC group and all of these [other pro-reform businesses] were like the chorus in *Medea*—not absolutely essential, but an important force in amplifying the basic themes and messages [of tax reform]."[29]

Moreover, if the balance of power among groups were decisive, then tax reform and deregulation would never have occurred. The pro-reform groups were outnumbered and outspent by the anti-reform groups, a fact that interviewees for this study reiterated. The preponderance of organized businesses (and of interest groups generally) clearly opposed tax reform, including such resourceful and well-established organizations as the Chamber of Commerce, National Association of Manufacturers, and Business Roundtable. If policymakers simply responded to the demands voiced by organized interests, they would have gone along with the far more numerous and resourceful anti-reform forces.

The same can be said of trade policy. Milner's findings—that increased export dependence and multinationality of American industry created an active and influential antiprotectionist constituency—should be kept in perspective. The overwhelming proportion of U.S. industry in the 1970s remained neither export-dependent nor multinational. For about 80 percent of U.S. industry, such factors cannot be said to affect their policy preferences.[30] Even though the relative share of American industry predisposed to demand protection in the 1970s may have been less than in the 1920s, in both numbers and intensity demands for protection surged in the 1970s and accelerated in the 1980s. Moreover, antiprotectionist political activity of domestic and foreign groups, according to Destler, has been "hardly equal" to that of the groups seeking protection.[31] Furthermore, at least as important as any increase in industry preferences for open trade between the 1920s and the 1970s were the fundamentally different attitudes of policymakers toward protectionism. In the 1970s those attitudes were conditioned by Smoot-Hawley and the postwar position of the United States economically and militarily, which led to institutional arrangements that were inhospitable to protection. Congress devolved tariff setting to the executive branch and granted authority to the president for negotiating liberal trade agreements with other countries early in the postwar period, well before the onset of greater integration of U.S. industries in the international economy.

Finally, an issue context hospitable toward producers can keep off the agenda those issues that galvanize an organized opposition. For example, even if the organized opposition to farm subsidies had been significant, it could not have registered its influence during the 1980s because serious reform was kept off the agenda. Of course, it may be possible for organized opponents to help determine the agenda. But the examinations in chapters 2, 3, and 4 of what shaped the issue context, and therefore the agenda, reveal that organized opponents of producer groups played only a modest role. The issue context was shaped primarily by actors inside government (the president, legislative entrepreneurs, and bureaucrats) and in the media, who themselves were reacting to changes in the economy, effects of previous policy choices, and public opinion.

Coalition Building

The strongest support for a producer-group explanation of policy fortunes lies with the coalition-building capacity of the groups. Farm interests, for example, have forged long-standing logrolling relationships. The strength and permanency of those relationships are the truly distinctive features of farm politics, which set farm producers apart from the groups in the other policy areas. At the heart of the coalition are the farm commodity groups. They work closely with the seventy to eighty legislators from the farm bloc, which includes those districts where agriculture remains an important economic activity. The farm bloc engages in intercommodity logrolling, whereby legislators representing districts growing different commodities support one another's subsidy programs. Proponents of the separate commodities are rarely in conflict with one another, as they realize that the defeat of one of their brethren could easily unravel the entire coalition. For example, in key votes on the 1981 farm bill, according to one lobbyist, "You could see the peanut and grain and cotton and rice people all working the floor for dairy."[32]

Farm interests are not only internally united; they have also adroitly cultivated ongoing alliances with potential opponents. Because rural districts have been a shrinking minority in Congress, farm interests cannot build a majority simply through intercommodity logrolling. They must seek support from a sizable proportion of legislators representing nonrural districts, in particular from urban Democrats. These Democrats have regularly supported subsidies in exchange for rural support for the food stamp portion of the farm bill and for legislation of interest to labor, such as increases in the minimum wage and trade protection for certain industries.[33]

By the 1980s this coalition-building arrangement was firmly established. In 1981, on the key vote in the House on the farm bill, Food Stamp Subcommittee Chairman Fred Richmond successfully rallied urban support by telling his colleagues: "I want to support sugar . . . tobacco, rice, cotton, dairy, every one of these other commodities."[34] The coalition proceeded to defeat amendments to reduce price supports for dairy programs, a commodity that the Reagan administration had targeted for sharp reductions, and then turned back Republican attempts to tighten requirements for food stamps.[35] Similarly, when the sugar program came under attack in 1990, legislators from sugar-growing areas traded votes with labor, environmental, and pro-farm Democrats to defeat the amendment. "The sugar guys did a much better job in trading votes. . . . They used fundraising and other relationships and worked it very hard," according to Representative Tom Downey, the author of the amendment.[36]

The commodity interests also exploit their ties with organized labor by defining farm issues in terms that resonate well with the unions. In 1985, for instance, Agriculture Committee members deflected pro-consumer arguments by insisting that sugar supports assured a steady price to manufacturers and in the process protected U.S. jobs. "This will be the first vote on whether we protect American producers and manu-facturers this year," Agriculture Committee Chairman "Kika" de la Garza stated with protectionist ardor. "We have to fly the flag."[37] And again in 1990 he sounded the protectionist theme: "Vote 'no' on the Downey amendment [to cut the sugar price support level from 18 cents to 16 cents]. It is jobs U.S.A., jobs U.S.A., jobs U.S.A.! You cannot cut it anymore. . . . It is jobs, jobs, jobs in the U.S.A.!"[38] The amend-ment failed, 150–271.

The strength of this coalition was also the major impediment to the adoption of means-testing in 1990. The Armey-Schumer amendment to deny subsidies to farmers with farm incomes of more than $100,000 lost when the AFL-CIO came out against it. Members and aides suggested that pro-labor Democrats, who voted overwhelmingly against the amend-ment, were fulfilling their end of a trade: a vote against Armey-Schumer in exchange for farm-state support for the cargo-preference provision of the farm bill and a textile protection bill that would soon come to the floor. (The cargo-preference provisions require that half of all govern-ment-generated agricultural exports be shipped on U.S. flag vessels, in effect subsidizing U.S. merchant marine fleets.) In addition, several en-vironmental groups opposed the amendment, worried that if large farm-ers were excluded from the programs, they would no longer be required to comply with environmental regulations.

The tax case shows the importance of coalition building in fueling a rise in benefits and demonstrates how a crumbling coalition can contrib-ute to a decline in benefits. The Carter administration's attempt to reform the tax system in 1978 turned into a victory for a broad coalition of businesses seeking to open loopholes. "The defeat of President Carter's tax reform efforts signaled . . . the triumph of a broad coalition of busi-ness lobbyists who came together under the rubric of 'capital forma-tion.'"[39] The Carlton Group, named after the Washington hotel in which they met each Tuesday, and their research organization, the American Council for Capital Formation, championed the creation of new tax breaks for business and investors. The group's leader, Charls E. Walker, became Reagan's tax adviser during the 1980 campaign. After the election Walker convinced President Reagan to include the "accelerated cost recovery system"—a scheme to allow businesses to rapidly write off depreciations worth hundreds of billions of dollars—in the administration's proposal to cut individual tax rates. The coalition fueled the bidding war that broke out in Congress, with Republicans and Democrats falling over one another to see who could be more generous in providing special tax benefits. In the end, the Economic Recovery Tax Act of 1981 included not only the new cost recovery system but also several other expensive provisions, such as a lowered top tax rate on capital gains and generous real estate shelters.

The tax case also shows what happens when unity among producer groups breaks down. Compared with the cohesion of farm groups, cooperation among business groups is a transitory phenomenon arising out of particular issue contexts (as in the 1978 and 1981 tax bills). By the mid-1980s the Carlton Group had dissolved and businesses seeking to protect their tax breaks had failed to coalesce in the fight over tax reform. Each recipient of tax benefits focused exclusively on preserving those provisions that were central to its own interests and ignored other groups' concerns and the need to build alliances. As Richard Darman observed, producer groups "were brought down by the narrowness of their vision. . . . Precisely because they defined themselves as representatives of single special interests, they failed to notice their collective power."[40] Likewise, in fighting deregulation, "separate firms or segments of industries were inclined to insist on their own views of political strategy—even if doing so imperiled the effectiveness of the whole industry."[41]

Similarly, one of the reasons for the absence of widespread "legislated protectionism" is that firms seeking trade protection have not mobilized collectively in broad-based organizations, nor have they been very successful at logrolling. With a few exceptions, firms seeking protection have pursued their cause separately. The one cross-industry group that has favored protection—organized labor—has had only little direct impact on trade policy. Union weakness was reflected in the failure to win major trade policy battles from the 1970s to the 1990s.[42] As labor's position on trade has changed from supporter of liberalization in the early postwar years to proponent of protection, its organizational and political strength has declined. At the outset of the postwar period, about one-third of the nonagricultural work force was unionized. By the end of the 1980s, unions claimed less than one-fifth of that population. Finally, the strength of some of the oldest and most formidable protection-oriented industries—textiles and steel—has been waning.[43]

The Effect of Groups in Perspective

A case exists, therefore, for the argument that fluctuations in producer-group fortunes rest, at least in part, on their cohesion and coalition-building effectiveness. How important this capacity is must be kept in perspective, however.

First, producer groups are among several actors and forces that shape the issue context. Which issues will be salient and how they will be defined are determined by conditions in the environment, such as the state of the economy and previous policy choices and their consequences. For example, on most of the key policy developments in farm policy in the period under study, the farm groups' much-touted capacity to build coalitions was largely irrelevant. No coalition to raise subsidy spending in the 1980s was necessary because the design of the programs, coupled with a deteriorating farm economy, ensured automatic increases in payments to farmers. Similarly, no coalition was needed to defeat market reform in 1981 or 1985 because, given an issue context friendly to farm interests, the proposals never reached the agenda. The large revenue losses and "abuses" resulting from the rise in tax loopholes under the Economic Recovery Tax Act of 1981 lent credence to arguments about unfairness in the tax law and encouraged a split between those industries that benefited from ERTA and those that would benefit from a plan that closed loopholes and lowered corporate tax rates. The producer groups were thus put on the defensive early on and were never able to offer a more compelling definition of the issues in tax policy. Likewise, the lingering discredit attached to protectionism in the wake of Smoot-Hawley and the perceived success of liberal trade policies afterwards dampened the mobilization and effectiveness of protectionist coalitions. Producers seem to be shaped by the issue context as much as they shape it.

Groups may also be helped or hindered by the decisions of politicians, the mass media, and other actors who shape the issue context. Farm producers have been helped, for example, by the media's inattention to the cost and inequity of farm programs and by the sympathetic portrayal of farmers during tough economic times; they have been aided also by the apparent lack of incentives for leading politicians to adopt market-oriented agricultural reform as a priority.[44]

In the case of deregulation, Martha Derthick and Paul J. Quirk show how deregulation was an idea initially pushed by experts, which eventually captured the imaginations of some key politicians and finally became a powerful symbol and fashionable policy innovation that permeated the policy arena.[45] As the idea of deregulation and the issues surrounding it gathered momentum, the regulated industries were put under stress and on the defensive, which greatly weakened their ability to muster political resistance and pursue an effective strategy.

Just as important, institutional arrangements and actors in all four cases have been crucial in either facilitating or impeding cohesion and coalition building among producer groups.[46] Thus the unity and logrolling success of farm groups have depended on institutions that nurture and accommodate farming interests. The agriculture committees in Congress are the principal venues for logrolling among the different commodity groups and between them and labor and environmental groups. The full committee cuts deals with the different commodity groups as well as the nonfarm interests, so its legislation is reported to the floor with a firm majority in place.[47]

The committees act as receptive hosts for logrolling because they are constituency-oriented. Members who serve on those committees have reelection as their primary goal. As John Mark Hansen has shown, the influence of the commodity groups in the agriculture committees depends on their access to members. Access, in turn, rests on the committee members' judgment of the groups' ability to meet their reelection needs—in particular, by providing specialized electoral information and propaganda.[48] By contrast, committees like Ways and Means are less prone to logrolling. Because their members pursue goals beyond reelection and occupy safe seats, they have less incentive to accommodate producers, especially when the issue context is unfavorable.

Agriculture committee members have organized themselves so as to maximize access for commodity groups. They are among the most decentralized committees in Congress, with subcommittees organized on a commodity-by-commodity basis. A committee member gravitates to that subcommittee whose commodity is critical to the member's district. As William P. Browne puts it, "Situationally, . . . commodity groups do benefit more than any others from the procedural aspects of agricultural policymaking in Congress and the USDA."[49] They benefit not only in a positive sense, in that their programs fall under the jurisdiction of those legislators who are most likely to be solicitous of them, but in a negative sense as well. That is, the subcommittee structure limits the agricultural policy agenda to a set of narrowly focused issues pertaining to subsidies. The subcommittees "persist in making policy on a commodity basis when agriculture's problems are, in fact, much broader." Thus there exists no fundamental debate over the appropriate goals for agricultural policy because "this dispersion of power . . . presently restricts agricultural policy reform."[50] With the subcommittees as gatekeepers, it is hardly surprising that major reforms that might reverse the fortunes of farm producers have had such a difficult time reaching the agenda.

John Ferejohn has argued that logrolling between farm legislators (mainly southern Democrats) and proponents of the food stamp program (urban Democrats) is inherently unstable; it is sustainable only under specific institutional arrangements. Presumably, Republicans would rather join either urban or rural Democrats in passing either food stamps or farm subsidies than see a coalition of the two Democratic factions pass both programs. The GOP would therefore be motivated to form a majority with urban or rural Democrats by offering a deal better than one that logrolling between urban and rural Democrats could produce.[51] Nevertheless, Ferejohn shows, urban and rural blocs of Democrats have been able to forestall defections to the Republicans, and thus preserve their logrolling arrangement, because the institutional arrangements of committees in Congress allow "opportunities for exchanges of support that span different stages of Congressional action."[52] That is, institutional means exist to strike a deal and, more important, to keep it intact throughout the legislative process. Two institutional arrangements in particular have facilitated and preserved the logroll between supporters of farm subsidies and food stamps: placing food stamps under the jurisdiction of the agriculture committees and using various restrictive procedures—the committees' gatekeeping powers, floor rules, conference committees, and rules governing consideration of conference reports—to prevent separate consideration of food stamps and of farm subsidies.

Institutional actors and arrangements affect the prospects for logrolling in other ways as well. First, leaders committed to resisting and challenging producers can short-circuit logrolling, as Dan Rostenkowski and Robert Packwood did in the tax reform case. Second, leaders can preclude logrolling by making logrolling itself the problematic issue. Logrolling thrives mainly when issues are defined in terms that do not suggest a high level of competition among political interests over how to distribute resources—that is, when the issue simply calls for enlarging a pool of benefits enough to produce a legislative majority. Logrolling is less easily undertaken when the dominant issue is whether one group or set of groups (in this case, resourceful and reputedly influential industries) is legitimately benefiting at the cost of another group (in this case, the public).

In the tax and regulatory cases, leaders managed to make the producer groups themselves and how they operated part of the issue: producers' *modus operandi*—logrolling, lobbying, and the like—constituted proof of their selfish motives. This redefinition of the issue put producer groups on the defensive at the outset and constrained their attempts to logroll. By contrast, the absence of reform leadership in agriculture meant that farm interests had free rein to logroll. In sum, the relatively good fortune of farm producers is attributable at least as much to extant institutional arrangements as it is to their own political capacities.

Institutional change can serve to accelerate or to brake the influence of producer groups. As discussed in chapter 2, the growth of tax expenditures over the early 1970s to the early 1980s was abetted by reforms in Congress that made it easier for producer groups to influence the process. Before that time the House Ways and Means Committee had been tightly controlled for years by a powerful and skilled chairman, Wilbur Mills, who helped to contain pressures to enact revenue-losing measures.[53] The Senate Finance Committee too had been dominated by a few senior (and fairly conservative) lawmakers. Procedures like the closed rule, which prevented amendments on the floor to Ways and Means bills, indicated the degree of power and deference that the parent chamber bestowed upon the committee. This institutional resistance to pressure for tax expenditure growth eroded, however, beginning in the first half of the 1970s, when Congress adopted a series of institutional reforms that decentralized authority, which opened the process to wider scrutiny and made it easier for individual legislators to pursue their own agendas. While the more open procedures of the reformed Congress were advertised as "more democratic," they offered the best access to those interests with the greatest resources and highest stakes in the outcomes. The result was the loss of control over agenda setting and decisionmaking by the chairmen, and thus a weakening of institutional restraints on tax expenditure growth.[54]

By the 1980s much of the Ways and Means Committee's strength and autonomy had been restored.[55] The early reforms were blamed for making it more difficult to lead and for crippling the Democratic majority's ability to develop and legislate coherent policy positions.[56] In addition, the huge budget deficits in the 1980s and the need for high-level bargaining between Congress and the Reagan administration had fostered greater centralization of decisionmaking and constrained the influence of producer groups.

In time, conditions changed to elicit a return to the stronger, more directive leadership that had characterized Ways and Means in the pre-reform era. Leaders of the tax-writing committees took advantage of closed committee markups, made frequent use of party caucuses to develop partisan majorities on the committees, molded legislation to take into account the concerns of committee members, changed the rules to keep packages intact on the floor, and bargained and consulted widely on legislation. In addition, the replacement of Al Ullman with Dan Rostenkowski (a strong chairman, reminiscent of Mills's style) and President Carter with President Reagan, along with sustained guidance from Finance Committee chairmen (Robert Dole and then Robert Packwood), brought to the fore individuals capable of skilled leadership.[57]

One reason producer groups seeking trade protection have not been able to mobilize collectively and logroll the way they did under Smoot-Hawley has to do with the kinds of institutional channels available to them to influence policymakers. As chapter 3 pointed out, demands for relief from foreign competition are handled outside the normal logrolling arena—Congress—and are processed on an industry- or firm-specific basis. Congress remains once-removed from granting benefits to specific constituencies; instead of acting directly, Congress pressures the executive branch or alters the criteria and procedures for granting relief to those producers complaining of unfair competition. Industries too large to ignore have been bought off by special deals cut outside the legislative process and trade agreements, while smaller industries have been channeled into a supposedly depoliticized regulatory process. Each battle to aid a specific industry must be mounted separately and in isolation from other battles, thus precluding the kind of coalition building among industry interests that is the hallmark of legislative logrolling.

Similarly, each of the industries targeted for deregulation was taken on separately, by different regulatory commissions at different times.

Furthermore, before the regulated industries could mobilize their forces in Congress, the independent commissions and the courts unilaterally took action. The swiftness and unpredictability of these policy changes put the regulated industries under pressure from the beginning and created a sense of *fait accompli*. Under such circumstances, industries were put in the position of favoring legislation that could, at best, moderate the decisions of the largely autonomous commissions and courts. Institutional arrangements thus vitiated the possibility of cooperation among the regulated industries in order to preserve the status quo.

Conclusion

There is only limited support for the notion that variations in levels of producer-group mobilization, their resources, and their membership exclusivity correspond to changes in producer-group fortunes. Although higher levels of mobilization coincide with rising benefits, such levels do not appear to be determinative when other conditions are favorable to reducing or to containing benefits.

There is more support for the proposition that the existence of an organized opposition is detrimental to producers' fortunes. And the relationship of producer-group cohesion and coalition-building capacity to policy outcomes is strong, suggesting that group fortunes are enhanced if producers remain cohesive and build coalitions with each other and with nonproducer interests.

Yet the notion that producer groups largely determine their own policy fortunes should be kept in perspective. To the extent that a producer-group explanation is persuasive, it constitutes not so much an *alternative* as it does an *adjunct* to the explanation already developed in this study. The impact of producer groups on policy outcomes seems contingent on a host of other variables that come into play, particularly those subsumed under the institutional and issue contexts. Policy fortunes are the result of complex, dynamic, and interdependent relationships among an array of forces and actors in the policymaking process.

CHAPTER SIX

Issues, Institutions, and Public Policy

THE QUESTIONS posed in this book lie at the intersection of political interests, issues, institutions, and public policy. The book began with the observation that the fortunes of producer groups vary over time and across policy areas. In some periods and in some areas fortunes are on the rise while in others they are declining. In still others, producer fortunes rise but are contained, and sometimes fortunes are maintained in the face of a threatened decline.

These outcomes result from variations in the kinds of issues and issue definitions that are salient at particular historical junctures and from the organizational features and behavior of the principal institutional actors who make policy. Under favorable issue contexts, the opportunities for producers to enjoy a rise in benefits (as well as to fend off efforts to reduce them) are enhanced. Conversely, when the issue context is unfavorable, it is more likely that policymakers will resist policies with concentrated benefits and diffuse costs, that they will launch challenges against those that already exist, and that they will succeed in their efforts. An institutional context favorable to producer-group interests is one in which institutional actors lack the capacity, incentives, and commitment to resist and challenge policies with concentrated benefits and diffuse costs; an unfavorable context is one in which such actors are willing and able to resist and challenge such policies.

This chapter summarizes findings and assesses the relative importance of the issue and institutional contexts as well as their interdependence. It

165

then goes on to acknowledge, as does other recent work, the importance of institutions in the policymaking process, but it also cautions that the impact of institutions on policy should not be assumed to be automatic; rather, it is contingent. Finally, the chapter concludes by asking whether this book confirms the prevailing view that American politics has moved from "clientelism" to "neopluralism."

Issues, Institutions, and Group Fortunes

Table 6-1 summarizes the basic findings from the preceding chapters. It divides each of the four policy areas into two time periods. The second and third columns show whether the issue and institutional contexts were favorable or unfavorable toward producer interests in each policy area. The fourth column indicates whether or not the policy decisions or outcomes generally favored the groups.

In the three cases where both the issue and institutional contexts were unfavorable to producer groups (trade policy before the 1970s, tax reform after 1981, and anticompetitive regulation since the 1970s), policy fortunes declined—that is, policy decisions went against producers' interests and their benefits diminished. In the three cases where producers' fortunes rose (agricultural policy in the 1980s, tax policy from the 1970s to 1981, and anticompetitive regulation before the 1970s), the opposite situation prevailed—both issue and institutional contexts strongly favored the producers. Where the issue context favored producers but institutional actors remained largely committed to opposing them (trade policy, 1970s and 1980s), containment was the outcome. Producers' fortunes rose modestly, but no more than that. This outcome is scored as unfavorable in terms of policy fortunes because a highly favorable issue context for producers was not translated into anything more than an incremental gain. Finally, where producer interests faced an unfavorable issue context but institutional actors' commitment or capacity to challenge them was low, producers' existing programs and benefits were largely maintained (agricultural policy in the 1990s). This is scored as favorable because, in the context of an increasingly unfavorable issue context, efforts that might have led to a significant decline in benefits failed or never materialized.

One might logically wonder whether one of the two contexts is more important than the other, but the question is akin to asking whether the human heart is more important than the brain, or whether legs are more

Table 6-1. *Effects of Issues and Institutions on Policy Fortunes*[a]

Policy area	Period	Issue context	Institutional context	Status of policy fortunes
Trade protection	Pre-1970s	−	−	− (Declining)
Trade protection	1970s and 1980s	+	−	− (Contained)
Agricultural subsidies	1980s	+	+	+ (Rising)
Agricultural subsidies	1990s	−	+	+ (Maintained)
Tax expenditures	1970–81	+	+	+ (Rising)
Tax expenditures	Post-1981	−	−	− (Declining)
Anticompetitive regulation	Pre-1970s	+	+	+ (Rising)
Anticompetitive regulation	1970 to present	−	−	− (Declining)

a. A plus sign (+) means favorable to producers; a minus sign (−) means unfavorable to producers.

vital than arms. Both are obviously important but for different reasons. The issue context determines the kinds of problems that get on the agenda and how they get defined as well as the kinds of coalitions that are likely to emerge in response. The institutional context determines whether producers' interests or those of their opponents tend to prevail on those issues that reach the agenda for decision. In short, both issues and institutions are crucial in their own right, and any analysis that omits either one is likely to be inadequate.

The issue and institutional contexts are interdependent to some degree. It is not pure coincidence that in six of the eight cases in table 6-1 the two contexts held the same implications, either favorable or unfavorable for producer interests. One reason for this is that key institutional actors take account of the issue context in deciding their stance toward producers' interests. They will be emboldened by an unfavorable issue context because it signals that producer interests are politically vulnerable. Such were the cases in tax reform and deregulation. Conversely, an issue context favorable to producers is likely to discourage a commitment to challenging or resisting producers, and it may persuade institutional actors to accommodate or even champion producer interests. Reform prospects in agriculture were stymied in part by tepid presidential leadership and the absence of leadership in the Senate on the issue, which reflected an issue context that cast farmers as victims deserving help from government. Furthermore, over the longer term institutional arrangements adjust, even if only gradually and partially, to changes in the issue context. As new issues and issue definitions emerge and take hold and new coalitions form in response to them, so too should organizational rules, procedures, and relationships among actors in the policymaking process.

Yet, even though the issue and institutional contexts certainly are related, changes in one do not necessarily produce or correspond to changes in the other. There is no guarantee that the two will be synchronized, as the trade policy (1970s and 1980s) and agricultural (1990s) cases show. This is because "institutions, once created, live substantially beyond the mandate they originally served," as Judith Goldstein argued in the case of trade policy.[1] Institutions embed the reigning issue definitions, preferred solutions, and supporting coalitions that emerged at earlier times.

Even where the two contexts are consistent (that is, when both are favorable or unfavorable for producers' fortunes), the nature, timing, and extent of change in one context are shaped by more than the other context. Issues change with shifts in economic conditions, the effects of previous policy choices, and a host of other changes and choices that are independent of institutions. How and whether institutions will adjust to a new issue context, how long it will take to make the adjustments, and to what degree institutional reforms or other changes will accommodate changes in issues are all to a significant degree under the control of institutional actors themselves, and reforms may be put in place without any precipitating change in the issue context.

The Issue Context as Policy Predictor

It is possible that one or the other of the two contexts is a better predictor of policy outcomes. Table 6-1 shows that in six of the eight cases the issue context predicts correctly. A favorable issue context in tax policy before the mid-1980s allowed for a rise in tax expenditures, just as it allowed one industry after another to receive the benefits of anticompetitive regulations in the decades preceding the 1970s. In the case of tax policy, poor economic performance, much of it blamed on government involvement in the economy, led to concern with the needs of business and sympathy with the business community's argument for relief through more generous tax incentives. In the case of deregulation, relatively good economic performance before the mid-1970s meant that there was little reason to challenge anticompetitive regulations, despite growing academic criticism of regulation. For those who cared about the existing policy (the regulatory commissions, the relevant committees in Congress, and, of course, the regulated industries themselves), regulation was regarded as intellectually defensible and politically advantageous.

Because subsidies for producer groups have diffuse, externalized costs, they can accumulate over long periods of time. Yet because these policies have few obvious diffuse benefits, they have little support among the public. As a result, they become enticing targets for elimination when problems that entail diffuse economic burdens become salient. Starting in the 1970s, these problems included inflation, slower economic growth, high taxes, and a vague concern with big government. The distributive problems associated with business-oriented tax incentives, especially unfairness and middle-class tax burdens, worsened over time and became salient in the wake of abuses publicized after the 1981 tax law passed. Similarly, regulation was linked in clear and plausible ways to inflation, anticonsumer behavior, slower growth, and the energy crisis.

Neither economic conditions nor previous policy choices by themselves, however, guaranteed that pro-reform coalitions would emerge. Tax reform as a policy prescription had to be refashioned to maximize political viability and to build a broad-based, pro-reform coalition. Deregulation was supported by an unassailable body of analysis and evidence that not only showed the benefits to be gained from reform but also allayed fears and uncertainty that deregulation would produce unwanted consequences. Both prescriptions were congruent with the evolution of conservative and liberal thinking and policy goals in the areas of taxes and regulation. With the widespread perception that a decision on the merits meant supporting these reforms, and with the glare of media attention focused on the issue (especially in the tax reform case), momentum built for the reforms. This set of circumstances altered (though did not determine) the electoral calculus of the average member of Congress; incentives were tipped in the direction of supporting constituents' diffuse interests.

The issue context in trade policy for much of the post–World War II period was conducive to a sharp decline in tariff levels and kept the adoption of new trade barriers at a minimum. The tragic experience with Smoot-Hawley during the 1930s made a long-lasting impression on a generation of U.S. policymakers. Protectionism was roundly discredited, and a commitment to freer trade came as close to being a bipartisan issue as any other policy did in this period. The pursuit of freer trade in turn coincided with (and was given partial credit for) growing global economic prosperity in which U.S. producers faced little foreign competition; moreover, a more open world economy helped contain communism. Furthermore, the prosperity for which liberalization was given some credit meant that the political pressures for trade protection were relatively modest. It was therefore possible to hold together a solid elite consensus behind trade liberalization.

Although the cost, waste, and inequitable distribution of farm subsidies became salient issues in the 1980s, they were overshadowed and displaced by the severe economic problems many farmers experienced during these years. Building the kind of strong, broad-based, pro-reform coalitions that emerged in the tax and regulatory arenas was not possible in the 1980s, because the problem was defined as the farmers' plight—victims of economic forces and events largely out of their control—and not as out-of-control farm subsidies. The poor economic conditions of the farm were joined with a symbolically powerful agrarian myth. The portrayal of farmers and of farming as the embodiment of widely shared American values amplified public concern and sympathy for the producers, resulting in the widespread perception that farmers needed and deserved help from the government.

The Reagan administration ignored this situation when it put forward its radical reform proposals. The Democrats, who have traditionally supported farm interests for logrolling as well as for ideological reasons, used the farm crisis as a populist rallying cry, putting the Republicans on the defensive. This electoral strategy turned out to be effective in the Senate, where rural interests have greater institutional leverage and where party majorities are precarious. In the tax and regulatory cases, by contrast, reformers did not have to contend with competing issues in which the producer groups could be portrayed as victims. Nor could the producer groups draw upon symbols and myths that could cast them in a sympathetic light. Instead they were portrayed as selfish interests whose policy demands increasingly disadvantaged the public.

The Institutional Context as Policy Predictor

Table 6-1 shows that the institutional context predicts producer-group fortunes better than the issue context does. In every case the institutional context predicted the policy fortunes correctly. Each time the institutional context favored the groups' interests, so did the policy outcomes; whenever the institutional context was unfavorable to producer groups' interests, so were the policy outcomes.

In the two cases for which the issue context did not correctly predict the policy outputs, the institutional context alone was decisive in the outcome. Since the 1970s the issue context in trade policy has become much more hospitable for a rise in producer-group fortunes and consequently in protectionism. The United States has experienced greater economic difficulty (slower growth, lower productivity, and a strong dollar in the 1980s) at the same time that it has faced the challenge of vigorous international competition. As more industries have been adversely affected, producer groups have mobilized for protection. Simultaneously, bipartisan support for free trade has eroded.

Nevertheless, protectionism's advance has been less than what might plausibly have been expected, given these political and economic changes. The institutional arrangements that so effectively reduced protectionism before the 1970s and 1980s have remained largely in place and continue to contain protectionism in the new era.[2] Key institutional actors have stayed committed to resisting pressures that threaten a return to rampant legislated protectionism. Congress continues to refrain from industry-specific protectionism and to delegate to the executive branch broad authority to negotiate reductions in trade barriers with other nations. It also continues to divert protectionist pressures to a depoliticized administrative process that, while not as unfriendly to granting relief as in earlier years, is more insulated than the legislative arena from those pressures. Instead, Congress has given the executive branch encouragement and leeway to cut special deals with industries too powerful to ignore. Moreover, major legislation to liberalize trade continues to gain passage in Congress. Strong, committed leadership on the part of committees like Ways and Means, which regained much of its autonomy by the 1980s, has kept protectionist initiatives from coming to a vote. Vigorous leadership from chairmen of the trade committees (along with the adoption of new mechanisms such as the fast-track procedure) has restored much of the insulation of the legislative process from producer-group pressures.

Similarly, continued presidential support for trade agreements and skilled special trade representatives have effectively built coalitions in Congress in favor of free trade. Although support for free trade has eroded among House Democrats, bipartisanship is still the rule in the Senate, where many of the protectionist initiatives from the House have been deflected. In addition, most members of Congress remain comfortable with an arrangement that allows them to take positions sympathetic to the plight of distressed constituents while relieving them of responsibility for either the distress itself or the risks entailed in actions that would injure trade relations. Finally, although support for free trade among labor leaders has waned, support from other elites (executive branch officials, businessmen, and academics) remains strong.

The other case for which the issue context did not predict correctly is agricultural policy in the 1990s. Looking only at the issue context, one might have expected efforts to impose means-testing to succeed, but they did not. The farm economy had improved by that time, and means-testing (targeted against affluent farmers who do not fit the mythical image of struggling family farmers) reached the agenda. The deficit was more salient than the farm economy, and a bipartisan coalition had gained sufficient strength to bring the proposal up for a vote.

But an institutional commitment to challenge the producers was absent, and the result has been the maintenance of farm programs that are decades old. The Bush administration displayed even more ambivalence toward market-oriented reform than the Reagan administration had in the 1980s. Nor have bold initiatives come from the bureaucracy or Congress, where both the Agriculture Department and the agriculture committees are constituency-oriented. Leadership has been particularly lacking in the Senate; no legislative entrepreneur has stepped forward to champion reform, as occurred in the other cases. For leaders and potential policy entrepreneurs who must choose where to invest their political resources, the salience of the farm crisis and public sympathy for farmers probably made reducing farm subsidies a less attractive cause than other issues. Sympathy for the producers subsides with improvement in the farm economy, but so does the level of expenditures, which reduces the salience of the programs and their costs. Farm policy, encompassing a single sector, is also likely to be perceived as less central to the national economy than tax policy or regulation and therefore of less interest to the broad national audiences to whom leaders like to appeal. In addition, the growing internationalization of U.S. agriculture places constraints on presidential initiative, because building a consensus for cutting U.S. subsidies is predicated upon getting other nations to lift their restrictions on imports of U.S. products.

In the six cases where there is agreement between the issue context and the policy outcomes, the institutional context remains a part of the explanation for producers' fortunes. In the tax case, a weakened Ways and Means Committee, ineffective presidential leadership (from Carter), and an acquiescent president (Reagan) facilitated the great outpouring of tax expenditure provisions from 1978 through 1981. For the coalitions supporting tax reform and deregulation to consolidate and triumph over producer-group interests, certain institutional actors had to be committed to achieving reform. The Treasury Department played a key role in getting tax reform on the agenda, and the regulatory commissions accomplished much of the deregulation on their own. Had the missions of these agencies not been (or become) congruent with reform, the chances for policy change would have been much worse.

Tax reform and deregulation also became top priorities for presidents, committee chairs, and agency heads. Both reforms would have been unthinkable without strong leadership. Leaders were able to bring to bear the resources and other advantages of their positions to push vigorously for these reforms. Leaders' calculations were influenced by the opportunity to take credit for effecting major reforms over the opposition of reputedly powerful opponents—thus enhancing their prestige and prospects for influence in the future—and by the competitive and imitative dynamics of leadership. The same may be said of the role of institutions in the trade case. The executive-centered features of the trade policymaking process, combined with the committed and skilled leadership offered by executive officials and legislative committee chairmen, made it much harder to block trade-liberalizing legislation and to increase protectionism in the decades following World War II.

As important as institutional arrangements and actors have been, their roles have varied. They have not always been decisive. Sometimes they have merely contributed to an outcome or have even been irrelevant. For instance, the rise in farm subsidies in the 1980s and the failure of Reagan's reform proposals had more to do with the issue context than with the institutional one. The acuteness and salience of the farm crisis, the persistence of the agrarian myth in popular culture, and the entitlement features of the subsidy budget were the most direct and decisive factors in this case. Even with a radically different set of institutions and much more commitment to reform on the part of institutional actors, a different outcome would have been uncertain, at best. Tax reform and deregulation were not attempted (or pursued vigorously) in earlier years because institutional actors recognized that there would have been little chance of achieving reform then, or perhaps because they simply saw less reason to pursue those reforms until the issue context had changed. In the trade case, institutional resistance to protectionism—although always important since World War II—has been more critical since the 1970s, when the issue context changed in ways that produced far more pressures for protection than had been felt before. In short, the issue context limits and shapes the relevance of institutional actors and affects the timing of their responses to producer-group policies. The relationship, then, between the two contexts is complex, and the causal significance of each is variable.

Relationships among the Cases

Throughout this book change and continuity have been examined separately for the four policy areas. Yet perhaps opportunities for and constraints on producer groups in one policy area affected the fortunes of producers in one or more other areas. In his study of trade policy, Pietro Nivola suggests that just such a relationship exists. A principal reason, he argues, that policymakers have been willing to make it easier for producers to secure relief under unfair-trade laws and regulations is that they have been constrained in their ability to deliver particularized benefits through other policy tools: "In an era of budgetary austerity, domestic regulatory retrenchment, and a simplified tax code, all of which have constrained the flow of other selective preferences and protections, reliance on trade remedies has grown."[3]

Although this thesis is plausible and intriguing, empirical support for it is limited. The one instance where a clear connection between policy areas seems to exist is between trade policy and agricultural subsidies. As discussed in the chapter on farm policy, policymakers have increasingly offered trade protection and export assistance programs as means to cope with pressures to reduce spending on traditional farm commodity programs.[4] Moreover, one reason it was so difficult to reduce farm subsidies in the 1980s and early 1990s was that U.S. negotiators failed in their efforts to get European nations to reduce their agricultural trade barriers. The closure of markets abroad and the advantages other nations were giving their own producers strengthened the case for maintaining subsidy payments to U.S. producers.

But little else suggests that the fortunes of producers in one policy area are affected positively or negatively by developments in other areas. For one thing, the substance of policy issues for the other cases did not overlap much, and the degree to which various industries were affected by the different policies varied widely. The issues over which deregulation was fought, for instance, were not clearly, substantially, or directly related to those over which tax expenditures or farm subsidies were debated. Perhaps a more important reason for a lack of significant causal relationships among policy areas is simply the structure of the U.S. polity. Fragmented, pluralistic governing institutions militate against defining issues and building durable coalitions that encompass and coordinate activity across multiple policy areas.

Beyond Institutional Determinism

A noteworthy recent development in the study of politics is the "rediscovery of institutions" as important in their own right for understanding how government works and the policies it pursues.[5] Much of the rational-choice "neoinstitutional" literature views institutions as sets of rules and procedures that aggregate and order individual preferences. For example, policy outcomes may vary with the number of policy options that can be considered and how the alternatives are paired with one another; the sequence of decisionmaking steps; the prevailing organizational features of legislatures (the division and specialization of labor in committees, leadership organization, and party ratios, among others); and the procedures that legislatures follow (rules of debate and amendment, for example). Whatever the content or distribution of the preferences of the policymakers involved, alternative institutional features will lead to different policy decisions and, consequently, to different winners and losers.[6]

This shift in thinking about institutions is welcome. It advances the rational-choice approach to politics beyond an excessively atomistic conception of policymaking as simply the result of optimizing behavior and aggregating preferences. It also corrects the behavioralists' cramped view of institutions as mere shells filled by sociological categories.

Nevertheless, the redirection in political research presents a potential pitfall for students of public policy—namely, institutional determinism. Note, in the first place, that the content of political actors' preferences is taken as given and left unexplained, along with how and why those preferences might change over time. But if politics is about anything, it is about discovering one's preferences, deciding which are more important, and above all persuading others to change theirs.

Second, neoinstitutionalism tries to explain policy change (or the lack of it) by an exclusive emphasis on how institutions aggregate and order preferences. It therefore imparts to policymaking behavior a programmed quality, which tends to reduce policymakers to the status of laboratory rats running through a maze. Change the maze (that is, the institutional rules), and the rats' behavioral pattern changes with it. At its extreme, policy change could occur only in response to institutional change. In fact, many policy changes occur during periods of institutional stability, just as it is possible for policies to stay in place in periods of institutional innovation.

R. Kent Weaver and Bert A. Rockman offer a less deterministic perspective. In a recent volume on governmental institutions, they ask whether effective governance is linked more to certain institutional arrangements than to others. Two of the criteria they examine to judge effectiveness—the capacity to represent diffuse, unorganized interests and to impose losses on powerful groups—bear directly on the subject of producer-groups' fortunes. One of their conclusions is that although particular institutional arrangements provide opportunities for certain kinds of governmental actions, they do not guarantee them. "Although institutions affect governmental capabilities, their effects are *contingent*."[7] The findings in this volume confirm and elaborate upon that argument.

It is true, for instance, that federal agencies with capacities and incentives to maintain autonomy from producer groups (the Treasury Department, independent regulatory commissions, and tax-writing committees in Congress, for example) were more likely to represent diffuse interests and oppose producer-group interests than were those without such autonomy (for example, the Department of Agriculture and agriculture committees). Yet those propensities in no way *guaranteed* that these institutional actors would take positions favoring diffuse interests or that they would succeed in effecting policy changes in that direction. The very same Treasury Department and regulatory agencies that pushed for tax reform and deregulation, after all, either acquiesced in or actively promoted the rise in tax expenditures and anticompetitive regulations for several years.

Much the same can be said of other institutional actors. Those who occupy key formal leadership positions (that is, the president, committee chairs, agency heads, and sometimes party leaders), as well as informal leadership positions (legislative entrepreneurs), have greater incentives and capacities than nonleaders for defending diffuse interests against those of producers; these officials also often figure prominently in policy struggles that pit diffuse interests against those of producer groups. Here again, however, there is nothing automatic about the pattern of institutional behavior. Presidents, committee chairs, and other leaders did not always favor tax reform, deregulation, free trade, or farm subsidy reductions. Some have been hostile, or at least indifferent, to these policy changes. Even when leaders have favored these policies, their commitment to them has waxed and waned.

Part of the problem may lie in the misconceptualization of institutions. Thinking of institutions as only organizational "arrangements"—formal rules and procedures that distribute power and establish decisionmaking processes—constricts understanding of them. This truncated conception ignores the informal rules, norms, and relationships that, although not fully specified in an organization's formal scheme, clearly affect behavior. Neoinstitutionalists nonetheless choose to gloss over the informal aspects of institutions, perhaps because such sociological phenomena—wherein normative expectations gained through interaction with other individuals affect conduct—do not easily mesh with their concept of unadulterated, calculative, individual conduct.[8]

Second, an exclusive focus on the structural aspects of institutions overlooks the obvious fact that policymakers are themselves part of the institutions. As such, they do not simply operate within institutions but also give institutions their character as purposive actors. More important, neither policymakers' preferences nor their behavior is wholly conditioned by their institutional environment. Policymakers possess some measure of discretion, and their actions are influenced by noninstitutional actors and forces as well as by institutional ones. Institutional influences on policy are contingent rather than automatic because institutions rarely, if ever, dictate the specific policy preferences and choices of policymakers. They are merely one influence, albeit an important one, on preferences and choices. Institutions may make some outcomes more likely than others, but those who work in institutions have latitude to choose among alternative courses of action.[9]

Institutional roles, missions, rules, and norms shape political actors' goals, but whether those goals are translated into meaningful policy preferences and priorities depends on actors' assessments of issues and situations. They must decide which problems are most pressing and which are most amenable to correction, rate the ideological and intellectual appeal of proposed alternatives, and consider the lessons learned from previous policy choices.

Hence, the expectations for the role of president—that a president will represent diffuse interests and be responsible for national economic well-being, direct electoral appeals to wide national audiences in order to stay in power, and use the unique resources of the office to undertake such challenges—only partially account for active presidential leadership to promote deregulation and tax reform. Such leadership is conditioned also on the problems facing the nation at particular historical junctures (such as inflation, energy crises, and public concern with tax fairness and big government) and on the meshing of the president's willingness to address those problems with the availability of solutions that are ideologically appealing and intellectually sound. The shift over only a few years in politicians' thinking on tax breaks for business, from expansion of them to elimination of many of them, illustrates the malleability of policy preferences. What happened is that, as in the case of deregulation, institutions became sites for what Hugh Heclo called political learning.[10] In other words, behavior (in this case, public policy) altered in light of experience.

Even when policy outcomes remain relatively stable over time, as in the cases of farm and trade policies, it is often the design of the policies themselves, the ideas they embody, or the issue context that determines the behavior of institutional actors. Institutional arrangements have made it easier to resist group pressures in trade policy and harder to do so in farm policy, to be sure. Yet institutional resistance to trade protection has rested on a solid elite consensus in favor of free trade as a policy ideal and overarching prescription and on the discredit of the alternative, protectionism. This, in turn, was the result of lessons learned from the experience with protectionism before World War II. Indeed, the weakening of institutional resistance in the past decade or so (particularly in the area of administered trade protection) can be traced to a whole new set of experiences that created disenchantment with the free-trade ideal. Similarly, the lack of serious challenges to farm producers by the president, other leaders, and policy entrepreneurs is attributable partly to the disincentives arising out of the issue context in the 1980s, the design of farm programs, and the separation of agriculture from broader domestic policy concerns.

Skilled and committed actors will be able, of course, to shape the issue context and move toward consensus in a desired direction to some degree. But the policy preferences and priorities of institutional actors are in good measure extrainstitutional and situational. They are grounded partly in policymakers' own backgrounds and thinking about issues and in their interactions with interest groups, constituents, experts, and other sources of information. They are situational, and thus fairly malleable, because they are constrained by an issue context that is changeable and not altogether controllable. The polity was no more ready for tax reform in 1978 or deregulation in 1968 than it was for agricultural reform in the 1980s. It is doubtful that any plausible alternative set of institutional arrangements, missions, and even leadership commitment would have made a difference. Indeed, an issue context favorable to groups will discourage vigorous challenges from institutional actors who might have been inclined to act otherwise.

Finally, the direction of causality between institutions and policy may at times reverse. Policies and their consequences themselves can lead to alterations in institutional arrangements and orientations. The reconstitution of the trade policymaking process after World War II in the direction of a more insulated, executive-centered arrangement was the direct result of the lessons learned from Smoot-Hawley in the 1930s and the conversion of policymakers to the idea of liberal trade after postwar liberalization bore fruit. Likewise, the decline of the tariff and the rise of nontariff barriers as preferred policy instruments for trade protection led to the adoption of the fast-track procedure: the new procedure accommodated both Congress's need to approve trade agreements concluded with other nations and the executive's need for a speedy process that would be unlikely to unravel the agreements.

The experience of the Ways and Means Committee over the past few decades presents yet another illustration of how policy changes and institutional change are interactive processes. The congressional reforms of the early 1970s reduced the capacity of Ways and Means to resist tax expenditure and trade-restrictive proposals. The eventual realization that those reforms made governance more difficult—not to mention the specter of greater protectionism and the actuality of proliferating tax expenditures—brought reversals or revisions of many of the institutional reforms.

Clientelism, Pluralism, and Governmental Capacity

Clientelism, particularly in the 1950s and 1960s, was a dominant image of the American polity. A close, mutually beneficial working relationship was said to exist between public officials and particular interests in society.[11] Some of these interests were producer groups, which represented specific industries or sectors of the economy; others were simply loose coalitions of legislative districts. American politics, it was said, was not run by any single elite at the top but rather by multiple elites, each of which had carved out some segment of government for advancing and protecting its particular interests. Often these elites could be found thriving in stable "subgovernments" and "iron triangles."[12] What they sought (often with success) were various kinds of subsidies and protections from the government. The benefits of their capture of the public sector flowed to those involved in the relationship, while the costs were borne by everyone else. Even those who were not uncomfortable with this image, or who saw the process as far more open and competitive, admitted that the system responded better to narrow interests than to broad ones. "The making of governmental decisions," argued Robert A. Dahl, "is not a majestic march of great majorities united upon certain matters of basic policy. It is the steady appeasement of relatively small groups."[13]

Clientelism was viewed for the most part as problematic. A common complaint was that it corrupted the democratic process: because it benefited political minorities—producer groups—it undermined the concept of majority rule. Because these producer groups were narrowly based and privatistic, they worked against broader public interests. Groups with broader interests found it difficult to organize and compete in the pluralist arena. Their effective exclusion belied the pluralists' notion that American democracy produced a balance of competing interests.[14] Later clientelism was closely linked to rent-seeking behavior, which resulted in a bloated and inefficient public sector.[15] Moreover, since clientelism incubates in stable democratic regimes like the United States, the result can be an organizational sclerosis that reduces market efficiency and blocks the innovations necessary for sustained economic growth.[16]

But clientelism is no longer held up as the image that dominates much of American politics. The findings from this study confirm this conclusion. Although producer-group fortunes vary greatly across time and policy areas, on balance these groups now find themselves on the short end of the public policy stick as often as not.[17] In only one of the four policy areas examined in this book—agriculture—does the persistent, entrenched clientelism of old still hold sway. Certainly, little evidence exists of the stable, exclusive, invisible politics that mark subgovernments and iron triangles. Even in the case of agriculture, opposing interests have challenged producers on such issues as pesticides and nutrition, and budget constraints have increased the pressure to reduce subsidies. And it is not at all clear that the ability of farm interests to capture parts of the government was more important for the maintenance of agricultural programs than were public sympathy for family farmers and party competition in the Senate.

This conclusion will hardly seem startling to those who, for roughly the past fifteen years, have been alerting scholars to the emergence of actors who serve as counterweights to entrenched economic power. With clientelism diminished, American politics entered a period best described as "neopluralist" or "hyperpluralist."[18] The rise of public-interest organizations and social movements in the 1960s and 1970s,[19] followed by the countermobilization of business lobbies in the 1970s and 1980s,[20] and changes in Congress that encouraged legislative individualism,[21] all ushered in a more open, competitive, and pluralistic policymaking process. Loose and ephemeral issue networks replaced subgovernments;[22] "sloppy hexagons" supplanted iron triangles;[23] and neopluralism eclipsed clientelism.

What is somewhat more surprising is the fact that, in the cases studied here, the main source of countervailing power vis-à-vis entrenched economic interests has been actors in government rather than in society. The policy changes that have come about are not primarily the result of the pushing and hauling of organized interests. Why governmental actors? In part because diffuse interests are, despite the growth of public-interest groups, still quite difficult to organize. In part because policymakers, who must satisfy diffuse publics to stay in power, perceive producer-group demands as increasingly inconsistent with economic revitalization, tax fairness, lower tax burdens and deficits, and more efficient and less intrusive government. In addition, policies that benefit producers drain resources, either directly through the budget or indirectly through slower economic growth, from those programs that diffuse publics most cherish—entitlements.

The demise of one image (clientelism) in favor of another (neopluralism) has not been accompanied, however, by a more hopeful or happy verdict for democratic governance in America. Despite their differences, the old clientelism and the new pluralism have in common the image of a weak, debilitated government. More openness and more claimants— and more competition among them—along with weaker parties and a presidency weakened by Vietnam and Watergate, gave rise to "ungovernability," "overload," and an "atomized politics" in which coalitions must be "built in the sand."[24] Within government, "institutional combat" and divisive partisanship reign, resulting in stalemate, policy incoherence, and an inability on the part of governing elites to come to "authoritative policy closure" as policy endlessly gets made and remade.[25] At least the old subgovernments had the virtue of stable protocoalitions that could deliver authoritative policy choices and closure.

It would be incorrect to conclude that the United States no longer suffers from the disabilities of neopluralism, just as it would be to argue that clientelism has vanished from the political system. Yet the cases examined in this book suggest a government much more capable of building coalitions, making authoritative choices, and coming to closure than the one posited by the new conventional wisdom.[26] On the whole, this book's findings do not confirm a government stalemated or overloaded by competing interests any more than they confirm one captured by entrenched clients.

Some policies fit neither clientelism nor neopluralism very well. Trade policy reveals the remarkable capacity of elites in favor of free trade to sustain and enlarge liberalization efforts spanning several decades. Protectionist-seeking industries, while making headway in the past two decades, cannot be said to have returned the United States to its protectionist past. What is surprising is not that protectionist impulses have gathered strength, but that their progress has been so limited, given hospitable economic conditions and a government supposedly torn by conflicting interests and partisanship. Reversals of producer-group fortunes were more dramatic in anticompetitive regulation and tax policy, both of which have remained largely intact through succeeding Congresses and administrations. Consensus building for neither of these breakthroughs was easy, but broad coalitions and bold political leadership did develop.

Although neopluralism made governing more difficult in some ways, it facilitated it in others. Weaker parties and crumbling subgovernments may have undermined formerly reliable coalitions and diminished predictability in policymaking, but their decline also presented possibilities for forging new coalitions and opening new avenues for policymakers to challenge the status quo. In the more individualistic politics, policymaking became more atomized and chaotic, but it also afforded leaders greater maneuverability. As the various cases examined in this book show, greater pluralism and competitiveness need not permanently disable national policymaking institutions and may in fact inject fluidity into the process, which opens rather than closes possibilities for policy innovation.

Furthermore, there was no reason to expect that the conditions that gave rise to neopluralism, any more than those that cultivated clientelism, would continue indefinitely or that they would not be countered by opposing trends. Just as clientelism withered under economic and political changes beginning in the 1960s, so too did the freewheeling pluralism that took its place create the conditions for its own decline. The density and competitiveness that the proliferation of groups in the 1960s and 1970s spawned may have eventually diminished the policymaking impact of those groups. Crowding out one another for access and countering one another's claims might have given policymakers greater leeway to choose courses of action somewhat independent of group claims.

Other centrifugal tendencies of neopluralism have been halted or reversed as those in government perceived excesses and made corrective adjustments. Congress has moved in the direction of greater centralization and party cohesion; party leadership has grown in importance and visibility;[27] and the prestige and autonomy of key committees like Ways and Means and Finance have been restored.[28] Changes in the national agenda during the 1980s and 1990s (particularly the pressure of large deficits) have constrained the influence of interest groups that reforms in Congress had initially facilitated. With Vietnam and Watergate distant memories, more vigorous White House leadership reasserted itself under Reagan and in Clinton's first year. The lesson from the Bush years is that passivity in domestic affairs is untenable.

Governments do some things better than others. Many of the important domestic policy challenges that continue to defy consensus and closure do not reflect political conflict between diffuse publics and specific organized interests.[29] On issues such as taxes, deficits, health care reform, and entitlements, the conflict has been among competing and seemingly irreconcilable diffuse interests. Compared with its performance in reconciling competing majority preferences, the American government's capacity to manage and balance broader public interests with narrower private ones has been creditable. This observation underscores a humbling bit of truth: broad generalizations about American politics that hold up over time and across policies are not easy to come by.

Notes

Chapter One

1. The phrase *fluctuating fortunes* is from David Vogel's excellent study of shifts in the political power of American business, *Fluctuating Fortunes: The Political Power of Business in America* (New York: Basic Books, 1989). Although I borrow his alliteration, this work differs from Vogel's in several respects. First, Vogel looks at the fortunes of the business community as a whole; this book focuses on particular sectors or firms whose fortunes across different areas of public policy might vary considerably from the *overall* public policy fortunes of business. Indeed, from the mid-1970s to the mid-1980s—a period of "political resurgence of business," as Vogel characterizes it (pp. 193–239)—many businesses suffered dramatic defeats under deregulation and tax reform. Second, although the analytical frameworks of the two books share similarities, this one emphasizes the role of political institutions, whereas Vogel's stresses instead the importance of the political mobilization of business.

2. Many commentators have argued that political institutions and traditions in the U.S. encourage the proliferation and influence of these groups. For one of the earliest discussions of the political superiority of producer groups over larger ones with more diffuse interests, see E. E. Schattschneider, *Politics, Pressures and the Tariff* (Prentice-Hall, 1935), pp. 283–85. A system of fragmented and decentralized institutions, with comparatively weak national parties and constrained chief executives, is likely to foster a parochial orientation to policymaking. Members of Congress, for instance, attain reelection by paying greater attention to the interests that predominate in their geographical constituencies than to the broad, diffuse interests of the nation as a whole. See David R. Mayhew, *Congress: The Electoral Connection* (Yale University Press, 1974). The very structure of U.S. institutions, in turn, may reflect an ideology that equates democracy with private autonomy, with the latter believed to be best secured through de-

centralized political organization. See Grant McConnell, *Private Power and American Democracy* (Knopf, 1966). Theodore J. Lowi also stresses the importance of ideology—"interest group liberalism"—in his explanation for the political potency of private economic interests. Lowi, *The End of Liberalism* (W. W. Norton, 1969). Still another explanation is offered by Mancur Olson, who emphasizes the fact that the United States is one of the world's most stable democracies. Long periods of democratic rule, uninterrupted by war or antidemocratic regimes, he argues, serve as breeding grounds for such groups. See Mancur Olson, *The Rise and Decline of Nations* (Yale University Press, 1982).

3. Arthur F. Bentley, *The Process of Government* (Harvard University Press, 1967), p. 204.

4. E. E. Schattschneider, *The Semisovereign People: A Realist's View of Democracy in America* (New York: Holt, Rinehart, and Winston, 1960), pp. 23–24.

5. Although he does not use the term *producer groups*, Jack Walker identifies "organization[s] of small homogenous groups of people or institutions that share a distinct economic or professional interest" as one category of interest groups. They are distinguished from his other two categories, "organizations meant to represent the aspirations of many people involved in a broad social movement, and [organizations] willing to act as representatives for other, less fortunate or less competent members of the society." Jack L. Walker, Jr., *Mobilizing Interest Groups in America: Patrons, Professions, and Social Movements* (University of Michigan Press, 1991), p. 16.

6. James M. Buchanan, Robert D. Tollison, and Gordon Tullock, eds., *Toward a Theory of the Rent-Seeking Society* (Texas A & M University Press, 1980); and George J. Stigler, "The Theory of Economic Regulation," *Bell Journal of Economics and Management Science*, vol. 3 (Spring 1971), pp. 3–21.

7. James Q. Wilson characterizes such policies as involving "client politics." James Q. Wilson, *Political Organizations* (New York: Basic Books, 1973), pp. 333–34; and James Q. Wilson, ed., *The Politics of Regulation* (New York: Basic Books, 1980), pp. 369–70.

8. Olson, *Rise and Decline*, pp. 32–34, 41.

9. Trade barriers can fall into any of these three categories. Tariffs are clearly a tax on consumers of imports, but many nontariff trade barriers come in the form of spending subsidies and regulations.

10. This does not exhaust the number of policies appropriate for analysis, of course. Other policies involving a perceived trade-off between producer interests and those of the broader public are those with concentrated costs and diffuse benefits, or what Wilson calls "entrepreneurial" policies. See James Q. Wilson, *American Government: Institutions and Policies*, 4th ed. (Lexington, Mass.: D.C. Heath, 1989), pp. 432–33. Much "social regulation" (environmental policies, for example) falls into this category.

Many other policies, however, usually involve alternative distributive patterns of benefits and costs that would complicate the task. More difficult to incorporate in the analysis would have been health policy, for instance, in which the costs are diffuse (large groups pay for health care programs), but benefits are both concentrated—they are conferred on health care providers—*and* diffuse—they benefit large sections of the population, like the elderly. By choosing only cases whose distribution of costs and benefits are similar, I have tried to make the task of explaining fluctuations in producer fortunes easier by reducing the number of characteristics on which there is variation from case to case. Put another way, any fluctuations in the policy fortunes found among groups cannot be ascribed to variations in the cost-benefit distributions of the policies examined.

Any work that uses in-depth case studies is limited in the number of different cases that can practically be examined. It ought to be kept in mind that although only four policy areas are being looked at, more than four cases are observed because each area is studied over time. At any rate, it falls to future research to further test and strengthen the propositions advanced in this study by including additional cases.

11. Paul Peterson concluded recently that "special interests may have been steadily gaining influence throughout the 1960s and 1970s, but both during the Reagan years and during the initial years of the Bush administration, these groups lost much of the clout they had once acquired." Paul E. Peterson, "The Rise and Fall of Special Interest Politics," in Mark P. Petracca, ed., *The Politics of Interests: Interest Groups Transformed* (Boulder, Colo.: Westview Press, 1992), p. 326. Peterson's claim to be studying changes in the influence of interest groups is problematic, however, because he does not examine the relevant groups, whether they were active and attempted influence, and whether valid inferences about influence could be made even if we knew what the groups were doing. Rather, Peterson examines the changing fortunes of certain interests, using federal budget data to suggest that those programs benefiting special interests declined even though the budget as a whole grew in the 1980s. His definition of a "special interest" program is debatable, however. What the data do seem to suggest is not so much a decline in special-interest fortunes in general as a decline in the relative shares of the budget for certain interests (particularly those with programs in the nondefense, discretionary portion of the budget). Nor does Peterson examine trends in special-interest fortunes in the nonspending activities of government. For another general argument about the "decline of special interests," see Robert H. Salisbury, "The Paradox of Interest Groups in Washington—More Groups, Less Clout," in Anthony King, ed., *The New American Political System*, 2d ed. (Washington: American Enterprise Institute, 1990), pp. 203–30.

12. On the public-interest movement, see Jeffrey M. Berry, *Lobbying for the People: The Political Behavior of Public Interest Groups* (Princeton University Press, 1977); Andrew S. McFarland, *Public Interest Lobbies: Decision-Making on Energy* (Washington: American Enterprise Institute, 1976); and Richard A. Harris and Sidney M. Milkis, eds., *Remaking American Politics* (Boulder, Colo.: Westview Press, 1989). On the upsurge in nonelectoral forms of mass participation during this period, see Richard Brody, "The Puzzle of Political Participation in America," in Anthony King, ed., *The New American Political System* (Washington: American Enterprise Institute, 1978), pp. 287–324.

13. Some polling data suggest that the public increasingly believes that special interests have disproportionate influence in government. In 1964, when asked "Would you say the government is pretty much run by a *few big interests* looking

out for themselves or that it is run for the benefit of all the people?" a minority of Americans (30 percent) replied "a few big interests." This proportion rose steadily in following years; by 1992, 77 percent held this opinion. (The figure for 1964 is from Wilson, *American Government*, p. 86; the 1992 figure is from an ABC News/*Washington Post* poll.) Some care should be taken in interpreting these data. The question asked may simply tap into a vague, generalized discontent with or mistrust of government, which is elicited even by questions that make no reference at all to organized interests. It is also possible, however, that one of the sources of the growth of public distrust with government and politics generally is a belief that organized interests exert disproportionate influence.

14. Aaron Wildavsky, *Speaking Truth to Power: The Art and Craft of Policy Analysis* (Little, Brown, 1979), p. 4.

15. See Olson, *Rise and Decline*.

16. On incrementalism, see Charles Lindblom, "The Science of Muddling Through," *Public Administration Review*, vol. 14 (Spring 1959), pp. 79–88; on the garbage-can model, see John W. Kingdon, *Agendas, Alternatives, and Public Policies* (Little, Brown, 1984).

17. Schattschneider, *Semisovereign People*, p. 66.

18. For a fuller critique of the garbage-can model's indeterminacy and randomness, see Gary Mucciaroni, "The Garbage Can Model and the Study of Policy Making: A Critique," *Polity*, vol. 24 (Spring 1992), pp. 459–82.

19. James Q. Wilson, "The Politics of Regulation," in Wilson, ed., *Politics of Regulation*, p. 393.

20. Christopher J. Bosso, *Pesticides and Politics: The Life Cycle of a Public Issue* (University of Pittsburgh Press, 1987). Other case studies that address producer-group interests in the policymaking process include Timothy J. Conlan, Margaret T. Wrightson, and David R. Beam, *Taxing Choices: The Politics of Tax Reform* (Washington: CQ Press, 1990); Jeffrey H. Birnbaum and Alan S. Murray, *Showdown at Gucci Gulch: Lawmakers, Lobbyists, and the Unlikely Triumph of Tax Reform* (Random House, 1987); Gary Mucciaroni, "Public Choice and the Politics of Comprehensive Tax Reform," *Governance*, vol. 3 (January 1990), pp. 1–32; Martha Derthick and Paul J. Quirk, *The Politics of Deregulation* (Brookings, 1985); Dorothy L. Robyn, *Braking the Special Interests: Trucking Deregulation and the Politics of Policy Reform* (University of Chicago Press, 1987); and I. M. Destler, *American Trade Politics*, 2d ed. (Washington: Institute for International Economics, 1992).

21. On subgovernments, see John Leiper Freeman, *The Political Process: Executive Bureau–Legislative Committee Relations* (Random House, 1955); Douglass Cater, *Power in Washington: A Critical Look at Today's Struggle to Govern in the Nation's Capital* (Random House, 1964); Grant McConnell, *Private Power and American Democracy* (Knopf, 1966); and Emmette S. Redford, *Democracy in the Administrative State* (Oxford University Press, 1969). On issue networks, see Hugh Heclo, "Issue Networks and the Executive Establishment," in King, ed., *New American Political System* (1978), pp. 87–124.

22. Theodore J. Lowi, "Four Systems of Policy, Politics, and Choice," *Public Administration Review*, vol. 32 (July–August 1972), pp. 298–310; Randall B.

Ripley and Grace A. Franklin, *Congress, the Bureaucracy and Public Policy* (Homewood, Ill.: Dorsey Press, 1976); and Wilson, *Political Organizations*, pp. 327–37.

23. Anticompetitive regulation at first glance would seem to fit into Lowi's regulatory category, but such regulation has been essentially self-regulatory and thus falls into Lowi's distributive category.

24. Recently, Frank R. Baumgartner and Bryan D. Jones suggested a conceptualization of the policymaking process very similar to the one adopted here. See *Agendas and Instability in American Politics* (University of Chicago Press, 1993), chap. 2. Their notion of a *policy image* corresponds to the way in which issues are defined in what I have called the issue context. Likewise, my reference to the institutional context includes what they label *policy venues*, although their conception of venues is somewhat narrower than my own term. By venue they are concerned with which institution(s) (for example, levels or branches of government, committees in Congress, and so on) control jurisdiction over policymaking in a certain area. My conception of the institutional context includes those organizational and jurisdictional aspects of institutions, but also stresses the importance of individual decisionmakers (especially leaders) and their goals, policy preferences, calculations, and strategies for reaching goals.

25. Addressing questions very similar to the ones in this book, R. Douglas Arnold focuses at the microlevel of analysis on the more or less direct and immediate influences on individual legislators' calculations and decisions as to how they will cast roll-call votes. R. Douglas Arnold, *The Logic of Congressional Action* (Yale University Press, 1990). This study, in contrast, places legislative decisions in a broader policymaking context, taking account of how issues evolve over time, how social and economic factors influence which issues become salient and how they get defined, and how alternative courses of action in response to those issues are formulated. This book does not start with the notion that policymakers behave differently depending upon the salience of issues to constituents. Instead, it explores how and why certain issues become salient in the first place, which requires a sensitivity to historical trends and events, shifts in economic thinking, political and economic geography, as well as to how political institutions change in response to changes in society.

26. Two other differences between Douglas Arnold's book and this one are instructive. First, whereas Arnold's study is of congressional decisionmaking, this one views the legislative branch as one political actor in a broader policymaking context. To have focused exclusively on Congress would have been to neglect other political actors, especially executive-branch agencies and officeholders, whose importance is sometimes greater than that of the legislative branch. In two of the cases examined here, regulation and trade policy, actors in the executive branch have frequently taken the lead in making policy decisions, with Congress acting only after the fact or in an ancillary role. As this research shows, fluctuations in producer-group fortunes arise in part out of variations in institutional settings, which requires placing the congressional role in the larger governmental context.

Second, although political leaders and policy entrepreneurs (what Arnold calls coalition leaders) figure in his analysis, he seeks to explain only one aspect of their work: how they "anticipate and respond to legislators' electoral needs when they are refining policy proposals and devising strategies to attract legislators' support" (Arnold, *Logic*, p. 8). This study, by contrast, examines also the incentives and capacities that affect leaders' decisions to address producer-group issues. As the evidence shows, leaders' choices of issues are shaped by more than their estimation of the electoral needs of rank-and-file legislators. Finally, the two studies do not completely overlap in the cases that they examine (energy policy and economic management in the Arnold volume, and farm and trade policy in this one).

27. Steven Kelman, *Making Public Policy: A Hopeful View of American Government* (New York: Basic Books, 1987), p. 252. On the need for minority interests to persuade majorities that their interests coincide with a *bona fide* public interest, see Wilson, ed., *Politics of Regulation*, pp. 363–65.

28. Schattschneider, *Semisovereign People*, p. 27.

29. For Charles E. Lindblom, this is the essence of the "privileged position of business" in the political system. See Lindblom, *Politics and Markets: The World's Political Economic System* (New York: Basic Books, 1977), chaps. 13, 14.

30. On problem definition, see Deborah A. Stone, *Policy Paradox and Political Reason* (Harper Collins, 1988), pp. 106–65; and David Dery, *Problem Definition in Policy Analysis* (University Press of Kansas, 1984). For a review of the literature, see David A. Rochefort and Roger W. Cobb, "Problem Definition, Agenda Access, and Policy Choice," *Policy Studies Journal*, vol. 21 (Spring 1993), pp. 56–71.

31. Schattschneider, *Semisovereign People*, p. 68.

32. Vogel, *Fluctuating Fortunes*.

33. For example, the 1986 tax reform act hit many older, declining manufacturing and "smokestack" industries (steel, for example) especially hard. Despite receiving the investment tax credit and other incentives for many years, these industries continued to decline, thus weakening their claim that the tax credit was needed for their revival.

34. Bosso, *Pesticides*, p. 235.

35. Schattschneider, *Semisovereign People*.

36. Ibid., chap. 1.

37. Olson, *Rise and Decline*, pp. 50–53.

38. James G. March and Johan P. Olsen, *Rediscovering Institutions: The Organizational Basis of Politics* (New York: Free Press, 1989); Kenneth Shepsle, "Studying Institutions: Some Lessons from the Rational Choice Approach," *Journal of Theoretical Politics*, vol. 1, no. 1 (1989), pp. 131–47; and R. Kent Weaver and Bert A. Rockman, eds., *Do Institutions Matter? Government Capabilities in the United States and Abroad* (Brookings, 1993).

39. On the more general concept of state autonomy, see Eric A. Nordlinger, *On the Autonomy of the Democratic State* (Harvard University Press, 1981); and Peter B. Evans, Dietrich Rueschemeyer, and Theda Skocpol, eds., *Bringing the State Back In* (Cambridge University Press, 1985). On the role of bureaucrats

and their agencies as driven by internal characteristics (such as organizational mission or professional training) rather than by pressure groups or other external sources, see Herbert Kaufman, *The Forest Ranger: A Study in Administrative Behavior* (Johns Hopkins University Press, 1960); Wilson, ed., *Politics of Regulation*; and Robert A. Katzmann, *Regulatory Bureaucracy: The Federal Trade Commission and Antitrust Policy* (MIT Press, 1980).

40. Richard F. Fenno, Jr., *Congressmen in Committees* (Little, Brown, 1973).

41. Derthick and Quirk, *Politics of Deregulation*, p. 103.

42. Ibid., pp. 106–11, 240–41.

43. References to benefit levels in this study refer only to absolute levels. Relative comparisons in levels would ultimately be arbitrary because no common yardstick exists that allows meaningful statements comparing, for instance, the value of tax expenditure benefits and anticompetitive regulations. Nor is it necessary to use a common yardstick to make valid comparisons that address the questions posed in this study. Moreover, actual policy decisions and nondecisions also must be examined to accurately gauge trends in group fortunes.

44. The rate of growth of benefits from these policies varied greatly from policy to policy, however. The rise in tax-expenditure benefits from the early 1970s to the early 1980s was rapid, as was the rise in farm subsidies from the early to late 1980s. After the period in which most economic regulation was enacted, from the late nineteenth century to World War II, benefits from anticompetitive regulation rose much more gradually.

45. It should be kept in mind that references to group fortunes as declining or rising apply exclusively to public policy fortunes, not to economic fortunes in general. Indeed, I have hypothesized that rising policy fortunes are more likely to occur when a producer is perceived to be experiencing bad economic times, and that declining fortunes often occur when a producer is experiencing no such difficulty.

46. Bentley, *Process of Government*; David B. Truman, *The Governmental Process* (Knopf, 1951); and Earl Latham, *The Group Basis of Politics: A Study in Basing-Point Legislation* (Cornell University Press, 1952). For a review of the literature on group theory, see J. David Greenstone, "Group Theories," in Fred I. Greenstein and Nelson W. Polsby, eds., *Handbook of Political Science* (Addison-Wesley, 1975), vol. 2, pp. 243–318.

47. It is worth noting that some group theorists present a more nuanced analysis of policymaking than they are often given credit for. Truman, for example, appreciated the role of institutions in channeling group pressures. But even his chief conclusion was that public policies were "the resultant of effective access by various interests." Truman, *Governmental Process*, pp. 322, 506–07.

Chapter Two

1. The term *tax expenditures* was coined by Stanley S. Surrey in *Pathways to Tax Reform: The Concept of Tax Expenditures* (Harvard University Press, 1973).

2. The cases of deregulation studied here are those in which industries sought to preserve regulation but were unable to do so. Not examined are cases in which

the regulated industry was a chief proponent of the policy change, as in banking. See Thomas H. Hammond and Jack H. Knott, "The Deregulatory Snowball: Explaining Deregulation in the Financial Industry," *Journal of Politics*, vol. 50 (February 1988), pp. 3–41.

3. On tax expenditures and the unlikelihood of reform, see John F. Witte, The *Politics and Development of the Federal Income Tax* (University of Wisconsin Press, 1985), p. 380; David G. Davies, *United States Taxes and Tax Policy* (Cambridge University Press, 1986), p. 287; Michael J. Graetz, "Can the Income Tax Continue to Be the Major Revenue Source?" in Joseph A. Pechman, ed., *Options for Tax Reform* (Brookings, 1984), p. 42; and Roger A. Freeman, *Tax Loopholes: The Legend and the Reality* (Washington: American Enterprise Institute, 1973), p. 90. On regulation, see George J. Stigler, "The Theory of Economic Regulation," *Bell Journal of Economics and Management Science*, vol. 2 (Spring 1971), pp. 3–21; Mark V. Nadel, *The Politics of Consumer Protection* (Indianapolis: Bobbs-Merrill, 1971); Louis M. Kohlmeier, Jr., *The Regulators: Watchdog Agencies and the Public Interest* (Harper and Row, 1969); Murray Edelman, *The Symbolic Uses of Politics* (University of Illinois Press, 1964); and Marver H. Bernstein, *Regulating Business by Independent Commission* (Princeton University Press, 1955).

4. Timothy J. Conlan, Margaret T. Wrightson, and David R. Beam, *Taxing Choices: The Politics of Tax Reform* (Washington: CQ Press, 1990), pp. 29–30. On the 1969 legislation, see also Henry S. Reuss, "Foreword," in Joseph A. Ruskay and Richard A. Osserman, *Halfway to Tax Reform* (Indiana University Press, 1970), p. vii. On the 1976 legislation, see Witte, *Politics and Development*, p. 194.

5. Witte, *Politics and Development*, p. 292; and Laurie McGinley, "The Treasury's Plan to Overhaul Tax Code Sparks Heated Debate," *Wall Street Journal*, April 3, 1985, p. 27.

6. For detailed examinations of the act's provisions, see Alan Murray, "Individuals' Top Rate Would Plunge to 28 Percent: Tax Break Curbs Offset Benefits to Wealthy," *Wall Street Journal*, August 18, 1986, pp. 6, 10; and Alan Murray, "Industry-by-Industry Review of Tax Bill Shows Loss of Special Deductions Offsets Rate Cut," *Wall Street Journal*, August 19, 1986, pp. 6, 8.

7. This figure is from Jeffrey H. Birnbaum and Alan S. Murray, *Showdown at Gucci Gulch: Lawmakers, Lobbyists, and the Unlikely Triumph of Tax Reform* (Random House, 1987), p. 288. See also Conlan, Wrightson, and Beam, *Taxing Choices*, pp. 3–6; and *General Explanation of the Tax Reform Act of 1986*, Joint Committee on Taxation, 99 Cong. 1 sess. (Government Printing Office, 1987). Other important changes made by the 1986 act include a reduction in the top tax rate for individuals from 50 percent to 28 percent and, for corporations, from 46 percent to 34 percent. In place of fourteen income brackets, the act legislated just two. The act also had important redistributive effects. It shifted $120 billion in tax liabilities from individuals to corporations, and it took about 12 million of the "working poor" off the tax rolls, lifting them above the poverty line. (Conlan, Wrightson, and Beam, *Taxing Choices*, p. 6.) It is also important not to overstate

the extent of tax reform. The tax code was not simplified much; it remains an arcane, complex tangle of rules and regulations. Some tax expenditures were largely untouched, such as those for the oil and gas industries. Many of the most popular deductions used by the public were also preserved (see appendix 2A-1).

8. Given the continued growth in the value of those tax expenditures that were not repealed by the 1986 act, the decline in tax expenditures between 1985 and 1989 is less than the $300 billion in loophole closing achieved by the act. The $300 billion represents savings in the sense that losses in revenue from tax expenditures would have been $300 billion higher without the 1986 act.

9. Middle-class tax expenditures were not left unscathed, however. Repealing only a few such provisions (second-earner deductions and deductions for sales taxes and consumer interest, for example) and trimming back a few more (deductions for independent retirement accounts and other pension schemes, medical deductions, and employee business expenses, among others) achieved substantial revenue gains.

10. Joseph A. Pechman, *Federal Tax Policy*, 5th ed. (Brookings, 1987), pp. 40–41.

11. Allen Schick, *The Capacity to Budget* (Washington: Urban Institute Press, 1990), pp. 139–40.

12. Witte, *Politics and Development*, p. 236.

13. Proposition 13, also known as the Jarvis-Gann initiative, limited property tax rates in California to 1 percent of assessed valuation, rolled back assessed values to what they had been in 1975–76 (for properties that had not changed hands since then), limited annual increases in assessment to 2 percent (except upon sale), and prohibited new property taxes. It also forbade local governments from imposing new taxes without the approval of local voters. See Terry Schwadron, ed., *California and the American Tax Revolt: Proposition 13 Five Years Later* (University of California Press, 1984), p. 7.

14. Birnbaum and Murray, *Showdown at Gucci Gulch*, p. 11.

15. David Vogel, *Fluctuating Fortunes: The Political Power of Business in America* (New York: Basic Books, 1989), pp. 193–239. See also Thomas Byrne Edsall, *The New Politics of Inequality* (W. W. Norton, 1984); and Thomas Ferguson and Joel Rogers, *Right Turn: The Decline of the Democrats and the Future of American Politics* (New York: Hill and Wang, 1986).

16. Witte, *Politics and Development*, pp. 204–17.

17. Ibid., chap. 11.

18. Quoted in William Greider, "The Education of David Stockman," *Atlantic Monthly*, December 1981, p. 35.

19. See Roper Organization, Inc., *The American Public and the Income Tax System*, vol. 1: *Summary Report* (Kansas City, Mo.: H & R Block, Inc., July 1978), p. 45; and Roper, *Third Annual Tax Study*, vol. 1: *Summary Report* (Kansas City, Mo.: H & R Block, Inc., July 1979), p. 37.

20. Witte, *Politics and Development*, p. 342.

21. David Shribman, "Growing Majority Believes Businesses Don't Pay Fair Tax Share, Poll Finds," *Wall Street Journal*, November 26, 1985, p. 20.

22. Birnbaum and Murray, *Showdown at Gucci Gulch*, p. 12.

23. When asked which problem they thought carried the most weight with policymakers generally, almost all of those interviewed for this study answered "fairness."

24. This perception was reiterated frequently by those interviewed.

25. On the importance of "focusing events," "policy windows," and political entrepreneurs, see John W. Kingdon, *Agendas, Alternatives, and Public Policies* (Little, Brown, 1984).

26. Interview responses invariably pointed to the role of anticipated voter reactions in getting members to decide in favor of taxpayers' diffuse interests. As Senator Packwood's top aide on the Finance Committee, Bill Diefendorfer, put it in a personal interview (May 1987):

They [members] would imagine nightmares of their opponent saying in the next election: "You opposed the bill that cut taxes for individuals by $120 billion and raised taxes for business by $120 billion, and took 12 million working poor off the tax rolls." These were pretty hard political charges. . . . The President's people and others told them, "If you don't support us, these are the things we're going to say," and they had no answer for them. Ultimately, while in the past they supported the same interest groups that managed to tilt the election in their favor, the President and others had so focused the political argument that they couldn't take the heat anymore, and retreated.

On electoral incentives to vote for deregulation, see Martha Derthick and Paul J. Quirk, *Politics of Deregulation* (Brookings, 1985), pp. 144–46. Electoral considerations were almost certainly more compelling in voting in favor of tax reform than they were in voting for deregulation, because tax policy was a more salient issue with more easily discernible impacts for the public and the media.

27. Witte, *Politics and Development*, pp. 326–30.

28. Ibid., p. 327.

29. Ibid., pp. 21–22.

30. Conlan, Wrightson, and Beam, *Taxing Choices*, pp. 25–38.

31. Harris poll reported in Timothy B. Clark, "Flat-Rate Income Tax Debate May Spur Attacks on Some Tax Breaks," *National Journal*, November 13, 1982, p. 1932.

32. Lower taxes were an article of faith for Reagan. Ever since his days as a highly paid Hollywood actor, he had harbored resentment toward the income tax.

33. Bradley's decision not to raise taxes on corporations to pay for tax cuts for individuals followed the same logic. Higher taxes on business should be separated from reform, so as to avoid arousing business opposition. As it turned out, Bradley was wrong. It *was* possible to increase the amount of taxes business would pay. In addition, the tax reform act was somewhat redistributive in that it took about 12 million of the working poor off the tax rolls.

34. Interview with Gina Despres, staff assistant to Senator Bill Bradley of New Jersey, August 1987.

35. Although to a lesser degree, the Senate Finance Committee too had been dominated by a few senior (and fairly conservative) lawmakers such as Russell Long.

36. John F. Manley, *The Politics of Finance: The House Committee on Ways and Means* (Little, Brown, 1970); and Richard F. Fenno, Jr., *Congressmen in Committees* (Little, Brown, 1973).

37. Witte, *Politics and Development*, p. 242.

38. See Catherine E. Rudder, "The Policy Impact of Reform on the Committee on Ways and Means," in Leroy N. Rieselbach, ed., *Legislative Reform: The Policy Impact* (Lexington, Mass.: Lexington Books, 1978), pp. 73–89; and Catherine E. Rudder, "Fiscal Responsibility and the Revenue Committees," in Lawrence C. Dodd and Bruce I. Oppenheimer, eds., *Congress Reconsidered*, 3d ed. (Washington: CQ Press, 1985), pp. 211–22.

39. Witte, *Politics and Development*, p. 334.

40. Randall Strahan, *New Ways and Means: Reform and Change in a Congressional Committee* (University of North Carolina Press, 1990), p. 90.

41. Steven S. Smith and Christopher J. Deering, *Committees in Congress* (Washington: CQ Press, 1984), p. 177.

42. Rudder, "Fiscal Responsibility," p. 221.

43. Strahan, *New Ways and Means*, p. 81.

44. Ibid., pp. 101–11. On the stronger role of congressional leaders in general in the 1980s, see Barbara Sinclair, "House Majority Party Leadership in an Era of Legislative Constraint," in Roger H. Davidson, ed., *The Postreform Congress* (New York: St. Martin's Press, 1992), pp. 91–111; and Roger H. Davidson, "The New Centralization on Capitol Hill," *Review of Politics*, vol. 50 (1988), pp. 345–64.

45. Roy Blough, *The Federal Taxing Process* (Prentice-Hall, 1952); and Manley, *Politics of Finance*.

46. Conlan, Wrightson, and Beam, *Taxing Choices*, pp. 252–55.

47. Steven V. Roberts, "How Tax Bill Breezed Past, Despite Wide Doubts," *New York Times*, September 26, 1986, p. 20; David E. Rosenbaum, "Senators Expect Approval in '86 of Tax Changes," *New York Times*, January 27, 1986, p. 1; and Timothy B. Clark, "Tax Focus," *National Journal*, January 4, 1986, p. 54.

48. Bill Bradley, *The Fair Tax* (New York: Pocket Books, 1984).

49. The stress here on the skill and persistence of individual leaders is consistent with accounts in Birnbaum and Murray, *Showdown at Gucci Gulch*; and Hedrick Smith, *The Power Game: How Washington Works* (Random House, 1988), pp. 498–500.

50. Quoted in Smith, *Power Game*, p. 498.

51. Robert W. Merry and David Shribman, "Reagan Opens Drive to Overhaul US Tax System," *Wall Street Journal*, May 29, 1985, p. 3.

52. Roberts, "How Tax Bill Breezed Past," p. 20.

53. Jeffrey H. Birnbaum, "House Committee Seeks Big Support for Tax Bill through Myriad Concessions to Small Interests," *Wall Street Journal*, November 21, 1985, p. 64.

54. Jeffrey H. Birnbaum, "How Three Legislators Wheeled and Dealed to Help Draft Tax Bill," *Wall Street Journal*, November 26, 1985, p. 20. The major concession Rostenkowski could not avoid was preserving the deduction for state and local taxes, an item that his fellow Democrats insisted upon. With the

Republicans in the minority, he was able to compensate for this by making draconian cuts in tax benefits for business, finance, and the affluent. In the compromise with the Senate over the final legislation, deductions for state income and property taxes (but not sales taxes) were retained.

55. It is misleading to view these as concessions forced upon the reformers or as evidence of some sort of failure on the part of reformers. After all, the granting of these rules was used as leverage for accomplishing comprehensive tax reform. While transition rules were crucial in giving leaders leverage over other politicians, granting them did not substantially diminish the degree of reform. They amounted to $10 billion–$15 billion, a fraction of the hundreds of billions of dollars in tax expenditure closure accomplished by the legislation.

56. Interview with Senator John Danforth, Republican of Missouri and member of the Finance Committee.

57. There is an extensive literature on the politics of economic regulation. One of the classic statements of the capture theory, which argues that many regulatory commissions came to be dominated by the very industries that they were intended to regulate, is Bernstein, *Regulating Business*. Perhaps the most cited academic work on regulation is Stigler, "Theory of Economic Regulation." Stigler argues that political incentives operated to encourage industries to acquire regulation and to ensure that it was designed and operated primarily for their benefit. More recent literature on economic regulation paints a more complicated and varied picture, arguing that the political influence and self-interested motivations of industries explain only part of the origins and operation of regulation. See, in particular, James Q. Wilson, "Regulation," in James Q. Wilson, ed., *The Politics of Regulation* (New York: Basic Books, 1980), pp. 367–72; and Marc Allen Eisner, *Regulatory Politics in Transition* (Johns Hopkins University Press, 1993).

58. In addition to setting rates, the ICC imposed restrictions on what kinds of goods could be shipped through regulated carriers. Some of the restrictions imposed were truly senseless and bizarre. Some truckers could carry empty ginger ale bottles but not empty cola or root beer bottles. Others were exempt from regulation if they carried frozen TV dinners, unless the dinners contained chicken or seafood. In one case, an exasperated competitor announced that it wished to carry yak fat from Omaha to Chicago. Even though yak fat was a nonexistent product, thirteen different companies filed protests challenging the competition. See Dorothy L. Robyn, *Braking the Special Interests: Trucking Deregulation and the Politics of Policy Reform* (University of Chicago Press, 1987), pp. 18–19.

59. See Michael Pertschuk, *Revolt against Regulation: The Rise and Pause of the Consumer Movement* (University of California Press, 1982).

60. For further discussion of the scale and impacts of deregulation, see Leonard W. Weiss and Michael W. Klass, eds., *Case Studies in Regulation: Revolution and Reform* (Little, Brown, 1981); and Leonard W. Weiss and Michael W. Klass, *Regulatory Reform: What Actually Happened* (Little, Brown, 1986).

61. Rogene A. Buchholz, *Business Environment and Public Policy: Implications for Management* (Prentice-Hall, 1992), pp. 155–56.

62. Anticompetitive regulation had few committed allies left, aside from the regulated industries themselves, whereas the more recent victories in social reg-

ulation were supported strongly by actors in and out of government. Furthermore, there was little chance of developing the type of bipartisan alliance between Democrats and Republicans to deregulate in the social area that developed around procompetitive deregulation. Democrats had come to a negative view of economic regulation that did not extend to social regulation, viewing the latter as protecting widely shared interests in society. The best that deregulation advocates in areas such as environmental policy could do would be to frame their issue as a struggle between competing diffuse interests—jobs versus a safe environment, for example. Even if defined as such a contest, however, building a broad coalition in favor of a wholesale elimination of social regulation would have been far more difficult than building one favoring the repeal of regulations that were perceived as benefiting narrow business interests at the expense of the public.

63. Derthick and Quirk, *Politics of Deregulation*, pp. 35–39; and Robyn, *Braking the Special Interests*, chap. 2 and pp. 89–90.

64. Robyn, *Braking the Special Interests*, chap. 4.

65. Ibid.

66. Derthick and Quirk, *Politics of Deregulation*, pp. 51–53, 238-39; and Robyn, *Braking the Special Interests*, pp. 95–109.

67. Derthick and Quirk, *Politics of Deregulation*, pp. 45–47.

68. Ibid., pp. 40–45.

69. Robyn, *Braking the Special Interests*, pp. 27–29.

70. Derthick and Quirk, *Politics of Deregulation*, p. 244.

71. Ibid., pp. 243–44. See also Robyn, *Braking the Special Interests*, pp. 29–34, 39–41.

72. Derthick and Quirk, *Politics of Deregulation*, pp. 102–04.

73. Robyn, *Braking the Special Interests*, p. 37.

74. To grasp the importance of having the right individuals in the right places at the right time, one has only to compare the performances of Reagan and Rostenkowski with the failed efforts at reform of Jimmy Carter and Al Ullman (Rostenkowski's predecessor on the Ways and Means Committee). On the 1970s, see Witte, *Politics and Development*, chaps. 9, 10.

75. Rudder, "Fiscal Responsibility," pp. 214–15. For further discussion, see Catherine E. Rudder, "Tax Policy: Structure and Choice," in Allen Schick, ed., *Making Economic Policy in Congress* (Washington: American Enterprise Institute, 1983), pp. 208–10.

Chapter Three

1. In addition, industrialized countries no longer need to raise revenue with tariffs (one of the major original reasons for imposing tariffs).

2. John M. Dobson, *Two Centuries of Tariffs: The Background and Emergence of the U.S. International Trade Commission* (Washington: U.S. International Trade Commission, 1976), p. 34.

3. The standard measure is the proportion of a nation's trade affected by NTBs. The problem with this measure is that it weighs moderate barriers more

heavily than severe ones. See I. M. Destler, "U.S. Trade Policy-making in the Eighties," in Alberto Alesina and Geoffrey Carliner, eds., *Politics and Economics in the Eighties* (University of Chicago Press, 1991), p. 276.

4. See Bela Balassa and Carol Balassa, "Industrial Protection in the Developed Countries," *World Economy*, vol. 7 (June 1984), pp. 179–96; Gary Clyde Hufbauer, Diane T. Berliner, and Kimberly Ann Elliott, *Trade Protection in the United States: 31 Case Studies* (Washington: Institute for International Economics, 1986); Julio J. Nogues, Andrzej Olechowski, and L. Alan Winters, "The Extent of Nontariff Barriers to Imports of Industrial Countries," World Bank Staff Working Paper 789 (Washington: World Bank, 1986); Sam Laird and Alexander Yeats, "Trends in Nontariff Barriers of Developed Countries, 1966–1986" (Washington: World Bank, 1988); and Andrew Stoeckel, David Pearce, and Gary Banks, *Western Trade Blocks: Game, Set, or Match for Asia-Pacific and the World Economy?* (Canberra, Australia: Centre for International Economics, 1990).

5. Robert B. Reich, "Beyond Free Trade," *Foreign Affairs*, vol. 61 (Spring 1983), p. 786.

6. It should be noted also that the United States has fewer NTBs than many other developed nations and uses them less strategically to gain trade advantages.

7. Destler, "U.S. Trade Policy-making," p. 277.

8. Some have argued that while increased protectionism has not reduced trade flows, the gains from lower transport and communications costs that have fueled trade expansion would have been greater had protection not increased. See Anne O. Krueger, "Comment," in Alesina and Carliner, eds., *Politics and Economics*, pp. 283–84.

9. Peter Morici and Laura L. Megna, *U.S. Economic Policies Affecting Industrial Trade: A Quantitative Assessment* (Washington: National Planning Association, 1983), p. 97.

10. I. M. Destler, *American Trade Politics: System under Stress*, 2d ed. (Washington: Institute for International Economics, 1992), p. 154.

11. Ibid., pp. 156–61. Unlike tariffs, export restraints not only protect domestic producers but also reward their foreign competitors by allowing them to collect rents from the higher prices they can charge on the reduced supply of their exports.

12. Ibid., p. 169.

13. Letter from I. M. Destler to the author, August 3, 1992.

14. Destler, *American Trade Politics*, pp. 6–7.

15. Ibid., p. 7.

16. Some claim that Americans are "ideological conservatives" and "programmatic liberals." Support for abstract principles like individual self-sufficiency and free enterprise exists alongside support for many forms of governmental intervention in the market and the provision of public services. See Herbert McClosky and John Zaller, *The American Ethos: Public Attitudes toward Capitalism and Democracy* (Harvard University Press, 1984), pp. 144–53.

17. For an analysis of congressional politics and Smoot-Hawley, see E. E. Schattschneider, *Politics, Pressures and the Tariff* (Prentice-Hall, 1935).

18. I. M. Destler, *American Trade Politics: System under Stress* (Washington: Institute for International Economics, 1986), p. 9.

19. Cordell Hull, *The Memoirs of Cordell Hull*, vol. 1 (Macmillan, 1948), p. 8; and Dobson, *Two Centuries of Tariffs*, pp. 56–66.

20. "Peril point" provisions required the U.S. Tariff Commission to estimate the point beyond which tariffs could not be reduced without "peril" to specific industries. They were intended to make it difficult for the president to negotiate rates below that level.

21. Robert E. Baldwin, "The Changing Nature of U.S. Trade Policy since World War II," in Robert E. Baldwin and Anne O. Krueger, eds., *The Structure and Evolution of Recent U.S. Trade Policy* (University of Chicago Press, 1984), p. 12.

22. Richard Fenno described the House Ways and Means Committee's handling of trade issues in the 1960s as consensual, the issue having "lost its partisan character nationally." Richard F. Fenno, Jr., *Congressmen in Committees* (Little, Brown, 1973), p. 207.

23. Congressional delegation of authority in this area can be traced back to 1897, when the president was allowed to impose countervailing duties against subsidized foreign exports. In the 1920s the president gained authority to levy antidumping duties and to impose duties on (or exclude) foreign goods in retaliation for unfair practices and discriminatory import policies on the part of other countries.

24. A comprehensive survey of trade laws is found in *Overview of Current Provisions of U.S. Trade Law*, House Committee on Ways and Means, Subcommittee on Trade, 98 Cong. 2 sess. (Government Printing Office, 1984), p. 62.

25. Destler, *American Trade Politics* (1986), pp. 112–13.

26. Ibid., p. 60.

27. Robert A. Pastor, *Congress and the Politics of U.S. Foreign Economic Policy, 1929–1976* (University of California Press, 1980), pp. 105–23.

28. Theodore C. Sorenson, *Kennedy* (Harper and Row, 1965), p. 460.

29. Congress did alter the bill in some important ways, however, including substituting a "Special Trade Representative" for the State Department in trade negotiations and providing for congressional representation in future negotiations.

30. Pastor, *Congress*, pp. 118–19.

31. This has been more the case in Congress than among the public. Poll results on the salience of trade as an issue with the public are mixed. Several polls in the 1980s revealed surprisingly little concern on the part of Americans about trade issues, and the trade imbalance with Japan in particular. On the other hand, decisive majorities were increasingly concerned about Japanese competition. The poll results are discussed in Destler, *American Trade Politics* (1992), pp. 180–82.

32. Pietro S. Nivola, *Regulating Unfair Trade* (Brookings, 1993), p. 19.

33. Opinion polls indicate that Americans have increasingly favored more restrictive trade actions. Between 1977 and 1983 Gallup reported that only 12

percent to 15 percent of Americans favored more imports, against 68 to 75 percent who favored more restrictions on imports, up from the figures reported earlier in this chapter for the 1950s. Also, 75 percent of Americans saw import competition as harmful to American workers, according to a 1983 Harris survey. See Destler, *American Trade Politics* (1992), pp. 180–82.

34. Twentieth Century Fund Task Force on the Future of American Trade Policy, *The Free Trade Debate* (New York: Priority Press, 1989), p. 77.

35. Nivola, *Regulating Unfair Trade*, p. 51.

36. Ibid., p. 131.

37. Except where otherwise indicated, much of this section summarizes Destler, *American Trade Politics* (1986), chap. 3.

38. These figures are calculated in constant dollars. The reasons for this trend include reductions in international transportation and communications costs, changes in consumer tastes, and the rise in oil import costs (which required foreign sales to pay for them). Destler, *American Trade Politics* (1992), pp. 44–46.

39. Figures are in current dollars. Ibid., p. 45.

40. What was positive about the trade imbalance was that it showed that Americans were using the funds earned from substantial overseas investments to buy goods that they could now afford.

41. Destler, *American Trade Politics* (1986), p. 45.

42. John E. Rielly, ed., *American Public Opinion and U.S. Foreign Policy, 1991* (Chicago Council on Foreign Relations, 1991), pp. 20, 22.

43. The European Economic Community is a part of the European Union (formerly the European Community).

44. Destler, *American Trade Politics* (1986), pp. 48–49.

45. American exporters were also harmed by the debt crisis among many developing nations, particularly in Latin America; Destler, *American Trade Politics* (1992), p. 60, n. 52.

46. Ibid., pp. 57–58.

47. According to Destler, when the world moved to floating exchange rates in the 1970s, it was expected that rate fluctuations would reflect gradual fluctuations in trade flows. Instead, rate fluctuations have swung much more erratically because they are responsive to capital flows rather than to trade flows. Investors shift capital in response to interest rate fluctuations and the anticipation of the value of a currency in the short term. Ibid., pp. 59–60.

48. Reich, "Beyond Free Trade," pp. 773–804.

49. Baldwin, "Changing Nature of U.S. Trade Policy," p. 12.

50. Ibid., p. 13.

51. Destler, *American Trade Politics* (1986), p. 144.

52. This was lower, however, than for all other legislation that comes under the jurisdiction of the committee, such as social security and taxes. Randall Strahan, *New Ways and Means: Reform and Change in a Congressional Committee* (University of North Carolina Press, 1990), p. 169. "Partisan" votes are those in which a majority of one party opposes a majority of the opposing party. Strahan also calculates an "index of partisanship" by subtracting the percentage of mem-

bers of one party voting for a bill from the percentage of members of the other party voting for the bill. Again, trade was the least partisan of the five issue areas that come under the Ways and Means Committee's jurisdiction, with a score of 43.

53. Quoted in "Trade Policy," *Congressional Quarterly Almanac*, vol. 41 (1985), p. 253.

54. Nivola, *Regulating Unfair Trade*, pp. 97–99.

55. See Catherine E. Rudder, "The Policy Impact of Reform of the Committee on Ways and Means," in Leroy N. Rieselbach, ed., *Legislative Reform: The Policy Impact* (Lexington, Mass.: Lexington Books, 1978), pp. 73–89; and Catherine E. Rudder, "Fiscal Responsibility and the Revenue Committees," in Lawrence C. Dodd and Bruce I. Oppenheimer, eds., *Congress Reconsidered*, 3d ed. (Washington: CQ Press, 1985), pp. 211–22.

56. Destler, *American Trade Politics* (1986), pp. 60–61.

57. Negotiators at the Uruguay round have agreed to phase out the MFA over the next ten years.

58. Nivola, *Regulating Unfair Trade*, chap. 5.

59. Destler points to the Zenith case as an extreme example; *American Trade Politics* (1986), p. 131.

60. Nivola, *Regulating Unfair Trade*, pp. 92–93. See also Richard Boltuck and Robert E. Litan, eds., *Down in the Dumps: Administration of the Unfair Trade Laws* (Brookings, 1991), chaps. 2, 3, 4, 5, 7.

61. For the numbers, see Destler, *American Trade Politics* (1986), p. 118.

62. Ibid., p. 120.

63. Nivola, *Regulating Unfair Trade*, pp. 93–94.

64. Destler, *American Trade Politics* (1986), pp. 121–23.

65. Ibid., p. 125.

66. Because it has been much easier for firms to secure relief under CVD and antidumping provisions of the trade laws, the number of escape clause petitions has declined to negligible levels. See Destler, *American Trade Politics* (1992), pp. 166–69.

67. Destler, *American Trade Politics* (1986), p. 125.

68. Destler, *American Trade Politics* (1992), p. 169.

69. Nivola, *Regulating Unfair Trade*, pp. 103–04.

70. See Carl J. Green, "Legal Protectionism in the United States and Its Impact on United States–Japan Economic Relations," in *Appendix to the Report of the Japan–United States Economic Relations Group* (Washington, April 1981), pp. 262–312.

71. Destler, *American Trade Politics* (1986), p. 132.

72. Destler, *American Trade Politics* (1992), p. 83.

73. Nivola, *Regulating Unfair Trade*, pp. 132–33.

74. Ibid., p. 104.

75. Judith Goldstein, "Ideas, Institutions, and American Trade Policy," *International Organization*, vol. 42 (Winter 1988), p. 215.

76. Destler, *American Trade Politics* (1992), p. 16.

77. Baldwin, "Changing Nature of U.S. Trade Policy," p. 15.

78. The VERs got around the rules that allowed American firms to secure trade relief through the International Trade Commission because they did not have to prove injury and were not subject to limits on the duration of protection. And since they were actions taken against foreign exports, they were not subject to the GATT provisions that allowed other nations to impose equivalent trade restrictions unless the United States offered compensation in the form of offsetting tariff reductions.

79. Destler, *American Trade Politics* (1992), pp. 26–27.

80. On blame avoidance, see R. Kent Weaver, "The Politics of Blame Avoidance," *Journal of Public Policy*, vol. 6 (October–December 1986), pp. 371–98.

81. David R. Mayhew, *Congress: The Electoral Connection* (Yale University Press, 1974).

82. Destler, "U.S. Trade Policy-making," p. 258.

83. Strahan, *New Ways and Means*, p. 90.

84. Steven S. Smith and Christopher J. Deering, *Committees in Congress* (Washington: CQ Press, 1984), p. 177.

85. Rudder, "Fiscal Responsibility," p. 242. See also Strahan, *New Ways and Means*, pp. 81, 101–11. On the strengthening of congressional leadership in the 1980s generally, see Barbara Sinclair, "House Majority Party Leadership in an Era of Legislative Constraint," in Roger H. Davidson, ed., *The Postreform Congress* (St. Martin's Press, 1992), pp. 91–111; and Roger H. Davidson, "The New Centralization on Capitol Hill," *Review of Politics*, vol. 50 (Summer 1988), pp. 345–64.

86. Goldstein, "Ideas, Institutions, and American Trade Policy," pp. 215–16.

87. Destler, *American Trade Politics* (1992), p. 16.

88. Ibid., p. 111.

89. Ibid., pp. 125–27.

90. Destler, *American Trade Politics* (1986), p. 108.

91. According to Destler, "The first Reagan administration developed a pattern of endorsing liberal trade in principle but tightening protection in practice." Ibid., p. 103.

92. For a critique of this strategy, see Jagdish Bhagwati and Hugh T. Patrick, eds., *Aggressive Unilateralism: America's 301 Trade Policy and the World Trading System* (University of Michigan Press, 1990).

93. Destler, *American Trade Politics* (1992), pp. 131–33.

94. Ibid., p. 88. On the leadership role of Brock, in particular, see "On Trade, a Happy Ending," *Washington Post*, October 12, 1984, p. A22.

95. Reagan vetoed the bill originally because it included a provision requiring prenotification of plant closings. Reagan later signed separate bills on trade and plant closing.

96. Destler, *American Trade Politics* (1992), p. 96.

97. Thomas Friedman, "Clinton Calls Trade Debate World Issue," *New York Times*, November 7, 1993, p. 1; and Douglas Jehl, "A Few Switch to Clinton's Side in the House," *New York Times,* November 17, 1993, p. 1.

98. Destler, *American Trade Politics* (1992), p. 182.

Chapter Four

1. The administration also called for ending most acreage reduction programs, overhauling the allotment and quota features of the peanut program, ending the sugar price support program, reducing lending programs for farmers and rural communities, and separating the authorization of the food stamp program from the rest of farm legislation.

2. David S. Cloud, "Logic Doesn't Always Apply to Multiyear Farm Bills," *Congressional Quarterly Weekly Report*, February 24, 1990, p. 582.

3. *Economic Report of the President, 1987*, pp. 147–78.

4. Farmers could collect multiple payments by breaking down their acreage into smaller parcels and rearranging their operations. David S. Cloud, "Farm Bloc on the Defensive as Bills Move to Floor," *Congressional Quarterly Weekly Report*, July 14, 1990, pp. 2209–12.

5. The notion that subsidies are primarily an economic stabilization tool has become harder to defend. As a consequence of the 1985 farm bill, a larger share of the agricultural budget has been devoted to income support payments. Price supports have receded in importance as they have been pegged below market rates. Thus, farmers now produce mainly for the market, while Congress maintains farmers' income by setting target prices above market prices, allowing farmers to collect deficiency payments. As a result, it is more transparent that farm subsidies are like simple income transfers from taxpayers to farmers. (Cloud, "Logic Doesn't Always Apply," p. 580.) Second, as the dependence of American producers on export markets has grown, market stabilization has become more difficult to maintain. It is difficult for any single country to stabilize prices or manage supplies unilaterally. (Jonathan Rauch, "Writing a Blank Check," *National Journal*, March 23, 1985, p. 629.) What is left, then, is the income maintenance justification—farmers deserve a minimum income or at least sufficient assistance to keep them in business. But once income maintenance is the primary purpose of farm policy, the case for means-testing becomes compelling.

6. Cloud, "Logic Doesn't Always Apply," p. 582.

7. Allen Schick, "The Budget as an Instrument of Presidential Policy," in Lester M. Salamon and Michael S. Lund, eds., *The Reagan Presidency and the Governing of America* (Washington: Urban Institute Press, 1984), pp. 107–09.

8. When price supports were the principal form of subsidy, many farmers benefited without actually joining the program and qualifying for deficiency payments. Since the government bought up most surplus crops, most farmers could simply take advantage of the artificially high prices. But when income subsidies became more important after 1985, farmers had to join the program to get the benefits.

9. Cloud, "Logic Doesn't Always Apply," p. 576.

10. Ibid.

11. Rekha Mehra, "Winners and Losers in the U.S. Sugar Program," *Resources*, vol. 94 (Winter 1989), p. 7; and I. M. Destler and John S. Odell, *Anti-Protection: Changing Forces in United States Trade Politics* (Washington: Institute for International Economics, 1987), p. 14.

12. Pietro S. Nivola, *Regulating Unfair Trade* (Brookings, 1993), pp. 53–55; International Trade Administration, *International Financing Programs and U.S. International Economic Competitiveness* (Department of Commerce, September 1990), pp. 17–18, 22–23; and Export-Import Bank of the United States, *Report to the U.S. Congress on Tied Aid Credit Practices* (April 1989), p. 25.

13. Subsidies retard economic adjustment to current world and domestic markets, diverting resources from more optimal uses. When loan rates and target prices are set above market prices, they encourage overproduction. This is compounded because the amount of subsidies received by farmers increases with the amount they produce. Maintaining artificially high prices makes U.S. farm products less competitive in international markets, diminishing export earnings and maintaining surpluses. The excess supply, in turn, drives market prices down further, increasing the gap between market and target prices and boosting the cost of deficiency payments. At the same time, target prices have to be maintained to attract farmers to participate in acreage reduction programs that are intended to get rid of the surpluses that farm programs created in the first place. But the higher prices only serve to stimulate production further. Higher price supports also encourage nonparticipating farmers to expand their production, thus offsetting participant reductions. Even participating farmers may not reduce their production much because they tend to idle their least productive land and have become adept at increasing yields on fewer acres. Finally, subsidies and restrictive trade and marketing practices offset the lower prices and productivity gains that result from government-sponsored research and innovation.

14. The average annual increase in the 1970s was about 17 percent, and for the 1980s about 23 percent, well above the increases in inflation during these periods.

15. Note that the figures discussed thus far pertain only to the costs of subsidies to taxpayers. They do not include costs to the consumer. Costs to consumers are difficult to calculate because they require determining what domestic and international market prices would be if the United States and other countries followed market-oriented agricultural policies. The estimates that do exist indicate that excess consumer costs in 1979 came to $8.4 billion and for 1982, to $13.2 billion. See D. Gale Johnson, Kenzo Hemmi, and Pierre Lardinois, *Agricultural Policy and Trade: Adjusting Domestic Programs in an International Framework,* Task Force Report to the Trilateral Commission (New York University Press, 1985), p. 23.

16. Rauch, "Writing a Blank Check," p. 625.

17. Ibid., p. 627.

18. Don E. Albrecht and Steve H. Murdock, "The Structural Characteristics of U.S. Agriculture: Historical Patterns and Precursors of Producers' Adaptations to the Crisis," in Steve H. Murdock and F. Larry Leistritz, eds., *The Farm Financial Crisis* (Boulder, Colo.: Westview Press, 1988), pp. 29–44.

19. The largest 10 percent of the farms that participated in the programs received average payments of $12,000, plus $6,000 in price benefits, and gave up about $5,000 in forgone income (for idling land). The smallest 50 percent of the

farms received a net cash gain of about $460 per farm, or about a thirtieth of what the largest 10 percent of the farms received.

20. Johnson, Hemmi, and Lardinois, *Agricultural Policy and Trade*, p. 79.

21. Cloud, "Farm Bloc on the Defensive," pp. 2209–10.

22. See Robert Emmet Long, ed., *The Farm Crisis: The Reference Shelf*, vol. 59, no. 6 (New York: H. W. Wilson, 1987).

23. *Farm Policy: The Politics of Soil, Surpluses, and Subsidies* (Washington: CQ Press, 1984), pp. 152–53.

24. Lance McKinzie, Timothy G. Baker, and Wallace E. Tyner, *A Perspective on U.S. Farm Problems and Agricultural Policy* (Boulder, Colo.: Westview Press, 1987), p. 61.

25. *Farm Policy*, p. 16.

26. Quoted in "Agriculture," *Congressional Quarterly Almanac, 1985*, vol. 41 (Washington: CQ Press, 1986), p. 515.

27. Steven V. Roberts, "Farm Issue: Headaches by the Hundredweight," *New York Times*, February 12, 1985, p. B8; and William P. Browne, *Private Interests, Public Policy, and American Agriculture* (University Press of Kansas, 1988), pp. 86–88.

28. Quoted in Christopher K. Leman and Robert L. Paarlberg, "The Continued Political Power of Agricultural Interests," in R. J. Hildreth and others, eds., *Agriculture and Rural Areas Approaching the Twenty-first Century* (Iowa State University Press, 1988), p. 36.

29. William Robbins, "Surge in Sympathy for Farmers Found," *New York Times*, February 25, 1986, p. 1, quoted in H. Wayne Moyer and Timothy E. Josling, *Agricultural Policy Reform: Politics and Process in the EC and the USA* (Iowa State University Press, 1990), p. 136.

30. Jonathan Rauch, "Farmers' Discord over Government Role Produces a Farm Bill that Pleases Few," *National Journal*, November 9, 1985, p. 2538.

31. James T. Bonnen and William P. Browne, "Why Is Agricultural Policy So Difficult to Reform?" in Carol S. Kramer, ed., *The Political Economy of U.S. Agriculture* (Washington: Resources for the Future, 1989), p. 12. See also "Opinion Outlook: Farm Aid," *National Journal*, December 10, 1988, p. 3157.

32. Brenda Jordan and Luther Tweeten, "Public Perceptions of Farm Problems," Research Report #P-894, Oklahoma State University, 1987; cited in Luther Tweeten, *Farm Policy Analysis* (Boulder, Colo.: Westview Press, 1989), pp. 77–79.

33. Robbins, "Surge in Sympathy," p. 1.

34. Bonnen and Browne, "Why Is Agricultural Policy So Difficult," p. 10. See also Paul B. Thompson, "The Philosophical Rationale for U.S. Agricultural Policy," in M. Ann Tutwiler, ed., *U.S. Agriculture in a Global Setting: An Agenda for the Future* (Washington: Resources for the Future, 1988); Luther Tweeten and Brenda Jordan, "Farm Fundamentalism: Support for Farmers Is Widespread, But It May Fade," *Choices*, vol. 3, no. 1 (1988), pp. 26–27; and William P. Browne and others, *Sacred Cows and Hot Potatoes: Agrarian Myths in Agricultural Policy* (Boulder, Colo.: Westview Press, 1992), pp. 5–16.

35. Don Paarlberg, *American Farm Policy: A Case Study in Centralized Decision-Making* (Wiley, 1964), p. 5.

36. An expanded program of crop insurance, for instance, could be expected to protect farmers from the unique risks they face with less expense and less intrusiveness in commodity markets than the existing subsidy programs.

37. For additional support for this argument, see Graham K. Wilson, *Special Interests and Policymaking: Agricultural Policies and Politics in Britain and the United States of America* (Wiley, 1977), pp. 147–53.

38. "Agriculture," p. 515.

39. On the House, see Steven V. Roberts, "House, in Rebuff for Reagan, Passes $141 Billion Farm Bill," *New York Times*, October 9, 1985, p. 1; on the Senate, see David Rapp, "Farm Bill Offers Limited 'Win' for All Sides," *Congressional Quarterly Weekly Report*, December 21, 1985, p. 2674.

40. Bureau of the Census, *Statistical Abstract of the United States, 1992*, 112th ed. (Department of Commerce, 1992), p. 650.

41. Demonstrating the power of the agrarian myth, reformers often couch their arguments for reducing subsidies in terms that are consistent with the myth. A principal argument that reformers employed for means-testing was that by making affluent farmers ineligible for subsidies, a greater proportion of subsidies would go to small, family-run operations that were "deserving."

42. Wesley McCune, *The Farm Bloc* (Garden City, N.Y.: Doubleday, Doran, 1943), pp. 262–63; and Grant McConnell, *The Decline of Agrarian Democracy* (University of California Press, 1953).

43. Steven S. Smith and Christopher J. Deering, *Committees in Congress*, 2d ed. (Washington: CQ Press, 1990), chap. 3.

44. In the case of tax reform, see Timothy J. Conlan, Margaret T. Wrightson, and David R. Beam, *Taxing Choices: The Politics of Tax Reform* (Washington: CQ Press, 1990), pp. 252–255; for deregulation, see Martha Derthick and Paul J. Quirk, *The Politics of Deregulation* (Brookings, 1985), pp. 102–04.

45. See the review of the Truman, Eisenhower, and Kennedy years in Willard W. Cochrane and C. Ford Runge, *Reforming Farm Policy: Toward a National Agenda* (Iowa State University Press, 1992), pp. 245–50.

46. Elizabeth Wehr and Ross Evans, "Senate Farm Bill Reflects Budget Pressure," *Congressional Quarterly Weekly Report*, September 19, 1981, p. 1806.

47. David Stockman, *The Triumph of Politics: The Inside Story of the Reagan Revolution* (New York: Avon, 1987), pp. 166–67, 416–18.

48. David S. Cloud, "Farm-State Senators Prepare for Partisan Showdown," *Congressional Quarterly Weekly Report*, June 9, 1990, p. 1784.

49. David S. Cloud, "House and Senate Resist Calls to Alter Course on Farm Bill," *Congressional Quarterly Weekly Report*, July 28, 1990, p. 2395.

50. Browne, *Private Interests, Public Policy, and American Agriculture*, p. 220.

51. David S. Cloud, "Administration's Farm Plans Unveiled—Sort Of," *Congressional Quarterly Weekly Report*, February 10, 1990, p. 384.

52. Some argue that commodity prices have little to do with failure to expand exports. Aside from lowering trade barriers, breaking into expanding markets (for example, East Asia) depends on such factors as quality, the distance between

the producer country and the consumer, and special trading arrangements (joint ventures, for example) between nations. Bruce Stokes, "Pyrrhic Victory?" *National Journal*, December 7, 1985, p. 2830.

53. David S. Cloud, "Old Ways Don't Work Anymore for Farm-State Politicians," *Congressional Quarterly Weekly Report*, June 2, 1990, p. 1723.

54. Peter T. Kilborn, "Iowa Farmers Rebel against Subsidies, Seeking New Setup," *New York Times,* July 25, 1994, p. A1.

55. For a fuller discussion of how these and other policy instruments work, see Bruce L. Gardner, *The Governing of Agriculture* (Regents Press of Kansas, 1981), chap. 2.

56. Roll-call voting data are from *Congressional Quarterly Almanac* (Washington: CQ Press, various years). Rural and agricultural measures are calculated from data from *Congressional Districts in the 1970s* (Washington: CQ Press, 1974), and *Congressional Districts in the 1980s* (Washington: CQ Press, 1983).

57. Wilson, *Special Interests and Policymaking*, pp. 147–53.

Chapter Five

1. Mancur Olson, *The Logic of Collective Action: Public Goods and the Theory of Groups* (Harvard University Press, 1965).

2. See Timothy J. Conlan, Margaret T. Wrightson, and David R. Beam, *Taxing Choices: The Politics of Tax Reform* (Washington: CQ Press, 1990), p. 25. Also, according to John Witte, "Major tax subsidies are often supported by powerful organizations. . . . Similarly, smaller-scale lobbying efforts representing much narrower groups are often successful in altering minor legislative provisions or IRS rulings." John F. Witte, *The Politics and Development of the Federal Income Tax* (University of Wisconsin Press, 1985), p. 285.

3. Jeffrey M. Berry, *The Interest Group Society* (Little, Brown, 1984), chap. 2; see also Kay Lehman Schlozman and John T. Tierney, *Organized Interests and American Democracy* (Harper and Row, 1986); and Mark P. Petracca, "The Rediscovery of Interest Groups," in Mark P. Petracca, ed., *The Politics of Interests: Interest Groups Transformed* (Boulder, Colo.: Westview Press, 1992), pp. 13–22. The political mobilization of business was a response to the defeats suffered by business in the 1960s and 1970s at the hands of environmental, consumer, and civil rights interests. See David Vogel, *Fluctuating Fortunes: The Political Power of Business in America* (New York: Basic Books, 1989).

4. I. M. Destler, *American Trade Politics: System under Stress* (Washington: Institute for International Economics, 1986), p. 42.

5. John E. Rielly, ed., *American Public Opinion and U.S. Foreign Policy, 1991* (Chicago: Council on Foreign Relations, 1991), p. 27.

6. Commenting on deregulation, Derthick and Quirk concluded, "Because of the political strength of the reform forces in Congress, it was in fact only . . . mildly favorable terms that could be obtained [by the industries]. In the end, all three industries made drastic concessions to procompetitive reform." Martha Derthick and Paul J. Quirk, *The Politics of Deregulation* (Brookings, 1985), p. 203.

7. Judith Goldstein, "Ideas, Institutions, and American Trade Policy," *International Organization*, vol. 42 (Winter 1988), p. 215.

8. Only when it became clear very late in the process that they were about to lose did some of the producers decide to join the tax reform and deregulation efforts as a way to influence the details of the final policy decision. See Jeffrey H. Birnbaum and Alan S. Murray, *Showdown at Gucci Gulch: Lawmakers, Lobbyists, and the Unlikely Triumph of Tax Reform* (Random House, 1987), pp. 236–37; and Derthick and Quirk, *Politics of Deregulation*, p. 151.

9. I. M. Destler, *American Trade Politics: System under Stress*, 2d ed. (Washington: Institute for International Economics, 1992), p. 207 (emphasis added).

10. Vogel, *Fluctuating Fortunes*, chap. 8.

11. Conlan, Wrightson, and Beam, *Taxing Choices*, pp. 139–40.

12. W. P. Welch, "Campaign Contributions and Legislative Voting: Milk Money and Dairy Price Supports," *Western Political Quarterly*, vol. 32 (December 1982), pp. 478–95; Henry W. Chappell, Jr., "Campaign Contributions and Congressional Voting: A Simultaneous Probit-Tobit Model," *Review of Economics and Statistics*, vol. 64 (Spring 1982), pp. 77–83; P. J. Feldstein and G. Melnick, "Congressional Voting Behavior on Hospital Legislation: An Exploratory Study," *Journal of Health Politics, Policy and Law*, vol. 8 (Winter 1984), pp. 686–701; and K. J. Mueller, "An Analysis of Congressional Health Policy Voting in the 1970s," *Journal of Health Politics, Policy and Law*, vol. 11 (Spring 1986), pp. 117–35. Other research has found at least some relationship between PAC contributions and voting; see Kirk Brown, "Campaign Contributions and Congressional Voting," paper prepared for the 1983 annual meeting of the American Political Science Association; John Frendeis and Richard Waterman, "PAC Contributions and Legislative Behavior: Senate Voting on Trucking Deregulation," paper prepared for the 1983 annual meeting of the Midwest Political Science Association; James B. Kau and Paul H. Rubin, *Congressmen, Constituents, and Contributors* (Boston: Martinus Nijhoff, 1982); and Laura I. Langbein, "Money and Access: Some Empirical Evidence," *Journal of Politics*, vol. 48 (November 1986), pp. 1052–62.

13. Quoted in Conlan, Wrightson, and Beam, *Taxing Choices*, p. 100.

14. Helen V. Milner, *Resisting Protectionism: Global Industries and the Politics of International Trade* (Princeton University Press, 1988), pp. 259–60; and Daniel C. Esty and Richard E. Caves, "Market Structure and Political Influence," *Economic Inquiry*, vol. 21 (January 1983), pp. 24–38.

15. John Mark Hansen, "Creating a New Politics: The Evolution of an Agricultural Policy Network in Congress, 1919–1980," Ph.D. dissertation, Yale University, 1987, p. 239. See also John Mark Hansen, *Gaining Access: Congress and the Farm Lobby, 1919–1981* (University of Chicago Press, 1991). Economic change, which reflected the increased specialization of agriculture according to product, also boosted the rise of commodity organizations. See William P. Browne, *Private Interests, Public Policy, and American Agriculture* (University Press of Kansas, 1988), p. 239; and Jonathan Rauch, "Farmers' Discord over Government Role Produces a Farm Bill that Pleases Few," *National Journal*, November 9, 1985, p. 2539.

16. Hansen, "Creating a New Politics," pp. 233–34.

17. Birnbaum and Murray, *Showdown at Gucci Gulch*, pp. 16, 112, 145, 161.

18. See Destler, *American Trade Politics* (1992), pp. 268–431.

19. For an interpretation of tax reform that emphasizes the importance of structural changes in the economy, lobbying on the part of businesses that would gain from reform, and their alliance with reform proponents in government, see Cathie J. Martin, *Shifting the Burden: The Struggle over Growth and Corporate Taxation* (University of Chicago Press, 1991), chap. 7.

20. Dorothy L. Robyn, *Braking the Special Interests: Trucking Deregulation and the Politics of Policy Reform* (University of Chicago Press, 1987), pp. 96–97, 234–35.

21. Ibid., p. 106.

22. Milner, *Resisting Protectionism*. Earlier empirical tests of the relationship of export dependence and multinationality to industry preferences for protection produced mixed results. Milner contends that these earlier studies were problematic because they looked only at the industries and not at the firms within them, and because they looked at the relationship between trade policy outcomes and export dependence and multinationality, skipping the intermediate step of establishing a link between the latter and industry demands. See Glenn Fong, "Export Dependence and the New Protectionism," Ph.D. dissertation, Cornell University, 1982; Robert E. Baldwin, *The Political Economy of U.S. Import Policy* (MIT Press, 1986); Réal P. Lavergne, *The Political Economy of U.S. Tariffs* (New York: Academic Press, 1983); William H. Becker, *The Dynamics of Business-Government Relations: Industry and Exports, 1893–1921* (University of Chicago Press, 1982); Peter Gourevitch, "International Trade, Domestic Coalitions, and Liberty," *Journal of Interdisciplinary History*, vol. 8 (Autumn 1977), pp. 281–313; Peter Gourevitch, *Politics in Hard Times* (Cornell University Press, 1986); G. K. Helleiner, "Transnational Enterprise and the New Political Economy of U.S. Trade Policy," *Oxford Economic Papers*, vol. 29 (March 1977), pp. 102–16; Gerald K. Helleiner, "Transnational Corporations and Trade Structure," in Herbert Giersch, ed., *On the Economics of Intra-Industry Trade* (Tübingen: Mohr, 1979), pp. 159–84; and Susan Strange, "Protectionism and World Politics," *International Organization*, vol. 39 (Spring 1985), pp. 233–60.

23. Milner, *Resisting Protectionism*, p. 247.

24. Destler, *American Trade Politics* (1992), p. 192.

25. Cited in ibid., p. 182.

26. Bruce Stokes, "A Divided Farm Lobby," *National Journal*, March 23, 1985, pp. 632–38. On agriculture as a classic subgovernment in the 1950s and 1960s, see Theodore J. Lowi, "How Farmers Get What They Want," in Theodore J. Lowi and Randall B. Ripley, eds., *Legislative Politics U.S.A.* (Little, Brown, 1973), p. 185; Ross B. Talbot and Donald F. Hadwiger, *The Policy Process in American Agriculture* (San Francisco: Chandler, 1968); and Don Paarlberg, *American Farm Policy* (Wiley, 1964), pp. 103–51. On the evolution of agriculture into a more pluralistic "issue network," see Christopher J. Bosso, *Pesticides and Politics: The Life Cycle of a Public Issue* (University of Pittsburgh Press, 1987); and Hugh Heclo, "Issue Networks and the Executive Establishment," in Anthony

King, ed., *The New American Political System* (Washington: American Enterprise Institute, 1978), p. 113.

27. Jeffrey M. Berry, "Consumers and the Hunger Lobby," in Donald F. Hadwiger and Ross B. Talbot, eds., *Food Policy and Farm Programs* (New York: Academy of Political Science, 1982), p. 74. As is often the case in agricultural politics, the more things change, the more they stay the same. Commenting on the greater pluralism, Browne states that "rather than competing to represent the same issues and policies, established organizations and most new groups occupy distinct policy niches. . . . This tendency is as old as the agricultural lobby itself." Browne, *Private Interests*, p. 39.

28. Derthick and Quirk have little to say in *Politics of Deregulation* about the role of organized opponents in trucking deregulation, either.

29. Interview with Gina Despres, aide to Senator Bradley, August 1987.

30. Milner's statistics show that the rise in export dependency and multinationality was quite large in the context of the low base of 2 percent in the 1920s. Her figures are 20 percent for both export dependence (measured as the value of industrial exports as a percentage of total industrial gross national product) and multinationality (measured as the value of all foreign assets of U.S. manufacturing as a percentage of total manufacturing assets) in the 1970s. See Milner, *Resisting Protectionism*, p. 246.

31. Destler, *American Trade Politics* (1992), p. 194.

32. Elizabeth Wehr, "Farm Coalition Regroups around House Bill," *Congressional Quarterly Weekly Report*, October 10, 1981, p. 1991.

33. The need to appeal to nonrural members stems from developments that have taken place over the past several decades. The productivity gains arising from technological innovation and the consequent mechanization of farming, as well as government-sponsored research, freed up workers to migrate to urban industrial centers. The pace of innovation accelerated during the first two postwar decades, and with it, the depopulation of rural areas. See Paarlberg, *American Farm Policy*, pp. 33–44. Second, the Supreme Court's application of the "one person, one vote" principle in the 1960s led to redistricting, and rural areas were left with substantially fewer House seats. Third, as the number of the agricultural workers declined in rural districts, "rural lawmakers elected in the 1960s and 1970s . . . were more inclined to . . . build bridges to an urban Congress." Hansen, "Creating a New Politics," p. 277. Finally, farm legislators in the 1960s could not count on urban and suburban support as they had in the past. Such support was forthcoming in the 1950s because farm legislators and nonfarm Democrats had a mutual interest in opposing the Eisenhower administration. Eisenhower's farm policy—to lower price supports—was opposed throughout much of the farm belt and as a result redounded to the electoral advantage of the Democrats. But with the Democrats back in the White House in the 1960s, this incentive for urban-rural cooperation evaporated. Instead urban liberals, chafed by opposition of conservative southerners on the agriculture committees to civil rights and social legislation, threatened to hold the farm program hostage. The tactic alarmed the farm coalition. It was clear that if they did not strike a bargain with food stamp proponents, the farm program would be in jeopardy.

Ever since, the food stamp program, which expanded dramatically in the 1960s, has been regularly included in the omnibus farm legislation that Congress passes every four years.

34. Wehr, "Farm Coalition Regroups," p. 1991.

35. Ibid.

36. David S. Cloud, "House and Senate Resist Calls to Alter Course on Farm Bill," *Congressional Quarterly Weekly Report*, July 28, 1990, p. 2395.

37. "Agriculture," *Congressional Quarterly Almanac, 1985,* vol. 41 (Washington: CQ Press, 1986), p. 531.

38. Cloud, "House and Senate Resist Calls," p. 2395.

39. Birnbaum and Murray, *Showdown at Gucci Gulch*, p. 16.

40. Quoted in ibid., p. 287.

41. Derthick and Quirk, *Politics of Deregulation*, p. 204.

42. Labor was defeated on the Burke-Hartke quota bill in 1971, on the Nixon-Ford trade bill of 1973–74, on domestic content legislation for automobiles in the early 1980s, and in its fight against the extension of trade preferences to developing countries in 1974 and 1984. Trade adjustment assistance was expanded in the 1970s but then was reduced drastically in the 1980s. Labor's efforts to derail fast-track negotiating authority for the North American Free Trade Agreement and to defeat NAFTA have failed as well. Labor's victories include a provision in the 1984 trade bill that forced firms to reinvest in steel facilities and worker training, and in 1988, plant-closing prenotification. Destler, *American Trade Politics* (1992), p. 191.

43. Ibid., pp. 192–96.

44. Some of the recent literature on the politics of agriculture has reached even stronger conclusions about limited importance of farm producers in setting the agenda. According to William Browne, "Despite the high incidence of their satisfaction with agricultural policy decisions, little evidence exists to show that organized interests dominate policymaking. . . . It would be necessary to reject any model of agricultural policymaking that portrayed government as little more than the reactive element in a political process in which narrow special interests defined acceptable policy alternatives." Browne, *Private Interests*, p. 213.

45. Derthick and Quirk, *Politics of Deregulation*, chap. 2.

46. Some group theorists themselves long ago recognized an important role for institutions. David Truman, for example, observed that institutions provide a "multiplicity of points of access" for groups, and that "factors peculiar to the institutions themselves" help to determine which groups gain more effective access. David B. Truman, *The Governmental Process* (Knopf, 1953), p. 506. "The formal institutions of government in the United States . . . mark some of [the] limits [of politics] . . . and designate certain points through which it must flow" (p. 322). Nevertheless, Truman's main argument was that group interests and activities are the chief determinants of public policy: "The product of effective access, of the claims of organized and unorganized interests . . . is a governmental decision. Government decisions are the result of effective access by various interests. These decisions may be more or less stable depending on the strength of the supporting interests" (p. 507).

47. Commenting on the defeat of means-testing and other proposals unfriendly to agriculture in 1990, one member of Congress observed that "the committee is well-organized and managed to make its deal with a variety of groups." Remarks of Representative Tom Downey, in David S. Cloud, "Let's Make a Deal," *Congressional Quarterly Weekly Report*, August 4, 1990, p. 2495.

48. Hansen, *Gaining Access*. Hansen also shows that farm organizations have not always enjoyed such access. In the years after World War II, access declined as committee members turned to more reliable sources of information about the preferences of their farmer constituents.

49. Browne, *Private Interests*, p. 214. See also Willard W. Cochrane, "A New Sheet of Music," *Choices* (premiere edition, 1986), pp. 11–15; and Clifford M. Hardin, "Congress Is the Problem," *Choices* (premiere edition, 1986), pp. 6–10.

50. William P. Browne, "The Fragmented and Meandering Politics of Agriculture," in M. Ann Tutwiler, ed., *U.S. Agriculture in a Global Setting: An Agenda for the Future* (Washington: National Center for Food and Agricultural Policy, 1988), pp. 143, 149.

51. The most preferred policy of Republicans, of course, would be to enact neither food stamps nor farm subsidies, but a majority coalition for this preference is impossible given their minority status in Congress.

52. John Ferejohn, "Logrolling in an Institutional Context: A Case Study of Food Stamp Legislation," in Gerald C. Wright, Jr., Leroy N. Rieselbach, and Lawrence C. Dodd, eds., *Congress and Policy Change* (New York: Agathon Press, 1986), p. 225.

53. Witte, *Politics and Development*, p. 242.

54. Ibid., p. 334.

55. Randall Strahan, *New Ways and Means: Reform and Change in a Congressional Committee* (University of North Carolina Press, 1990), p. 90.

56. Steven S. Smith and Christopher J. Deering, *Committees in Congress* (Washington: CQ Press, 1984), p. 177.

57. Strahan, *New Ways and Means*, p. 81. See also Catherine E. Rudder, "Fiscal Responsibility, Fairness, and the Revenue Committees," in Lawrence C. Dodd and Bruce I. Oppenheimer, eds., *Congress Reconsidered*, 4th ed. (Washington: CQ Press, 1989), pp. 211–22.

Chapter Six

1. Judith Goldstein, "Ideas, Institutions, and American Trade Policy," *International Organization*, vol. 42 (Winter 1988), p. 181.

2. As discussed in chapter 3, there has been some erosion of institutional resistance to protectionism in the area of administered trade protection, where mechanisms that had been used to deflect and deny most pressure have been turned increasingly into mechanisms for gaining relief and burdening competitors.

3. Pietro S. Nivola, *Regulating Unfair Trade* (Brookings, 1993), p. 19.

4. See chapter 4, p. 114; and Nivola, *Regulating Unfair Trade*, pp. 53–55.

5. For syntheses of this literature and discussions of how this approach differs from other perspectives in political science, see James G. March and Johan P. Olsen, *Rediscovering Institutions: The Organizational Basis of Politics* (Free Press, 1989). For a presentation that distinguishes rational-choice neoinstitutionalism from the approaches in political science that preceded it, see Kenneth Shepsle, "Studying Institutions: Some Lessons from the Rational Choice Approach," *Journal of Theoretical Politics*, vol. 1, no. 2 (1989), pp. 131–47. For a view of neoinstitutionalism that is historical, sociological, and cross-national, see Peter B. Evans, Dietrich Rueschemeyer, and Theda Skocpol, eds., *Bringing the State Back In* (Cambridge University Press, 1985).

6. An excellent example is Kenneth A. Shepsle and Barry R. Weingast, "The Institutional Foundations of Committee Power," *American Political Science Review*, vol. 81 (March 1987), pp. 85–104. In an effort to explain the power of congressional committees, Shepsle and Weingast formulate a rational-choice institutional model that focuses on the sequence of the legislation process. They show how committee power is rooted not only in the ability to set agendas by originating legislation but also in the "second chance" that committees get at the conference stage, when House and Senate committees resolve differences between their bills. Other examples include an analysis of how different voting rules lead to different winning candidates in William H. Riker, *Liberalism against Populism: A Confrontation between the Theory of Democracy and the Theory of Social Choice* (San Francisco: W. H. Freeman and Co., 1982). For how a seniority rule for determining committee chairs and alternative rules, such as party discipline, produce different outcomes, see Kenneth Shepsle, "Institutional Arrangements and Equilibrium in Multidimensional Voting Models," *American Journal of Political Science*, vol. 23 (February 1979), pp. 17–59.

7. R. Kent Weaver and Bert A. Rockman, "When and How Do Institutions Matter?" in R. Kent Weaver and Bert A. Rockman, eds., *Do Institutions Matter? Government Capabilities in the United States and Abroad* (Brookings, 1993), p. 446 (emphasis added).

8. Donald D. Searing, "Roles, Rules, and Rationality in the New Institutionalism," *American Political Science Review*, vol. 85 (December 1991), pp. 1239–61.

9. This point echoes David Truman: "The formal institutions of government in the United States do not prescribe all the meanderings of the stream of politics. They do mark some of its limits, however, and designate certain points through which it must flow." David B. Truman, *The Governmental Process* (Knopf, 1953), p. 322.

10. Hugh Heclo, *Modern Social Politics in Britain and Sweden: From Relief to Income Maintenance* (Yale University Press, 1974), p. 306.

11. Grant McConnell, *Private Power and American Democracy* (Knopf, 1966); Theodore J. Lowi, *The End of Liberalism: Ideology, Policy, and the Crisis of Public Authority* (Norton, 1969); George J. Stigler, "The Theory of Economic Regulation," *Bell Journal of Economics and Management Science*, vol. 2 (Spring 1971), pp. 3–21; and E. E. Schattschneider, *Politics, Pressures and the Tariff* (Prentice-Hall, 1935), pp. 283–85. Various explanations for clientelism have been

put forward. Decentralized political institutions, as in the United States, foster parochial and localistic orientations to policymaking. Policymakers are encouraged to pay greater attention to the interests that predominate in their geographical or functional areas than to broad, diffuse interests. And those institutions that do have national constituencies will be weak in the face of the centrifugal forces. Others see institutional arrangements that are conducive to clientelism as simply the manifestation of a deeper commitment by Americans to an ideology that legitimates the power of private groups. Lowi, for instance, stresses the pervasiveness of "interest group liberalism," and McConnell argues that American ideology equates democracy with private autonomy, which, in turn, is secured through decentralized political organization. From a rational-choice perspective, others have identified the source of clientelism in the self-interested rationality of rent-seeking behavior. Smaller groups have a superior ability to overcome obstacles to collective action, such as the free-rider problem, because the limited size, exclusivity, and homogeneity of these groups facilitate their ability to clearly define their economic aims, which makes them more fervent about their policy preferences. Others point to incentives that operate within government, among politicians and other suppliers of public goods for whom delivering benefits to targeted constituencies is an effective means for remaining in office and maintaining bureaucratic organizations.

Even in the heyday of clientelism, however, not everyone agreed that it accurately portrayed American politics or that it was as widespread as it was reported to be. See, for example, Raymond A. Bauer, Ithiel de Sola Pool, and Lewis Anthony Dexter, *American Business and Public Policy: The Politics of Foreign Trade*, 2d ed. (New York: Aldine-Atherton, 1972); Edward C. Banfield and James Q. Wilson, *City Politics* (Harvard University Press, 1963); Edward C. Banfield, *Political Influence* (Glencoe, Ill.: Free Press, 1961); and James Q. Wilson, *Political Organizations* (New York: Basic Books, 1973).

12. Emmette S. Redford, *Democracy in the Administrative State* (Oxford University Press, 1969); John Leiper Freeman, *The Political Process: Executive Bureau–Legislative Committee Relations* (Random House, 1955); Douglass Cater, *Power in Washington: A Critical Look at Today's Struggle to Govern in the Nation's Capital* (Random House, 1964); Roger H. Davidson, "Policymaking in the Manpower Subgovernment," in Michael P. Smith and others, eds., *Politics in America* (Random House, 1975); Harold Seidman, *Politics, Position and Power: The Dynamics of Federal Organization*, 2d ed. (Oxford University Press, 1975); and Eugene Lewis, *American Politics in a Bureaucratic Age: Citizens, Constituents, Clients and Victims* (Cambridge, Mass.: Winthrop, 1977).

13. Robert A. Dahl, *A Preface to Democratic Theory* (University of Chicago Press, 1956), p. 146. See also David B. Truman, *The Governmental Process: Political Interests and Public Opinion* (Knopf, 1971); and Earl Latham, *The Group Basis of Politics: A Study in Basing-Point Legislation* (Cornell University Press, 1952).

14. See McConnell, *Private Power*; and Lowi, *End of Liberalism*.

15. A central point of the analysis of rent-seeking in politics is that through organizing, lobbying, and logrolling, groups of individuals can secure benefits for

themselves while bearing little of their costs. They demand and receive a higher level of public provision than they would choose if they had to pay for it themselves in the private market. See William C. Mitchell, *The Anatomy of Public Failure: A Public Choice Perspective* (Ottawa, Ill.: Green Hill Publishers, Inc., 1978); Peter H. Aranson and Peter C. Ordeshook, "Public Interest, Private Interest, and the Democratic Polity," in Roger Benjamin and Stephen L. Elkin, eds., *The Democratic State* (University Press of Kansas, 1985), pp. 87–178; Kenneth A. Shepsle and Barry R. Weingast, "Legislative Politics and Budget Outcomes," in Gregory B. Mills and John L. Palmer, eds., *Federal Budget Policy in the 1980s* (Washington: Urban Institute Press, 1984), pp. 343–67; George J. Stigler, *The Citizen and the State: Essays on Regulation* (University of Chicago Press, 1975); and William A. Niskanen, Jr., *Bureaucracy and Representative Government* (Chicago: Aldine-Atherton, 1971).

16. See Mancur Olson, *The Rise and Decline of Nations* (Yale University Press, 1982).

17. Paul E. Peterson, "The Rise and Fall of Special Interest Politics," *Political Science Quarterly*, vol. 105 (Winter 1990–91), pp. 539–56; and Robert H. Salisbury, "The Paradox of Interest Groups in Washington—More Groups, Less Clout," in Anthony King, ed., *The New American Political System*, 2d ed. (Washington: American Enterprise Institute, 1990), pp. 203–30. The decline in producer-group fortunes has been accompanied by a decline in the budgetary resources devoted for projects and subsidies targeted toward congressional districts. Grants-in-aid to state and local governments and other "pork barrel" spending declined as a proportion of the budget in the 1980s. See John Ellwood, "Comments," in Mills and Palmer, eds., *Federal Budget Policy*, pp. 368–78; and Norman J. Ornstein, "The Politics of the Deficit," in Philip Cagan, ed., *Essays in Contemporary Economic Problems, 1985: The Economy in Deficit* (Washington: American Enterprise Institute, 1985), p. 311. According to R. Douglas Arnold, because members of Congress have competing concerns, they cannot be single-minded seekers of pork barrel benefits; see Arnold, "Local Roots of Domestic Policy," in Thomas E. Mann and Norman J. Ornstein, eds., *The New Congress* (Washington: American Enterprise Institute, 1981), pp. 250–87.

18. See Andrew S. McFarland, "Interest Groups and the Policymaking Process: Sources of Countervailing Power in America," in Mark P. Petracca, ed., *The Politics of Interests: Interest Groups Transformed* (Boulder, Colo.: Westview Press, 1992), pp. 58–79.

19. On the rise of countervailing groups in such areas as environmental and consumer protection and civil rights, where public-interest and other broad-based organizations have appeared, see Bruce A. Ackerman and William T. Hassler, *Clean Coal/Dirty Air* (Yale University Press, 1981); Norman J. Ornstein and Shirley Elder, *Interest Groups, Lobbying and Policymaking* (Washington: CQ Press, 1978); Charles O. Jones, *Clean Air: The Policies and Politics of Pollution Control* (University of Pittsburgh Press, 1975); Jeffrey M. Berry, *Lobbying for the People: The Political Behavior of Public Interest Groups* (Princeton University Press, 1977); Andrew S. McFarland, *Common Cause: Lobbying in the Public Interest* (Chatham, N.J.: Chatham House, 1984); Andrew S. McFarland, *Public*

Interest Lobbies: Decision-Making on Energy (Washington: American Enterprise Institute, 1976); Robert Cameron Mitchell, "Public Opinion and Environmental Politics in the 1970s and 1980s," in Norman J. Vig and Michael E. Kraft, eds., *Environmental Policy in the 1980s: Reagan's New Agenda* (Washington: CQ Press, 1984); Mark V. Nadel, *The Politics of Consumer Protection* (Bobbs-Merrill, 1971); David Vogel, "The Public-Interest Movement and the American Reform Tradition," *Political Science Quarterly*, vol. 95 (Winter 1980–81), pp. 607–27; Jo Freeman, *The Politics of Women's Liberation* (New York: McKay, 1975); and William P. Browne, *Private Interests, Public Policy, and American Agriculture* (University Press of Kansas, 1988), p. 240.

20. Jeffrey M. Berry, *The Interest Group Society* (Glenview, Ill.: Scott, Foresman, 1989); and David Vogel, *Fluctuating Fortunes: The Political Power of Business in America* (New York: Basic Books, 1989).

21. Burdett Loomis, *The New American Politician: Ambition, Entrepreneurship, and the Changing Face of Political Life* (New York: Basic Books, 1988).

22. Hugh Heclo, "Issue Networks and the Executive Establishment," in Anthony King, ed., *The New American Political System* (Washington: American Enterprise Institute, 1978), pp. 87–124; Christopher J. Bosso, *Pesticides and Politics: The Life Cycle of a Public Issue* (University of Pittsburgh Press, 1987); and Roger H. Davidson, "Breaking Up Those 'Cozy Triangles': An Impossible Dream?" in Susan Welch and John G. Peters, eds., *Legislative Reform and Public Policy* (Praeger, 1977), pp. 30–53.

23. Charles O. Jones, "American Politics and the Organization of Energy Decision Making," *Annual Review of Energy*, vol. 4 (1979), pp. 99–121.

24. Michael Crozier, Samuel P. Huntington, and Joji Watanuki, *The Crisis of Democracy: Report of the Governability of Democracies to the Trilateral Commission* (New York University Press, 1975), pp. 57–88; Anthony King, "Overload: Problems of Governing in the 1970s," *Political Studies*, vol. 33 (June–September 1975), pp. 285–96; and Anthony King, "The American Policy in the Late 1970s: Building Coalitions in the Sand," in King, ed., *New American Political System* (1978). See also Paul E. Peterson and John E. Chubb, eds., *Can Government Govern?* (Brookings, 1989).

25. Benjamin Ginsberg and Martin Shefter, *Politics by Other Means: The Declining Importance of Elections in America* (New York: Basic Books, 1990); and Bosso, *Pesticides*, chaps. 9, 10.

26. Starting sometime in the 1980s, it became popular to cite "divided government" rather than neopluralism as the main source of trouble plaguing American government. Upon close inspection, it turns out that there is not much evidence that divided partisan control in the executive and legislative branches has significant adverse effects on governmental performance. Comparing periods of divided government with ones of unified control, David Mayhew found that important legislation was just as likely to win enactment under divided party control as it was under unified control. He concluded that "it does not seem to make all that much difference whether party control . . . happens to be unified or divided." David R. Mayhew, *Divided We Govern: Party Control, Lawmaking and Investigations, 1946–1990* (Yale University Press, 1991), p. 198.

Divided versus unified control does not seem to be determinative in the policy fortunes of producer groups, either. One might have expected that significant declines in group fortunes would have been more difficult to accomplish under divided government, but this is not the case. Tax reform failed under unified government in 1978 but succeeded under divided control in 1986. Deregulation occurred under both unified and divided control, as did the decline in trade barriers in the decades after World War II. Undoubtedly the frequency of divided partisan control since the 1940s has contributed to the need to construct bipartisan coalitions, which have been an important element in bringing about declines in producer benefits (and in resisting pressures to increase benefits). But the larger point is that such coalitions do indeed form. Furthermore, it is not clear that more years of unified party control over the past few decades would have led to greater success in resisting or challenging producer interests.

27. Barbara Sinclair, "House Majority Party Leadership in an Era of Legislative Constraint," in Roger H. Davidson, ed., *The Postreform Congress* (St. Martin's Press, 1992), pp. 91–111; and Roger H. Davidson, "The New Centralization on Capitol Hill," *Review of Politics*, vol. 50 (Summer 1988), pp. 345–64.

28. Randall Strahan, *New Ways and Means: Reform and Change in a Congressional Committee* (University of North Carolina Press, 1990); and Catherine E. Rudder, "Fiscal Responsibility and the Revenue Committees," in Lawrence C. Dodd and Bruce I. Oppenheimer, eds., *Congress Reconsidered*, 3d ed. (Washington: CQ Press, 1985), pp. 211–22.

29. Other problems facing Washington are not properly diagnosed as failures of governance at all. Some involve intractable social problems or a lack of knowledge. Any government would have difficulty addressing these challenges.

Index

AFL-CIO. *See* American Federation of Labor–Congress of Industrial Organizations (AFL-CIO)

Agricultural Adjustment Act of *1933*, 109, 114

Agricultural Adjustment Act of *1985*, 109

Agricultural subsidies, 3, 166, 168, 181; capping payments to recipients, 108–10; comprehensive reform of, 108–09; and Congress, 23, 109, 113, 117, 124–27, 129–30, 133, 156, 172; costs of, 1, 5, 14, 18, 23, 107, 113, 115–18, 166; cotton, 111, 155; criticisms of, 115, 117–18, 132; dairy, 109–10; described, 107, 135–36; economic effects of, 117–18, 148; as entitlements, 14, 107, 112, 117, 133, 148, 173; and federal budget, 108, 112–13, 121; grains, 111, 113, 156; honey, 110, 134; income supports, 108–09, 112–13, 135; inequity of distribution, 14, 110, 118, 132; means-testing of, 5, 108–14, 110–11, 127, 133, 157, 172; mohair, 110, 134; peanuts, 109–10, 156; price supports, 109, 112–14, 118; production limits, 135–36; to promote exports, 114; prospects for reform, 134; reform failures, 5, 108–14, 122, 179; rice, 111, 113, 156; roll-call votes on, 124–25, 136–40; and Soviet grain embargo, 108, 122; soybeans, 110; sugar, 109–10, 114, 130, 156; tobacco, 109–10, 156; wool, 110, 134

Agriculture, 11, 23–26, 181; agrarian myth, 15, 123–24, 126, 132–33, 170, 172–73; agribusiness, 153; and anticompetitive regulation, 23, 107–08, 114, 119–20, 127–29, 131–34, 148–49, 170, 172; economic conditions in, 13–14, 23, 107, 112–14, 117–22, 127, 132, 159, 170, 172; exports, 117, 120–22, 131, 172; family farmers, 11, 13–15; farm bloc, 156, 161; farm population, 118, 149; institutional context for, 19, 23, 128–32, 160–61, 172, 178; intercommodity logrolling, 156; issue context for, 11, 13–15, 114–28, 130–33, 159–60, 170, 172, 178–79; leadership in, 23, 128–34, 167, 172, 177–79; and mass media, 122–25, 132, 159; partisan coalitions, 17–18, 110, 118–19, 124–27, 132, 134, 156–57, 159–61, 170; perception of farmers as deserving, 11, 13, 120, 122–23, 126–27, 130, 132–33, 159, 170, 172, 181; and public opinion, 122–23; and risk, 11, 111, 124; and tax policy, 23, 108, 114, 119–20, 127–29, 131–34, 148, 170; and trade policy, 107, 114, 132, 174

Agriculture committees (House and Senate), 20, 109, 112, 128, 133, 157, 160–61, 172, 176. *See also* Agricultural subsidies, and Congress

Agriculture, Department of, 19, 102, 128, 129, 130, 133–34, 153, 160, 172, 176; Commodity Credit Corporation (CCC), 114, 135; leadership of, 129, 130, 133

Aluminum Company of America, 151

American Airlines, 150

American Bankers Association, 151

American Conservative Union, 57

American Council for Capital Formation, 157

American Express, 151

American Farm Bureau Federation, 150

American Federation of Labor–Congress of Industrial Organizations (AFL-CIO), 86, 157

219